Quality Reading Instruction

in the Age of

Common Core Standards

Susan B. Neuman • Linda B. Gambrell

EDITORS

INTERNATIONAL
Reading Association
800 BARKSDALE ROAD, PO BOX 8139
NEWARK, DE 19714-8139, USA
www.reading.org

The International Reading Association attempts, through its publications, to provide a forum for a wide spectrum of opinions on reading. This policy permits divergent viewpoints without implying the endorsement of the Association.

Executive Editor, Publications   Shannon Fortner
Acquisitions Manager   Tori Mello Bachman
Managing Editors   Christina M. Lambert and Susanne Viscarra
Editorial Associate   Wendy Logan
Creative Services/Production Manager   Anette Schuetz
Design and Composition Associate   Lisa Kochel

Cover   Design, Frank Pessia; Photographs (from left), wavebreakmedia/Shutterstock.com, Andresr/Shutterstock.com, Thai Soriano/Shutterstock.com

Library of Congress Cataloging-in-Publication Data

Quality reading instruction in the age of common core standards / Susan B. Neuman and Linda B. Gambrell, editors.
        pages cm
    Includes bibliographical references and index.
    ISBN 978-0-87207-496-5 (pbk.) — ISBN 978-0-87207-498-9 (e-edition) 1.   Language arts—Standards—United States. 2.   Reading—United States.   I. Neuman, Susan B., editor of compilation.   II. Gambrell, Linda B., editor of compilation.
  LB1576.Q35 2013
  428.4—dc23

                                                                    2012048546

Suggested APA Reference

Neuman, S.B., & Gambrell, L.B. (Eds.). (2013). *Quality reading instruction in the age of Common Core Standards*. Newark, DE: International Reading Association.

CONTENTS

Susan B. Neuman is a professor in Teaching and Learning at the University of Michigan and New York University, specializing in early literacy development. Previously, she served as the U.S. Assistant Secretary for Elementary and Secondary Education. In her role as Assistant Secretary, she established the Early Reading First program, developed the Early Childhood Educator Professional Development Program, and was responsible for all activities in Title I of the Elementary and Secondary Act. She has served on the IRA Board of Directors (2001–2003) and other numerous boards of nonprofit organizations. She is currently the co-editor of *Reading Research Quarterly*, the most prestigious journal in reading research.

Susan's research and teaching interests include early childhood policy, curriculum, and early reading instruction, preK–grade 3, for children who live in poverty. She has written over 100 articles and authored and edited 11 books, including the *Handbook of Early Literacy Research* (Volumes I, II, III) with David Dickinson, *Changing the Odds for Children at Risk* (Teachers College Press, 2009), *Educating the Other America* (Paul H. Brookes, 2008), and *Multimedia and Literacy Development* (Taylor & Francis, 2008). More recently she published *Giving Our Children a Fighting Chance: Poverty, Literacy, and the Development of Information Capital* (Teachers College Press, 2012).

Linda B. Gambrell is Distinguished Professor of Education in the Eugene T. Moore School of Education at Clemson University, where she teaches graduate and undergraduate literacy courses. From 1999 to 2006, she was the director of the School of Education at Clemson University. Prior to coming to Clemson University in 1999, she was Associate Dean for Research in the College of Education at the University of Maryland, College Park. She began her career as an elementary classroom teacher and reading specialist in Prince George's County (Maryland) Public Schools. From 1992 to 1997, she was a principal investigator at the National Reading Research Center at the University of Maryland, where she directed the Literacy Motivation Project. She has served as president of the three leading professional organizations for reading: the International Reading Association, National Reading Conference/Literacy Research Association, and College Reading Association/Association of Literacy Educators and Researchers. She is currently the co-editor of *Reading Research Quarterly*, the most prestigious journal in reading research.

Linda's major research areas are literacy motivation, reading comprehension, and the role of discussion in teaching and learning. Her research has been published in major scholarly journals including *Reading Research Quarterly, Educational Psychologist, The Elementary School Journal,* and *Journal of Educational Research.*

Associate Editor

Chris L. Massey is a doctoral candidate at Clemson University, South Carolina. His areas of interest include adolescent content area literacy and reading motivation of lesbian, gay, bisexual, transgender, and questioning (LGBTQ) adolescents.

Marilyn Jager Adams holds a PhD in cognitive and developmental psychology from Brown University, where she is currently a visiting scholar in the Department of Cognitive, Linguistic, and Psychological Studies.

 Cheryl Burlingame is a doctoral student in the School Psychology program and a graduate research assistant for the ORCA Project at the University of Connecticut. She earned her Master of Arts in educational psychology from the University of Connecticut.

 Adriana Bus is professor of education and child studies at Leiden University in The Netherlands. She published meta-analyses in the area of reading and carried out experiments with an Internet environment to promote rich literacy experiences for young children.

 Julie Coiro is an assistant professor in the School of Education at the University of Rhode Island in Kingston, where she teaches graduate and undergraduate courses in reading. Julie has a doctorate in educational psychology from the University of Connecticut.

 James W. Cunningham, PhD, is emeritus at the University of North Carolina at Chapel Hill. He has taught at the elementary and secondary levels. He was a member of the Text Complexity Committee for the Common Core Standards in English Language Arts. He is in the Reading Hall of Fame.

 Brie Doyle is a doctoral student at the University of Maryland, College Park. She is an experienced elementary teacher and reading specialist. Her research interests include creating motivating literacy contexts targeted at improving vocabulary and comprehension for diverse struggling readers and English learners.

 Nell K. Duke is a professor of Literacy, Language, and Culture and faculty associate in the Combined Program in Education and Psychology at the University of Michigan. She focuses on early literacy development, particularly among children living in poverty. Among her books is *Reading and Writing Genre With Purpose in K–8 Classrooms* (Heinemann, 2012).

Elena Forzani is a doctoral student and Neag Fellow in Cognition and Instruction at the University of Connecticut, where she is a member of the New Literacies Research Lab. Prior to this, she taught first grade and high school English and reading. She earned her Master of Education in literacy from the University of Michigan.

 Linda B. Gambrell is Distinguished Professor of Education in the Eugene T. Moore School of Education at Clemson University, where she teaches graduate and undergraduate literacy courses, and she is currently the coeditor of *Reading Research Quarterly*. Her major research areas are literacy motivation, reading comprehension, and the role of discussion in teaching and learning.

 John T. Guthrie is professor emeritus at the University of Maryland, College Park. He has written extensively about cognitive and motivational aspects of reading and learning. He is the recipient of the Oscar Causey Award for Outstanding Reading Research and is a member of the Reading Hall of Fame. In 2004, he received the University of Maryland Regent's Faculty Award for research/scholarship/creative activity. In 2011, he was elected to the National Academy of Education, and in 2012, he was appointed to the International Reading Association Literacy Research Panel.

 Juliet L. Halladay, PhD, is assistant professor in the Department of Education at the University of Vermont, Burlington. Her work focuses on elementary reading, with a particular focus on text complexity, assessment, and the complex nature of interactions between readers and texts.

 Elfrieda (Freddy) H. Hiebert is president and CEO of TextProject Inc., a nonprofit aimed at increasing student reading levels through appropriate texts, and she is a research associate at the University of California, Santa Cruz. She has worked in the field of early reading acquisition for over 40 years, first as a teacher's aide and teacher of primary-level students in central California and, subsequently, as a teacher educator and researcher at the universities of Kentucky, Colorado-Boulder, Michigan, and California-Berkeley.

 Clint Kennedy is a doctoral student in Cognition and Instruction, a Neag Fellow, and a member of the New Literacies Research Team at the University of Connecticut (UConn) in Storrs. He also is the chief technology officer for Branford Public Schools. He earned his master's in educational psychology from UConn and his undergrad degree in engineering at the University of Pennsylvania.

Erin Kramer is a master's student in the Reading Specialist program at Rutgers, The State University of New Jersey and a second-grade teacher in the Morris Plains School District in Morris Plains, New Jersey, where she was teacher of the year for 2011–2012.

Jonna M. Kulikowich, PhD, is professor of education at Penn State, University Park. Her interests include academic development in mathematics/statistics, applied statistics, and measurement of variables in reading research.

Donald J. Leu, PhD, is the Neag Endowed Chair in Literacy and Technology and professor of education in the Neag School of Education at the University of Connecticut, Storrs, where he directs the New Literacies Research Lab (www.newliteracies .uconn.edu).

Anne McGill-Franzen, PhD, is professor of education in the Department of Theory and Practice in teacher education and director of the Reading Center at the University of Tennessee, Knoxville. She has written extensively on reading disabilities and instructional interventions to mitigate the problems faced by struggling readers and their classroom teachers.

Jennifer McPeake is a curriculum designer and professional development specialist on the Concept-Oriented Reading Instruction (CORI) research team. She was formerly a classroom teacher and literacy trainer with the Children's Literacy Initiative. Jennifer holds a bachelor's degree in education from the State University of New York, College at Oswego.

Lesley Mandel Morrow, PhD, is a Distinguished Professor of Literacy at Rutgers, The State University of New Jersey, where she directs the Center for Literacy Development. Lesley is past president of the International Reading Association, a member of the Reading Hall of Fame, and the IRA recipient of the William S. Gray Citation of Merit for research. She has published numerous research articles, book chapters, and books.

Susan B. Neuman is a professor in Teaching and Learning at the University of Michigan and New York University, and the coeditor of *Reading Research Quarterly*. She has served as the U.S. Assistant Secretary for Elementary and Secondary Education. Her research and teaching interests include early childhood policy, curriculum, and early reading instruction, prek–grade 3, for children who live in poverty.

P. David Pearson, PhD, is a faculty member in the programs in Language and Literacy and Cognition and Development at the Graduate School of Education at the University of California, Berkeley, where he served as dean from 2001–2010. He is the founding editor of the *Handbook of Reading Research*, now in its fourth volume; he edited *Reading Research Quarterly* and the *Review of Research in Education*; and he has served on the editorial review board for some 20 educational journals.

 D. Ray Reutzel, PhD, is the Emma Eccles Jones Distinguished Endowed Chair of Early Childhood Education at Utah State University in Logan. He is author of more than 200 publications and past editor of *The Reading Teacher*. Ray is an elected member of the Reading Hall of Fame.

 Theresa Roberts, PhD, is an educational consultant and professor emeritus of child development at California State University, Sacramento. Her research interests include alphabet and vocabulary learning, classroom instruction experiments, and family engagement in literacy. She has collaborated with preschool and elementary school teachers, administrators, and districts to promote early literacy development.

 Kathleen Roskos teaches courses in reading assessment and instruction at John Carroll University, University Heights, Ohio. She studies early literacy development, teacher learning, and the instructional design of professional development for educators, and has published research articles, chapters, and books on these topics.

 Nell Sedransk received her PhD in statistics from Iowa State University, Ames. Currently she is associate director of the National Institute of Statistical Sciences and professor of statistics at North Carolina State University, as well as an elected member of the International Statistical Institute and fellow of the American Statistical Association.

 Rebecca Silverman, EdD, is an associate professor at the University of Maryland, College Park. Her research focuses on language and literacy development and instruction for children at risk for reading difficulties, particularly children from low-income and English learning backgrounds, in early childhood and elementary school classrooms.

Daisy Smeets, PhD, works in the Department of Education and Child Studies at Leiden University, The Netherlands. She studies how technology (i.e., electronic storybooks) affects early literacy development.

 Kandy Smith is a school consultant for the Tennessee State Personnel Development Grant and a doctoral candidate in literacy studies at the University of Tennessee, Knoxville. Effective implementation of Response to Intervention is the focus of both her dissertation research and her work as a consultant in school districts.

 Dorothy S. Strickland, PhD, is the Samuel DeWitt Proctor Professor of Education Emerita of Rutgers, The State University of New Jersey and Distinguished Research Fellow at the National Institute for Early Education Research. A former classroom teacher and learning disabilities specialist, she is a past president of the International Reading Association.

 Alfred W. Tatum, PhD, teaches in the Literacy, Language, and Culture program at the University of Illinois at Chicago (UIC), where he also directs the UIC Reading Clinic. His research focuses on the literacy development of African American males.

PREFACE

The Common Core State Standards for English Language Arts represent the culmination of an extended, broad-based effort led by the National Governors Association Center for Best Practices (NGA Center) and the Council of Chief State School Officers (CCSSO) to help ensure that all students are college and career ready. These standards define general, cross-disciplinary literacy expectations that are designed to be grade-level expectations that help prepare students to enter college and the workforce ready to succeed.

Our intention in this book is to bring these standards to life, highlighting the 10 College and Career Readiness Anchor Standards for Reading (see Table P.1) that define the literacy skills and understandings that all students must demonstrate. The 10 anchor standards, along with the more specific grade-level standards, are necessary complements— with the anchor standards providing broad standards and the grade-level standards providing additional specificity. The anchor standards, like the more specific grade-level standards, are presented in the following four categories: Key Ideas and Details, Craft and Structure, Integration of Knowledge and Ideas, and Range of Reading and Level of Text Complexity.

Throughout the book, scholars address the critical design issues of these standards and provide helpful guidance on the implementation of classroom practices. Chapters emphasize learning progressions in reading, writing, speaking, listening, and language, starting with kindergarten all the way through high school. To help promote this, each chapter includes useful "Try This!" techniques. Additionally, recognizing that these standards are a shared responsibility within schools, chapters also include discussion questions designed to support conversations and considerations about the interdisciplinary nature of literacy.

It is a time of great challenge and opportunity for the reading profession. These standards will challenge all of us to help students advance throughout the grades as we work collectively to increase reading achievement and student proficiency. It is also a time of opportunity to ensure that all students, regardless of their economic circumstances, develop the competence, desire to read, and skills necessary to actively participate as readers and writers of the 21st century. It is a worthy mission, and one that our profession is uniquely qualified to accomplish.

Susan B. Neuman and Linda B. Gambrell
Editors

Table P.1. Overview of the College and Career Readiness Anchor Standards for Reading

Category	Standards
Key Ideas and Details	1. Read closely to determine what the text says explicitly and to make logical inferences from it; cite specific textual evidence when writing or speaking to support conclusions drawn from the text.
	2. Determine central ideas or themes of a text and analyze their development; summarize the key supporting details and ideas.
	3. Analyze how and why individuals, events, and ideas develop and interact over the course of a text.
Craft and Structure	4. Interpret words and phrases as they are used in a text, including determining technical, connotative, and figurative meanings, and analyze how specific word choices shape meaning or tone.
	5. Analyze the structure of texts, including how specific sentences, paragraphs, and larger portions of the text (e.g., a section, chapter, scene, or stanza) relate to each other and the whole.
	6. Assess how point of view or purpose shapes the content and style of a text.
Integration of Knowledge and Ideas	7. Integrate and evaluate content presented in diverse media and formats, including visually and quantitatively, as well as in words.
	8. Delineate and evaluate the argument and specific claims in a text, including the validity of the reasoning as well as the relevance and sufficiency of the evidence.
	9. Analyze how two or more texts address similar themes or topics in order to build knowledge or to compare the approaches the authors take.
Range of Reading and Level of Text Complexity	10. Read and comprehend complex literary and informational texts independently and proficiently.

Note. From *Common Core State Standards for English Language Arts and Literacy in History/Social Studies, Science, and Technical Subjects* (p. 10), by the National Governors Association Center for Best Practices and the Council of Chief State School Officers, 2010, Washington, DC: Authors.

CHAPTER 1

Challenges and Opportunities in the Implementation of Common Core State Standards

Susan B. Neuman & Linda B. Gambrell

The Common Core State Standards (CCSS; National Governors Association Center for Best Practices & Council of Chief State School Officers [NGA Center & CCSSO], 2010) for English Language Arts represent a shared and consistent vision of what students should know and be able to do. These Standards are designed to foster higher achievement among U.S. students, allowing them to compete more successfully in our global society, and striving toward equitable educational opportunity for all of our students. They represent a high bar but one that we should reach for in the field of reading and literacy learning for students across the grade levels.

Certainly there will be challenges in their implementation. By 2014–2015, current state assessments will be replaced by one of two consortia—Smarter Balanced, or Partnership for Assessment of Readiness for College and Careers (PARCC)—that will include new methods of assessments with new expectations for proficiency and achievement levels. Curricula will be needed to address these new Standards because they reflect different theories of reading comprehension and differentiated instruction than past standards, as well as a different style and organizational structure, which will make them more challenging for schools to implement. At the same time, while these Standards demand more from teachers and far more from students, they are essential if we are to enable students to be successful in developing 21st-century skills.

Simply put, this means that we will need to understand these challenges and create opportunities for students to learn. In this chapter, we highlight a number of these challenges and provide suggestions for how we can turn these issues into professional development opportunities that may ultimately lead us to a richer and more thorough understanding of the reading process and higher quality instruction in reading.

Quality Reading Instruction in the Age of Common Core Standards, edited by Susan B. Neuman and Linda B. Gambrell. © 2013 by the International Reading Association.

Key Design Changes

Designers of the CCSS began their effort to create world-class standards by developing a working definition of what it means to be college or career ready. Their portrait included both important skills and dispositions: Students must demonstrate independence in learning; build strong content knowledge; and respond to the varying demands of audience, task, purpose, and discipline in their communication. They need to comprehend well, value evidence in their oral and written interpretation of text, and understand other perspectives and cultures. Most reading educators would strongly endorse this view.

Based on their definition, designers then "back-mapped" to the lower grades, identifying specific targets at various grade-level spans. For example, in the Reading Standards for Informational Text K–5, fifth-grade students are expected to "integrate information from several texts on the same topic in order to write or speak about the subject knowledgeably" (NGA Center & CCSSO, 2010, p. 14). Looking at this same standard in kindergarten, students are expected to "with prompting and support, identify basic similarities in and differences between two texts on the same topic (e.g., in illustrations, descriptions, or procedures)" (NGA Center & CCSSO, 2010, p. 13). Given that more than half of children in the United States will not have received the benefit of high-quality preschool, and that many states do not have mandatory kindergarten, or that many kindergartens are still only half-day (Barnett, Carolan, Fitzgerald, & Squires, 2011), one could argue that this Standard stretches all credulity for many children, particularly for low-income children. While it is important to support challenging goals for children, at the same time, the goals must be achievable.

Back-mapping has been seriously criticized as an approach to identifying targets because it often leads to developmentally inappropriate goals or unrealistic expectations (National Association for the Education of Young Children, 2003). Rather, as professionals, we need to carefully examine these Standards from the other direction, starting first at kindergarten to identify the requisite skills children will need to have to meet these Standards. School professionals and curriculum developers will need to "unpack" many of these Standards and create instructional opportunities with appropriate scaffolds in place to reach these targets.

Furthermore, these Standards will require a greater breadth of knowledge in literacy. Although they are divided by grade level, there is the assumption that teachers will understand the learning progressions of a skill. This term—*learning progression*—describes the path that children might follow as instruction helps them move from initial learning to more sophisticated understanding (Nichols, 2010). This means that teachers will need to understand the antecedent skills that are necessary for developing more complex skills. For example, it is impossible to teach problem-solving skills without the requisite knowledge of inquiry and comprehension. Similarly, teachers will need to know how to build upon important skills to support higher order thinking in all domains. This means that we will all have to become more proficient in understanding the full spectrum of skills and strategies in reading to promote career- and college-ready thinking among our students.

Challenging Text

In the past, the conventional wisdom was to gear the text to the student's current reading level. Teachers would strive to find a book that was on children's *instructional level,* assuming that if students could read about 95 out of 100 words, they could successfully use the context of the paragraph to gain its meaning (Durrell & Catterson, 1980). If the text proved too difficult to comprehend, teachers would find a slightly easier text, one that would include shorter sentences and less complex words, easing students over time as they became more successful into more difficult text. *Leveled text* (Fountas & Pinnell, 2006) was based on the same premise: teachers would select text based on students' current skill levels in efforts to help them gain proficiency and move up the reading ladder.

In the CCSS, the notion is that students should grapple with grade-level texts, with a specified definition of *text complexity* clearly identified in Reading Standard 10 (NGA Center & CCSSO, 2010, p. 10; see also Cunningham and Hiebert chapters, this volume, for more detail). Text complexity is measured across three factors:

1. A qualitative evaluation of the text (e.g., its levels of meaning, knowledge demands)
2. A quantitative evaluation (e.g., lexile levels or other readability measures)
3. The matching of reader to text and task (e.g., motivation, knowledge, purpose for reading)

Here, the view is that teaching children with more challenging text than before will stretch their capabilities and engage them to meet the demands of reading more difficult text.

We have been down this road before. Previous experiences suggest that we could run the risk of alienating students to the degree that they lose all motivation to read. No one likes to be placed in a position where they feel like a failure. Consequently, we must take the concept of "close reading" seriously. The CCSS assert that students must acquire the habits of reading independently and closely and undertake the attentive reading that is essential for deep understanding of text, which are essential to their future success. The term *close reading* also implies efforts on our part to help students pay close attention to the text and to provide evidence for their interpretations. For example, Neuman and Wright (in press) recently worked with a group of students who were having difficulty understanding a complex text. In this study, text was broken into paragraphs, and students and the teacher engaged in a think-aloud task. After each paragraph, students shared their understandings of what the text was about. They focused on what expert readers do, creating a working hypothesis about what the text was about, looking for evidence to confirm or disconfirm their developing understanding, modifying their hypothesis if necessary with additional information, and finally coming up with a coherent interpretation of text. Notice in this description that students were strongly guided to use the text as evidence for understanding. This is in contrast to relying on prior knowledge, or generalized procedures like comprehension strategies that are thought to be transferable across different texts. In this response, each text reading is a unique experience that requires close reading of the text and supporting evidence, weighing such things as the author's diction, grammar, and organization to make meaning from the text.

Informational Text

Probably one of the most profound changes involved with implementing the CCSS is the shift toward greater emphasis on informational text. Duke and her colleagues (Chapter 4, this volume; Duke & Bennett-Armistead, 2003) have written extensively about the paucity of informational texts in the elementary grades in particular. The focus on informational books is an important one because it signals that book reading builds knowledge through text (Marinak & Gambrell, 2009; Mazzoni & Gambrell, 1996). At the same time, we must be careful of the pendulum shifting too much in one direction over the other. Many storybooks, beloved by young and old alike, contain information that is highly memorable in ways that these expository texts could never convey (Malloy & Gambrell, 2013; Neuman & Roskos, 2012).

The CCSS emphasize the importance of engaging children with informational texts on an equal basis with literary texts in grades K–5; attention to literature then falls to 25% in the upper grades. This means that elementary teachers need to raise their comfort level for working with informational text. It also will require adjustments in the read-aloud strategy. For example, depending on the book and its features, teachers may chose not to read a book from beginning to end, but instead might select certain sections or pages for a close reading. Teachers working with preschool and kindergarten children often read only several pages at a time, recognizing that the density of information and the vocabulary load may call for a greater focus on discussion and interpretation (Malloy & Gambrell, 2011).

Studies have shown that informational (or expository) books tend to differ from traditional storybooks in the diversity of vocabulary they include (Price, Bradley, & Smith, 2012). Informational books will generally contain more technical words associated with a topic (e.g., *echo-location*), and will often include generic nouns that represent categories of objects and things (e.g., *puppies bite*). They will have certain types of visual and design features like graphs, scale diagrams, and glossaries, all of which are intentionally linked to convey meaning to readers. These features, therefore, will need to be taught more deliberately if we are to make the most of these types of texts. Given that children are likely to be less familiar with these texts—even when they come from homes where shared reading is a familiar routine (Yopp & Yopp, 2006)—it will be important to highlight these features during our read-aloud activities.

Disciplinary Literacy

For years, we have attempted to convince content area specialists that *every* teacher is a reading teacher, recognizing that content text places high demands on the reader, especially those who struggle in reading. Most anecdotal accounts suggest that we have been less successful than we would like in this endeavor—content area teachers still believe that their responsibility is to teach content, not reading per se. Consequently, reading instruction has been left to the reading teacher or the literacy coach, particularly at the middle and upper grades.

The past emphasis in these instructional contexts, then, had been to help students develop strategies that they could then apply to any content area text. Studies, for example, focused on text structures, and how these could be applied to science, social studies, and other disciplines (Armbruster, Anderson, & Osterag, 1987). However, recent studies suggest that these skills may not be all that transferable (Clark, Kirschner, & Sweller, 2012). Rather, different disciplines require specialized reading emphases in certain content domains such as history/social studies, science, and other technical subjects.

This means that the content Standards will need to be shared with subject-matter specialists, not necessarily to ensure that all teachers are reading teachers but to enable all teachers to provide instruction that will enhance students' knowledge of the domain. There is the recognition that the CCSS are actually disciplinary standards, and that to meet these benchmarks of content, students will need to understand the unique uses of literacy required by the disciplines.

This will represent a challenge for all educators. It will require us to engage more fully with disciplinary specialists, and to determine collectively how their approaches to disciplines may be translated into instruction for secondary students. In a recent study, Shanahan and Shanahan (2008) reported the benefits of having conversations among disciplinary experts, literacy experts, high school teachers, and teacher educators. Instead of trying to convince disciplinary teachers of the value of general reading strategies developed by reading experts, they formulated new strategies that would directly and explicitly address the specific and highly specialized disciplinary reading demands of chemistry, history, and mathematics. Such a strategy benefits all constituencies, especially the students as learners.

The Integration of Knowledge and Ideas

As adult readers, we are likely to read multiple accounts of important events that especially interest us. Each account helps to build our knowledge in ways that allow us to broaden and deepen our understanding of the world. Given its focus on developing knowledge through text, the CCSS recognize that the interpretations of multiple texts throughout all the grade levels are integral to this process. Children will need to be able to delineate and evaluate specific claims in a text, including its veracity, as well as the relevance and sufficiency of its evidence.

From the beginning, children are expected to review arguments in texts and to create intertextual linkages between them. For example, they will be asked to analyze how two or more texts that address similar themes or topics compare and contrast to one another. Furthermore, they will be expected to develop some understanding of genre features in the course of making these comparisons. Even in the early grades, students are expected to understand the relationship between illustrations and the story, why certain illustrations are depicted, and in what moment they are depicted.

There are a number of important ways in which we can enhance the likelihood that our students will succeed with such challenging tasks.

First, underlying these Standards is the assumption that students will need to acquire story grammar (Stein & Glenn, 1979), an understanding of the essential features of a story, early on. It will facilitate their ability to compare and contrast the advances and experiences of characters if they can easily identify the settings and the characters of a story, sets of events, and the resolution of a well-structured story. In addition, it will be critically important for teachers to identify ideal models of stories. For example, some text illustrations may not enhance story comprehension or contribute to what is conveyed by the words in a story. Beck and her colleagues many years ago found that there is sometimes a mismatch between the words on the page and the context of the illustrations (Beck, Omanson, & McKeown, 1982). Third, as students begin to compare and contrast across genres, it will be important to clearly identify genre features as critical markers in interpreting text. It is clear, therefore, that teachers will have to consider building knowledge of genre and across genres early on. Approximately 10% of the Standards mention multiple texts in particular.

To support these goals, teachers will need to rely on text sets—collections of books that focus on a particular concept or a topic. For example, a recent study used text sets to engage children in learning about the life sciences as a way of integrating reading and science instruction (Neuman & Wright, in press). The intention was to spend two weeks on the topic, focusing on the content-rich vocabulary and the big ideas associated with the topic of living things.

Text sets are unified by the topic they explore (Neuman & Roskos, 2012). At the same time, they are differentiated by their genre and their format. The topic of flight, for instance, can be a focal point for a collection of books that could include a biography of the Wright brothers as well as an informational book on the basics of aerodynamics of flight. Text sets need to be coherent—narrowly focused on a set of key ideas to ensure that children will have repeated opportunities to hear and develop an understanding of a common set of words and concepts throughout the readings (see examples in Figure 1.1).

Text sets are organized to engage children with increasingly complex text and to learn some of the key genre features of each type of book. This is accomplished through scaffolding children's experiences with text, starting with more familiar genres before introducing the less familiar genre. Because we work with young children, we often start with a predictable book on a topic, which typically has a memorable rhyming or repetitive word pattern that enables children to anticipate words, phrases, and events in the story. We then move toward introducing storybooks, and focus on the story grammar features of the book. We can then compare

Figure 1.1. An Example of a Text Set

Topic: Weather

Concepts to Teach
- Weather conditions are constantly changing.
- There are weather patterns associated with each season.
- Various types of weather conditions are associated with temperature, precipitation, and wind conditions.
- There are tools to measure temperature, precipitation, and wind speed.
- Meteorologists use weather patterns to forecast weather.

Text Set

• Predictable
Cotton, C., & Steptoe, J. (2008). *Rain play.* New York: Henry Holt.
A group of children are playing in the park when it starts to rain. They stay to enjoy some rainy-day fun.

• Fiction
Koscielniak, B. (1995). *Geoffrey Groundhog predicts the weather.* New York: Houghton Mifflin.
When Geoffrey oversleeps on Groundhog Day and misses his forecast, nobody in town knows what type of weather to expect.

• Informational (Narrative)
Singer, M. (2000). *On the same day in March: A tour of the world's weather.* New York: HarperCollins.
This book explores the weather on a single day in locations around the world.

• Informational (Expository)
Weather Watchers series
This series of simple informational texts published by Looking Glass Library includes *It's a Thunderstorm* (Higgins & Ward, 2010) and *It's Hailing* (Higgins & Ward, 2010). Each book includes accurate information about weather patterns, including what they are like and how they form. Books have engaging illustrations and fun facts.

• Informational (Expository)
Gibbons, G. (1992). *Weather words and what they mean.* New York: Holiday House.
Using engaging illustrations, this text provides information about key terms related to weather, including *temperature, air pressure, moisture,* and *wind.*

---

and contrast across these two types of books. Following a number of examples of storybooks, we then move toward informational books. We find that informational book reading at this point becomes deeper and more meaningful because children now have at least a beginning network of words and concepts from which to draw. Combining genres in text sets gives children a rich opportunity to engage in learning the vocabulary, concepts, and information in many different contexts, building new knowledge about the similarities and differences between texts on the same topic. A recent study using this scaffolding procedure reported striking gains in children's vocabulary, concepts, and knowledge about the topic (Neuman & Wright, in press). In addition, the scaffolding of text enabled children to learn the genre features of informational text significantly better than children in the control group.

In the CCSS, students are also expected to write about the ideas learned from text. Traditionally in elementary school years, teachers have placed greater emphasis on personal writing and opinion pieces (Stotsky, 1995). However, the Standards shift from children writing stories to writing about what they learn from text. This means that writing becomes more closely integrated with reading comprehension by helping to consolidate children's views and understandings. It will also place greater emphasis on synthesizing information in one's own words, and in using the text to make an argument or opinion.

Technology

We have often assumed that technology will have a prominent place in education. Regardless of the technology (e.g., radio, television, computers), those who are advocates have sometimes claimed a "new literacy" (Compaine, 1983); on the other hand, Luddites have forecasted the "death of print" (McLuhan, 1962). Neither projection has rung true. In fact, as Cuban (1993) reported in his influential book, there has been more talk than action. Even though the technologies exist, it has hardly revolutionized teaching or learning.

As most teachers would attest, the emphasis on technology has been minimal in the past standards. Rather, it was assumed that the skills and strategies children developed through traditional print could be applied to other contexts or technologies. In other words, technology was seen merely as the delivery mechanism without any inherent benefits.

This time it may be different. Today, the sheer quantity of mediated information that is available has increased by an order of magnitude from about 100 mediated words per minute in 1960 to about 1,000 words per minute in 2007 (W.R. Neuman, 2010), available through the Internet at any time in any place where a Web connection is available. As Leu and Kinzer (2000) have argued, there are new affordances created by this technology that we have only begun to imagine. In this new technological world, students will need to be their own reference librarian: they will need to know how to search, read, evaluate, and use information drawn from the Internet. And here, the digital divide that persists virulently in low-income communities is likely to place many of our poor students at a disadvantage (Neuman & Celano, 2012). For example, Neuman and Celano (2012) found only three computers available after school in public areas for every 100 students in these low-income communities. Internet throughout these areas in homes was sporadic, with little opportunity for students to complete their homework assignments other than the library, which closed at 6:00 P.M.

We must also recognize that many students lack the reading skills to use these online resources effectively. In the Neuman and Celano (2012) study, for example, one teacher asked the students to do a Google search of an African American hero. However, what had been intuitive for the teacher was not intuitive for the students, who struggled with the assignment and had difficulty even with the rudimentary skills we would assume to be natural. Therefore, we need to step back and consider the skills and strategies children will need to use the technology for information gathering. Some students, for example, still struggle with word processing and will need other technological supports in their writing.

Consequently, these new literacies need to build on more foundational literacy skills. We must also not take for granted that students will know how to use these new tools wisely. Considering the wide range of experiences that students are likely to have outside of school, we must prepare them more deliberately in school to take advantage of these astonishing new resources.

Conclusions

The challenging new Common Core Standards represent the culmination of an extended, broad-based reform effort to identify the skills students need to become career and college ready. Surely there will be bumps along the road. Successful implementation of the CCSS will require a good deal of new teacher preparation and professional development, as well as quality materials to support these new instructional practices. However, we believe it is an exciting time for the field of reading. These new Standards support the development of content knowledge and learning through text. They recognize that children need to read increasingly complex text and be able to read closely, looking for evidence to support their contentions and understandings. In our knowledge-based economy, the CCSS convey that students will need to adapt their ability to communicate in relation to audience, task, purpose, and the particular disciplines they address. Perhaps for the first time, we have standards that embrace technology, recognizing that digital media can support learning in ways that we've never considered before. Rather than the "push" of previous technologies, these new digital technologies focus on "pull"—creating platforms that help people to mobilize appropriate resources when the need arises. If we do our job well, it will encourage children to develop self-learning techniques that will support their independence as readers and as lifelong learners.

TRY THIS!

- Using Figure 1.1 as a guide, come up with your own topic for a text set you can use in your classroom. Then, come up with at least four items for concepts to teach. For each category of the text set, list at least one example of an appropriate book.

- Again, use Figure 1.1 as a guide. Now, brainstorm and come up with at least 20 topics for possible text sets. List the pros and cons of each. Once complete, you should have at least 10–15 possible topics for text-set lessons. Continue the steps in the first "Try This!" idea for one or two of your ideas.

DISCUSSION QUESTIONS

1. Neuman and Gambrell assert that "while it is important to support challenging goals for children, at the same time, the goals must be achievable." Discuss how the CCSS can be a double-edged sword; that is, on the one hand, pushing students to read complex texts is good, but on the other, if these texts are inaccessible to students, the benefits are lost.

2. Discuss how technology can assist students in reading more complex texts as advocated by the CCSS.

REFERENCES

Armbruster, B.B., Anderson, T.H., & Osterag, J. (1987). Does text structure/summarization instruction facilitate learning from expository text? *Reading Research Quarterly, 22*(3), 331–346. doi:10.2307/747972

Barnett, W.S., Carolan, M.E., Fitzgerald, J., & Squires, J.H. (2011). *The state of preschool 2011.* New Brunswick, NJ: National Institute of Early Education Research.

Beck, I.L., Omanson, R.C., & McKeown, M.G. (1982). An instructional redesign of reading lessons: Effects on comprehension. *Reading Research Quarterly, 17*(4), 462–481. doi:10.2307/747566

Clark, R.E., Kirschner, P.A., & Sweller, J. (2012). Putting students on the path to learning: The case for fully guided instruction. *American Educator, 36*(1), 6–11.

Compaine, B.M. (1983). The new literacy. *Daedalus, 112*(1), 129–142.

Cuban, L. (1993). *How teachers taught: Constancy and change in American classrooms, 1890–1990.* New York: Teachers College Press.

Duke, N.K., & Bennett-Armistead, V.S. (2003). *Reading & writing informational text in the primary grades: Research-based practices.* New York: Scholastic.

Durrell, D.D., & Catterson, J.H. (1980). *Durrell analysis of reading difficulty* (3rd ed.). New York: Psychological Corporation.

Fountas, I.C., & Pinnell, G.S. (2006). *Leveled books, K–8: Matching texts to readers for effective teaching.* Portsmouth, NH: Heinemann.

Leu, D.J., & Kinzer, C.K. (2000). The convergence of literacy instruction with networked technologies for information and communication. *Reading Research Quarterly, 35*(1), 108–127. doi:10.1598/RRQ.35.1.8

Malloy, J.A., & Gambrell, L.B. (2011). The contribution of discussion to reading comprehension and critical thinking. In A. McGill-Franzen & R. Allington (Eds.), *Handbook of reading disability research* (pp. 253–262). New York: Routledge.

Malloy, J.A., & Gambrell, L.B. (2013). Reading standards for literature. In L.M. Morrow, K.K. Wixson, & T. Shanahan (Eds.), *Teaching with the Common Core Standards for English Language Arts, grades 3–5* (pp. 22–49). New York: Guilford.

Marinak, B., & Gambrell, L.B. (2009). Ways to teach about informational text. *Social Studies and the Young Learner, 22*(1), 19–22.

Mazzoni, S.A., & Gambrell, L.B. (1996). Text talk: Using discussion to promote comprehension of informational text. In L.B. Gambrell & J.F. Almasi (Eds.), *Lively discussions! Fostering engaged reading* (pp. 134–148). Newark, DE: International Reading Association.

McLuhan, M. (1962). *The Gutenberg galaxy.* Toronto, ON, Canada: University of Toronto Press.

National Association for the Education of Young Children. (2003). *Early childhood curriculum, assessment, and program evaluation* (position statement). Washington, DC: Author.

National Governors Association Center for Best Practices & Council of Chief State School Officers. (2010). *Common Core State Standards for English language arts and literacy in history/social studies, science, and technical subjects.* Washington, DC: Authors. Retrieved from www.core standards.org/assets/CCSSI_ELA%20 Standards.pdf

Neuman, S.B., & Celano, D.C. (2012). *Giving our children a fighting chance: Poverty, literacy, and the development of information capital.* New York: Teachers College Press.

Neuman, S.B., & Roskos, K. (2012). Helping children become more knowledgeable through text. *The Reading Teacher, 66*(3), 207–210.

Neuman, S.B. & Wright, T.S. (in press). *All about words: Integrating vocabulary in the Commom Core classroom, preK–grade 2.* New York: Teachers College Press.

Neuman, W.R. (Ed.). (2010). *Media, technology, and society: Theories of media evolution.* Ann Arbor: University of Michigan Press.

Nichols, P.D. (2010). What is a learning progression? *Test, Measurement & Research Services, 12,* 1–2.

Price, L.H., Bradley, B.A., & Smith, J.M. (2012). A comparison of preschool teachers' talk during storybook and information book read-alouds. *Early Childhood Research Quarterly, 27*(3), 426–440. doi:10.1016/j.ecresq.2012.02.003

Shanahan, T., & Shanahan, C. (2008). Teaching disciplinary literacy to adolescents: Rethinking content-area literacy. *Harvard Educational Review, 78*(1), 40–59.

Stein, N.L., & Glenn, C.G. (1979). An analysis of story comprehension in elementary school children. In Freedle, R.O. (Ed.), *New directions in discourse processing* (Vol. 2, pp. 53–120). Norwood, NJ: Ablex.

Stotsky, S. (1995). The uses and limitations of personal or personalized writing in writing theory, research, and instruction. *Reading Research Quarterly, 30*(4), 758–776. doi:10.2307/748197

Yopp, R.H., & Yopp, H.K. (2006). Informational texts as read-alouds at school and home. *Journal of Literacy Research, 38*(1), 37–51. doi:10.1207/s15548430jlr3801_2

CHAPTER 2

Linking Early Literacy Research and the Common Core State Standards

Dorothy S. Strickland

I n recent years, the literacy education of young children has received increased attention, both in the public policy arena and in the classroom. This can be attributed to a large body of research evidence showing the links between successful achievement in early literacy and later school success. This chapter connects an emergent and integrated view of early language and literacy development with the key considerations for curriculum offered by the Common Core State Standards (CCSS; National Governors Association Center for Best Practices & Council of Chief State School Officers [NGA Center & CCSSO], 2010). Connections will also be made to several current and ongoing early learning initiatives. Implications for policy, practice, and research will be offered throughout. The chapter concludes with some observations about the need for high-quality professional development for *all* of those involved in the education of young children, so that existing and future research findings might be shared and implemented in ways that better support learning and teaching.

Examining Connections Between Early Literacy Research and the CCSS

Early childhood education has a long and rich history of research in the area of early literacy learning and teaching, and both policy and practice have evolved considerably due to that research. Until the late 1980s, *reading readiness* was the approach used by most early literacy educators. Lapp and Flood (1978) define reading readiness as the necessary level of preparation children should attain before beginning formal reading instruction, which typically began in first grade. Teale and Yokota (2000) suggest that reading readiness was pursued along two different paths by

Quality Reading Instruction in the Age of Common Core Standards, edited by Susan B. Neuman and Linda B. Gambrell. © 2013 by the International Reading Association.

educators. Educators who were convinced that readiness was essentially a result of maturation or "neural ripeness" went down one path, whereas those who believed appropriate experiences created readiness or helped to accelerate it went down the other path. Extreme views on either side might result in some programs that involved little or no intentionally planned literacy education and others that devoted a considerable amount of time addressing the predictors in highly regimented ways. Alphabet knowledge, word recognition, vocabulary knowledge, and visual discrimination were cited as possible predictors of reading readiness.

More recently, scholars have examined reading and writing (literacy) development in the everyday lives of children from their earliest years (Teale & Yokota, 2000). The concept of early literacy suggests that children begin to acquire knowledge about oral and written language long before starting school. Some basic tenets of early literacy include (a) literacy learning starts early and persists throughout life; (b) oral language is the foundation for literacy development; (c) the development of oral language and literacy is interrelated and interdependent; and (d) children's experiences with the world and with books and print greatly influence their ability to comprehend what they read (Strickland & Riley-Ayers, 2006).

While on the surface, reading readiness and early literacy approaches appear to be highly disparate, the key distinction between the two approaches may not lie in what children should know and be able to do, but in how learning occurs and is best taught. For example, *Developing Early Literacy: The Report of the National Early Literacy Panel* (National Institute for Literacy, 2008) confirmed that alphabet knowledge, phonological awareness, oral language, and writing/name writing demonstrated by 4- and 5-year-old children are, in fact, among the best predictors of later success in literacy achievement. In traditional readiness programs, prescribed skills in these areas are directly taught to get children "ready" to read. However, while these competencies are also included among the foundational skills listed in the CCSS (NGA Center & CCSSO, 2010, pp. 15–17), the CCSS are aligned with recent early literacy research in that they promote the *integration* of these skills across the language arts and content areas, with an emphasis on helping children "think with" and "respond to" a variety of types of texts.

The key design considerations offered in the CCSS (NGA Center & CCSSO, 2010, p. 4) provide clarity about how these standards should be implemented. No doubt, the effectiveness of standards-based instruction will depend on how well early childhood educators understand what the standards are, what they are not, and how that knowledge best informs the learning opportunities offered to young children. The CCSS design considerations suggest the following for those planning early literacy curricula:

1. An integrated model of literacy
2. A cumulative model of expectations
3. Shared responsibility for students' literacy development
4. Research and media skills blended into the standards as a whole
5. Greater use of on-grade-level texts

Each of these design considerations will be discussed in connection with early literacy instruction and the CCSS, followed by recommendations for supportive policy and practice and research possibilities.

An Integrated Model of Literacy

The language arts—listening, speaking, reading, and writing—should be integrated with each other and across the curriculum. Students should be asked to read or listen to texts read aloud and respond critically through discussion and in writing. Response may take the form of written or oral explanation and argument. Emphasis should be placed on critical thinking, problem solving, and collaboration with peers.

Supportive policy and practice would encourage the development of a curriculum that includes a series of inquiry-based, experiential learning endeavors that focus on both the key content goals relevant to what students are expected to learn or know at the end of a unit and the key language arts and literacy goals and expectations based on the CCSS. For example, an investigation of "how plants grow" would involve thoughtful pre-planning by teachers regarding the content information children would be expected to acquire as a result of the project. Hands-on activities that involve planting seedlings and documenting their growth might be involved. At the same time, language arts activities—such as read-alouds from books about how plants grow, shared/interactive reading and writing activities, and collaborative projects that include discussions focused on the topic—would be designed to address both the content and the literacy standards in a coherent and meaningful way (Strickland, 2012).

Research possibilities include an examination of the various ways in which project- and inquiry-based instruction are conducted and the extent to which they promote content knowledge, foundational skills, and higher order thinking skills as described in the CCSS.

A Cumulative Model of Expectations

Instruction should address grade-specific standards in tandem with the broader goals of eventual college and career readiness. This concept, sometimes referred to as *spiraling,* involves similar standards expressed with increasing complexity from grade to grade.

Supportive policy and practice stress the importance of linking developmentally appropriate practice to grade-level standards. For example, the first College and Career Readiness (CCR) Anchor Standard for Reading listed under the heading of Key Ideas and Details states, "Read closely to determine what the text says explicitly and to make logical inferences from it; cite specific textual evidence when writing or speaking to support conclusions drawn from the text" (NGA Center & CCSSO, 2010, p. 10). At first glance, that standard may appear to be far over the heads of kindergarten and primary-grade children. However, a second look at the standard indicates that it actually does reflect the type of teacher–student interaction that is very much within the scope of "teaching for thinking" fostered by effective teachers during the early learning years. When appropriate, such teachers will pause strategically at key points during a read-aloud selection and ask, "What do you think will happen next?"; after accepting responses from one or more students, they will follow up with a "What made you think so?" prompt (if necessary) to elicit a rationale that is based on the text—that is, a response that is grounded in what the children actually heard during the read-aloud or saw in the pictures. Given such opportunities, it becomes quite obvious that even very young children can be encouraged to support their responses with evidence from the text. Moreover, they are also provided with opportunities to orally "explain" their thoughts and observations—another important element of the integration of the language arts.

Research possibilities include an examination of classroom-based, developmentally appropriate practices that link to children's attainment of and ability to demonstrate critical-thinking and problem-solving, and collaboration skills with others in ways that indicate that the skills are not only learned, but also sustained and applied appropriately in new contexts.

Shared Responsibility for Students' Literacy Development

During the early years, teachers generally work in self-contained classrooms in which they are solely responsible for the instruction of a particular group of students. Collaborative planning among groups of teachers at all levels is increasingly viewed as a supportive process.

Teachers benefit from sharing ideas for instruction, the selection and use of materials, and the organization and management of the school day.

Supportive policy and practice would include the development of a cohesive curriculum that spans prekindergarten through grade 3 (also discussed later in this chapter as a key current initiative). For example, teachers would collaborate across grade levels to examine the CCSS in conjunction with their existing standards and guidelines for instruction and assessment.

Research possibilities include an examination of various models of long-term, embedded professional development that bring together teachers at the same age or grade levels and teachers at contiguous levels on a regular basis to share, plan, and reflect on curriculum and practice that support the CCSS during the early learning years.

Research and Media Skills Blended Into the Standards as a Whole

Critical thinking with texts in all forms of media and technology is emphasized in the CCSS. Forms may be combined for a specific goal or purpose. A balance of literary and informational texts is desirable.

Supportive policy and practice would include the development of a long-term plan for the expansion of the types of texts and media to which young children are regularly exposed in the classroom. Emphasis would be placed on the acquisition of more informational texts related to planned topics of inquiry and the greater inclusion of technology to support meaningful experiences and exposure to content under study along with the application of language arts and literacy strategies. Particular emphasis would be placed on fostering teachers' abilities to select and use a variety of media, as well as their abilities to plan for their use in ways that are integrated into the overall organization of the day.

Research possibilities include an examination of various types of texts that potentially can be used for instruction, including a variety of media and text types, particularly for the uses described previously. This includes their purposeful and intentional use for the exposure to relevant content as well as the development of higher order thinking skills.

Greater Use of On-Grade-Level Texts

During the early years, emphasis is placed on supporting students' abilities to become proficient in reading complex texts independently and in a variety of content areas. Effective instruction typically includes the use of developmentally appropriate complex texts for the purposes of reading aloud to students; using closely guided or interactive instruction to build background knowledge, vocabulary, and concepts; and modeling how good readers approach difficult texts. Texts representing a range of complexity should also be available for independent reading and response.

Supportive policy and practice would involve providing classrooms with a variety of types and levels of texts. Teachers would be supported in their abilities to plan and implement instruction that includes (a) exposure to texts that are above students' reading levels but within their listening comprehension levels; (b) guided, small-group reading instruction that is differentiated according to students' reading levels; and (c) many opportunities for independent reading at students' individual reading levels. The key is to help teachers plan instruction so that students are exposed to rich vocabulary and concepts, while at the same time progressing according to their individual abilities, with increasingly greater fluency and comprehension.

Research possibilities include an investigation of how teachers are best helped to gain competence in the selection and use of various types and levels of texts for selected purposes. The purposes may be linked to specific standards or adjusted to the specific needs of children to differentiate instruction effectively.

Early Learning Initiatives With Links to the CCSS: Opportunities and Challenges

Upon examination, the connections between an integrated concept of early language and literacy development and the key considerations for curriculum offered by the CCSS become increasingly clear. However, an examination of how those links might be applied in the real world of emerging policies and practices deserves further attention. The following section provides brief descriptions of several current and ongoing education initiatives that are directly connected to early learning and the influence of the CCSS. Possible implications for future policy, practice, and research will be offered, with a focus on opportunities for professional development.

A Cohesive Early Learning Continuum From Preschool Through Grade 3

Educators, policymakers, and the general public have become increasingly aware of the importance of the early years of schooling. Support for the early learning years is viewed as a strategic investment in the future of children, particularly those considered to be at risk. Even in the face of budget crises, many states have maintained or even increased funding for prekindergarten education, in particular. The hope, of course, is to mitigate serious learning gaps that are often evidenced by grade 3 and that tend to persist throughout the later grades.

It is not surprising, however, that as interest in early learning has expanded, issues of quality and sustainability have begun to surface. It has become increasingly clear that simply providing access to prekindergarten was not enough. To replicate the gains demonstrated by model programs, prekindergarten programs must be of high quality. Indeed, even early gains may dissipate unless preschool is followed by consecutive years of quality schooling in the early years (Haynes, 2008).

Supportive policy and practice that builds on this initiative would include greater coordination and articulation among educators at all levels across prekindergarten to grade 3, increased coordination with education and family support agencies throughout the state and community systems, and increased support and coordination with the families involved.

Research possibilities include studies of how states and districts are implementing these goals. Issues of time and intensity of professional development should be explored, and teachers' understanding of the standards that relate to the level at which they teach as well as the levels that come before and after should be evaluated. Special attention might be given to the notion of spiraling (as described earlier in this chapter) to determine how teachers are interpreting what a standard might "look like" instructionally at different grade levels and within the same grade level in terms of differentiated instruction.

Early Childhood Assessments

The number of early childhood programs offered to our nation's young children has increased dramatically in the past several decades. Many of these programs were motivated by the abundance of research evidence linking long-term student achievement to high-quality early childhood education (Barnett, 1998). As the programs have increased, so has the need for measures aimed at accountability, especially those programs receiving public funds. School systems and government agencies are asked to set goals, establish standards, track progress, analyze strengths and weaknesses in programs, and report on their achievements, with consequences for unmet goals (National Research Council, 2008). Needless to say, the development of language and literacy is invariably included as a key component of these assessments.

A relatively new and important outcome of the attention given to early childhood assessment has been a growing interest in assessing children as they enter kindergarten, known as Kindergarten Early Assessment (KEA). The hope is to identify and meet the needs of children entering kindergarten to influence their development throughout the later grades and to assist, where needed, in planning for prevention and intervention. Snow (2011) reported that nearly half of the states had already instituted some form of kindergarten entry or readiness assessment by 2011.

Supportive policy and practice that builds on this initiative would include a system of long-term professional development that focuses on the need for prekindergarten and kindergarten teachers to learn and exchange ideas about the collection and use of assessment data. Special emphasis would be placed on a shared understanding of how the learning environment can support or restrict children's development and how this is linked to the early learning standards that guide teachers' efforts. Based on the work of the National Early Childhood Accountability Task Force, Schultz (2008) outlines a series of helpful suggestions for developing a comprehensive assessment system for prekindergarten through grade 3, including a call for states to take steps to align standards, curricula, and assessments; build the capacity to share data; and support the study and use of assessment information across these grade levels (p. 10).

Research possibilities include an examination of what should be measured, how it should be measured, and what types of assessments or combinations of assessment types should be used. The development of research-based models of professional development that serve both new and experienced teachers is needed.

Reading by Grade 3

Many in the field of early literacy have acknowledged the importance of *reading to learn*, even in the earliest years, as students are read to from informational books and encouraged to discuss ideas and information about topics of interest and importance to them. Likewise, the CCSS encourage the integration of content with language and literacy from the earliest years. The need for children to gain sufficient competency in reading during the primary grades in order to comprehend a variety of types of texts for a variety of purposes throughout the middle grades and beyond is well established among educators and confirmed by the research.

A recent study on this topic by Hernandez (2011) serves as a reminder that the literacy achievement gap starts early and persists throughout the grades. Key findings of the study include the following: (a) one in six children who are not reading proficiently in third grade do not graduate from high school on time, a rate four times greater than that for proficient readers; (b) the rates are highest for the low, below-basic readers; (c) 23% of these children drop out or fail to finish high school on time, compared with 9% of children with basic reading skills and 4% of proficient readers; and (d) graduation rates for black and Hispanic students who are not proficient readers by third grade lag far behind those for white students with the same reading skills.

Supportive policy and practice that builds on this initiative would include greater availability of high-quality prekindergarten programs; greater attention to the alignment of curriculum, standards, and instruction across prekindergarten through grade 3; higher standards for early childhood teachers and improved professional development; and improved school–family partnerships. A clear focus of the professional development would involve promoting teacher awareness and recognition that reading comprehension largely depends on the background knowledge a reader brings to the text to make sense of it. Indeed, even the decoding of print involves going beyond sound and symbol relationships to the use of contextual clues involving semantics and syntax. This is particularly important in situations where well-meaning teachers, who work with children considered to be at risk, may mistakenly focus on isolated skills alone in the hope that comprehension will automatically follow.

Research possibilities include the development of models of early literacy instruction that focus on broadening the background knowledge of children along with their literacy skills. This is exceedingly important in situations where children may lack the breadth and depth of background experiences generally expected of most children their age.

Technology and Early Education

It has already been noted that the CCSS emphasize critical thinking with texts in all forms of media and technology. The use of technology as a tool for learning and teaching and the media habits of young children have become growing sources of interest among educators, researchers, and those in the media industry. A study by the Joan Ganz Cooney Center at the Sesame Street Workshop indicates that today's young children have more access to all kinds of digital media and are spending more time during the day with them than ever before (Gutnick, Robb, Takeuchi, & Kotler, 2011). Additional findings include the following: (a) television continues to exert a strong hold over young children, who spend more time with this medium than any other; (b) access to newer digital technologies is largely dependent on family income; (c) lower income Hispanic and African American children consume far more media than their middle class and white counterparts; (d) children appear to shift their digital media habits around age 8 as their awareness of the wide world of media grows; (e) mobile media appears to be the growing choice of young children as they prefer to use their media on the go (p. 5).

Implications and cautions about the use of technology in early childhood education settings were addressed in a joint position statement by the National Association for the Education of Young Children and the Fred Rogers Center for Early Learning and Children's Media (2012). The report contains several key messages to early childhood teachers: (a) when used intentionally and appropriately, technology is an effective tool to support learning and development; (b) it is important to limit children's use of technology and media; and (c) teachers must ensure equal access to technology and model good digital citizenship (Parikh, 2012).

Supportive policy and practice that builds on this initiative should include a commitment to intensive, ongoing professional development that provides teachers with the information and resources they need to be able to select appropriate technology and integrate its use into the curriculum. The selection of technology for use with infants and toddlers should receive special attention.

Research possibilities include investigations of how educators might be helped to better understand how young children use and learn with technology and identify short- and long-term effects. Also, there is a need to help teachers better plan for and integrate technology into classroom routines in ways that serve curriculum and instruction.

Educator Evaluation

Throughout the United States, numerous efforts are underway to improve educator evaluation systems at the state and local levels. Much of that effort has focused on teachers and with good reason. Research indicates a teacher's contribution to student learning matters more than any other single factor, including class size, school size, and the quality of after-school programs (Rivkin, Hashek, & Kain, 2005). Obviously, the ultimate goal of educator evaluation, whether it focuses on teachers or school leaders, is to improve teaching and learning for children. In public school systems, all teachers in the early learning continuum, from prekindergarten through grade 3, are subject to an evaluation system, and that process is inevitably linked to both standards and assessment. Some have suggested that today's early education system is weakened by discrepancies between standards and measurement tools used for

K–12 teachers and those that are used for professionals in child care and prekindergarten programs. The use of the same observation tools across prekindergarten and K–12 settings would help to bridge this gap (Guernsey & Ochshorn, 2011).

Virtually all models used for measuring teacher effectiveness include many of the teacher competencies discussed earlier in this chapter. For example, a teacher's knowledge and application of standards-based practice will, no doubt, be subject to the scrutiny of evaluators. The use of developmentally appropriate instructional practices and assessment procedures will also be examined. According to Goe (2011), three major areas of teacher effectiveness are generally covered:

1. Evidence of growth in student learning and competency. This may include the kinds of classroom-based measures discussed earlier in this chapter.
2. Evidence of instructional quality. This includes classroom observations, an examination of lesson plans, and evidence of the documentation of student learning, such as portfolios.
3. Evidence of professional responsibility. This may include reports by administrators and supervisors as well as parent surveys.

Supportive policy and practice that builds on this initiative would involve a deliberate attempt to provide an environment in which teachers and administrators view the evaluation process as one that is fair and thoughtfully designed with the ultimate goal to improve the quality of teaching and learning. This includes the use of evaluation information to plan ongoing professional development that supports teachers' abilities and needs and the improvement of the evaluation competencies of those who observe and assess various aspects of teacher practice.

Research possibilities include pilot projects that involve teachers, administrators, and supervisors in an examination of existing practices and the development or the adoption of new models of educator effectiveness that fit their needs. Special emphasis should be given to examinations of the validity and reliability of existing teacher observation tools in a variety of settings with children of various backgrounds.

Summary and Implications

Upon reflection, it is clear that all of the elements discussed in this chapter are linked with each other and with the CCSS. Planning a cohesive early learning continuum from preschool through grade 3, using corresponding assessments that help to inform that process, and dedicating appropriate attention to fostering high-quality learning and teaching will *all* be essential to the mix. Research that looks not only at outcomes but also to the processes that led to those outcomes is required. Throughout the literature, *quality* appears to be the operative word. Research that identifies valid indicators of high-quality early literacy education while simultaneously assisting educators and policymakers to recognize and support those indicators will be critical.

TRY THIS!

- Before reading Gail Gibbons's *Fire! Fire!* to students, bring in a smoke detector. Press the test button to make the detector sound its alarm. Then, ask students what the sound means. After listing their suggestions on a whiteboard or chalkboard, read *Fire! Fire!* Finally, have students check their predictions of what happens when a smoke detector's alarm sounds against details from the text.

- In contemplation of reading Claire Liewellyn's *Earthworms*, have students go outside to search for earthworms by digging up soil and placing soil and earthworms in a plastic container. Then, once back in the classroom, ask the students questions about their newly found earthworms that require students to use various text features (e.g., heading, table of contents, glossary, index). For example, you could ask them, "Where is the earthworm's mouth?" To get the answer, students should open the book's index and turn to the page where the information is found.

DISCUSSION QUESTIONS

1. Strickland lists five CCSS design considerations for the curriculum. What are the five considerations, and how do they impact teachers' classrooms?

2. Strickland discusses the components of a cohesive early learning continuum for preschool through third grade. How are these components linked to CCSS?

3. Hernandez's (2011) report *Double Jeopardy* reminds us that literacy achievement begins early in students' academic careers and extends at least through high school. Given this fact, how do the CCSS attempt to address literacy achievement in all grades?

REFERENCES

Barnett, W.S. (1998). Long-term effects on cognitive development and school success. In W.S. Barnett & S.S. Boocock (Eds.), *Early care and education for children in poverty: Promise, programs, and long-term results* (pp. 11–44). Albany: State University of New York Press.

Goe, L. (2011, March). *Evaluating teacher and principal effectiveness*. Paper presented at the Legislative Conference, Council of Chief State School Officers Legislative Conference, Washington, DC.

Guernsey, L., & Ochshorn, S. (2011). *Watching teachers work: Using observation tools to promote effective teaching in the early years and early grades* (Policy paper). Washington, DC: The New America Foundation.

Gutnick, A.L., Robb, M., Takeuchi, L., & Kotler, J. (2011). *Always connected: The new digital media habits of children*. New York: The Joan Ganz Cooney Center Sesame Workshop.

Haynes, M. (2008, June). Building state early learning systems: Lessons and results from NASBE's Early Childhood Education Network. *The State Education Standard*, 13–16.

Hernandez, D.J. (2011). *Double jeopardy: How third-grade reading skills and poverty influence high school graduation*. Baltimore: Annie E. Casey Foundation.

Lapp, D., & Flood, J. (1978). *Teaching reading to every child*. New York: Macmillan.

National Association for the Education of Young Children & Fred Rogers Center for Early Learning and Children's Media. (2012). *Technology and interactive media as tools in early childhood programs serving children from birth through age 8* (Joint position statement). Washington, DC; Latrobe, PA: Authors.

National Governors Association Center for Best Practices & Council of Chief State School Officers. (2010). *Common Core State Standards for English language arts and literacy in history/social studies, science, and technical subjects*. Washington, DC: Authors. Retrieved from www.core standards.org/assets/CCSSI_ELA%20 Standards.pdf

National Institute for Literacy. (2008). *Developing early literacy: Report of the National Early Literacy Panel*. Washington, DC: Author.

National Research Council. (2008). *Early childhood assessment: Why, what, and how? Report of the National Research Council of the National Academies*. Washington, DC: National Academies Press.

Parikh, M. (2012). Technology and young children: New tools and strategies for young learners. *Young Children, 67*(3), 10–11.

Rivkin, S.G., Hashek, E.A., & Kain, J.F. (2005). Teachers, schools, and academic achievement. *Econometrica, 73*(2), 417–458. doi:10.1111/j.1468-0262.2005.00584.x

Schultz, T. (2008, June). Tackling PK-3 assessment & accountability challenges: Guidance from the National Early Childhood Accountability Task Force. *The State Education Standard*, 4–11.

Snow, K. (2011). *Developing kindergarten readiness and other large-scale assessment systems: Necessary considerations in the assessment of young children*. Washington, DC: National Association for the Education of Young Children.

Strickland, D.S. (2012, February/March). Planning curriculum to meet the common core state standards. *Reading Today, 29*(4), 25–26.

Strickland, D.S., & Riley-Ayers, S. (2006). *Early literacy: Policy and practice in the preschool years* (Report #10). New Brunswick, NJ: National Institute for Early Education Research.

Teale, W., & Yokota, J. (2000). Beginning reading and writing: Perspectives on instruction. In D.S. Strickland & L.M. Morrow (Eds.), *Beginning reading and writing* (pp. 3–21). Newark, DE: International Reading Association; New York: Teachers College Press.

CHAPTER 3

Critical Issues for the Implementation of the Common Core State Standards in Early Literacy Language Development: Research and Practice

Lesley Mandel Morrow & Erin Kramer

E arly literacy has been a critical issue for educators for many years. The importance of the early years was underestimated for a very long time, but we know now that it is crucial for young children to be exposed to appropriate literacy experiences as early as infancy. There are many critical issues of concern related to the Common Core State Standards (CCSS; National Governors Association Center for Best Practices & Council of Chief State School Officers [NGA Center & CCSSO], 2010) in English language arts and early literacy. In this chapter, we will discuss some of the CCSS in kindergarten through grade 2 that deal with language and provide vignettes from teachers in the classroom that illustrate how these standards have been interpreted into practice. The area of language development has been neglected in early childhood with few intentional lessons. Using the goals of the CCSS and engaging children in activities in this area will enhance their receptive and expressive language.

Putting the Speaking and Listening Standards Into Practice

Speaking and listening in early childhood build the foundation for literacy development and academic success in the future (Dickinson & Tabors, 2001; Roskos, Tabors, & Lenhart, 2009). Proficiency in speaking and listening involves the child's ability to acquire a large number of new vocabulary words weekly, use correct syntax or grammar of our language, and understand the social aspects of language, including

Quality Reading Instruction in the Age of Common Core Standards, edited by Susan B. Neuman and Linda B. Gambrell. © 2013 by the International Reading Association.

when it is appropriate to speak and what is appropriate to say in a given situation. Throughout the early childhood years, a main objective must be for children to learn vocabulary and syntax so that they are able to learn to have a coherent conversation with others and comprehend text.

The kindergarten through grade 2 Common Core State Standards for Speaking and Listening are divided into two categories. The first category is Comprehension and Collaboration and the second is Presentation of Knowledge and Ideas.

Presentation of Knowledge and Ideas refers to students' ability to talk about people, places, ideas, feelings, and events in their lives. Children in kindergarten through grade 2 are expected to be able to tell stories, provide descriptions, give explanations, and ask and answer questions that require clarification or more information. Presentation of Knowledge and Ideas includes not only oral presentations in the form of read-alouds and participation in plays, but also drawings, photos, videos and digital literacies. Children are encouraged to participate in these activities in a large or small group with the teacher. Eventually after practice guided by the teacher, Comprehension and Collaboration occurs—children should be able to collaborate with each other and tell stories and ask and answer each other's questions.

There are many things for children to learn that fall under this category. For example, there need to be discussions about what topics are appropriate to talk about in the classroom, on the playground, and with adults. These discussions have to do with developing children's practical knowledge about the use of language. Children with practical knowledge of appropriate language know "when" to say "what," "how much" to say, and to "whom" (Gillam & Reutzel, 2013). Children must be able to ask and answer questions about the oral language they hear to confirm that they understand or show that they are able to get clarification, if needed. Some comprehension questions asked of children relate to explicit information stated in oral discourse or written text and others require children to generate inferences. In both instances, children must listen carefully to new information and remember it. Children need to retrieve the information from their background knowledge to answer questions when asked. Their listening and speaking development is expected to increase in complexity over time.

In the sections that follow, we provide types of experiences young students should have in early childhood to achieve CCSS in Speaking and Listening under these two specific categories (NGA Center & CCSSO, 2010, p. 23). We discuss the Standard and then provide classroom vignettes that describe experiences demonstrating the mastery of the Standard.

Comprehension and Collaboration

Second-Grade Vignette for Speaking and Listening Standard 2: Recount or describe key ideas or details from a text read aloud or information presented orally or through other media. This marking period, the entire school is studying tolerance as a part of a schoolwide character education theme. This topic was introduced during an assembly, which featured a Zumba dance demonstration and excerpts from the book *My Friend With Autism* by Beverly Bishop. At the end of the quarter, the school will hold a Zumba dance-a-thon to raise money for a nonprofit organization that funds research on autism.

Throughout the marking period, teachers moderate discussions and conduct activities on tolerance. Today, Ms. Lynn's second-grade class is listening to a song written and performed by peace educator John Farrell titled "How Would You Feel?" The students sit in a circle and each have a copy of the lyrics downloaded from his website, www.johnfarrell.net. The class iPod sits in the center of the circle ready to go.

Ms. Lynn: The song I'm about to play for you is based on real-life events—real things that happened to real people. Let's listen carefully and follow along on the page to find out what this song has to do with our tolerance theme.

The students listen quietly and follow along on the lyrics page. This helps them focus on the message of the song. Afterward, they hold a discussion that focuses on Standard 2 in Speaking and Listening, giving the students practice recounting key ideas and details from the song. Ms. Lynn begins the discussion, referring to posters of two keywords introduced during the assembly.

Ms. Lynn: Remember, we define *tolerance* as a willingness to accept people who are different than you. Fairness is doing what is right to make sure others are not treated badly. What were some details in the song that match these definitions?

Jervane: The first part of the song tells the story of a boy getting his candy stolen on Halloween by some big kids. That's for fairness. They are not treating him with fairness.

Bitty: Yeah, they push him over. That's the opposite of "doing what is right to make sure others are not treated badly."

Reina: I know, it's like doing what is wrong to make sure others are treated badly.

Ms. Lynn:	Yes, you've got that right! What's another detail from the song that matches?
Terra:	Well, in the next line a girl is always picked last for the game. I think she kinda stinks at sports.
Ms. Lynn:	OK, so what does that have to do with our theme?
Connor:	Well, it says with her on the team it's harder to win. So why would they want her? I know, I know, it's not fair, but still. It makes sense she doesn't get picked.
Terra:	It's not about winning, Connor! They're playing a game to have fun. It's not fun for you *ever* if you aren't wanted. That's not right.
Ms. Lynn:	Right, how about the last example?
Hope:	The last one's a good example for tolerance. She dressed differently and talked weird, but they ask her to be their friend.

From the discussion, Ms. Lynn can tell that the students have a solid understanding of the song. They talked about the most important details and related it to their topic of study.

First-Grade Vignette for Speaking and Listening Standard 3: Ask and answer questions about what a speaker says in order to gather additional information or clarify something that is not understood.

Mr. Hershall's first graders are building concepts of time for their social studies unit, with a focus on the difference between the past and present. For homework, Mr. Hershall has created a VoiceThread for his students to watch and comment on. This online slideshow is a collection of photographs and videos depicting objects used in the past and those used today. VoiceThread is an excellent tool for young learners because users can make video or audio comments in addition to standard written comments. For their homework, the children use the comment feature to record a question on one of the slides. In addition to learning about the past and present, the students are developing an ability to ask questions to gain further information or clarify, which is necessary to satisfy Standard 3.

Mr. Hershall reviews these comments and responds by posting his own comments. During centers, his students will watch the VoiceThread again and listen to Mr. Hershall's comments. The following is a transcript of a series of audio and video comments from their VoiceThread. Mr. Hershall uses codes instead of names for his student accounts to protect their privacy.

Mr. Hershall:	This is an iPod touch, one of the many MP3 players out there today that people use to listen to music. On this device you download music from iTunes to save to your music library.
S11:	It has apps, too. I love playing games.
Mr. Hershall:	Yes, it does a lot more than just play music! You still need to add a question.
Mr. Hershall:	This is a phonograph. It was invented in the year 1877 by Thomas Edison. It not only played music, but was able to record sound, too!
Video:	[music playing]
S4:	Is the flower the speaker?
Mr. Hershall:	Yes, the flower is called the "horn." That is where the sound comes out.
Mr. Hershall:	This is a laptop. Today people often use word-processing programs on their computer, like Microsoft Word, to type.
S5:	Is this a MacBook?
Mr. Hershall:	No, it is made by HP.
Mr. Hershall:	This is a typewriter. People in the past used it to type. It prints right on a piece of paper as you push the keys.
Video:	[someone typing]
S13:	Did you have one when you were a kid?
Mr. Hershall:	No, I've had a computer since I was your age. My dad had an old one that I used to play with though.
S1:	How old is it?
Mr. Hershall:	This one is from the 1960s.
S8:	Who invented typewriters?
Mr. Hershall:	The first typewriter was made by Henry Mill in 1714, but not much is known about his invention. It is likely that none were ever sold. The next typewriter was made in 1808 by Pellegrino Turri for the blind. The first typewriter that uses keys in the same position they are today was made in 1878. It was invented by Christopher Latham Sholes and Carlos Glidden.
Mr. Hershall:	Cars are used today to help us get around.
S2:	What kind of car do you have?

Mr. Hershall:	This is a picture of a Prius. It's not my car, but that is the same kind of car I have.
Mr. Hershall:	This is an old advertisement for a company that varnishes, or paints a finish on, horse-drawn carriages. You can see the many different types of carriages there were.
S17:	When did people use carriages?
Mr. Hershall:	This advertisement is labeled circa 1878. *Circa* means around. So it's from somewhere around that time. In 1913 Henry Ford was able to make cars quickly on his assembly line, which made them affordable to some people and much more widely used than cars had been in the past.
S6:	How fast can they go?
Mr. Hershall:	It's probably not smart to have the horse go as fast as it can when it's pulling a carriage full of people. I'd guess they usually went around 5–8 mph, which is considered a trot.
S16:	Why didn't they just ride the horse?
Mr. Hershall:	Well, I guess there are probably a handful of reasons why. I would think you can get sweaty and dirty riding a horse. Riding in the carriage would keep you clean. You can also travel with a small group of people in the same carriage.

Most students did a great job on this homework assignment. They demonstrated an ability to ask questions to gain further information or clarify points.

Presentation of Knowledge and Ideas

Second-Grade Vignette for Speaking and Listening Standard 4: Tell a story or recount an experience with appropriate facts and relevant, descriptive details, speaking audibly in coherent sentences. Five students in Ms. Rine's class have decided to start a book club using a Judy Moody book they selected. Ms. Rine has found multiple copies of *Judy Moody Saves the World* (McDonald, 2002) for the group. The group members work mostly on their own, but their teacher helps them get organized to ensure that these students are benefitting from this experience. Together they decide that the members of the book club group will read a designated portion of the book during silent reading, which is to be completed before their scheduled book club meeting at center time. Each member will take turns leading the discussion. The job of the leader is to first summarize the chapter and then pick the first person to make a comment.

For their first session, Ms. Rine suggests the students focus on the connections they are making as they read. They are each given a pad of sticky notes to write down quick words and phrases as they read to remind them of what they were thinking. Making connections and note-taking procedures are familiar to the students, allowing them to complete this activity independently. The nature of this task gives each group member a chance to practice sharing a story or experience with the group for Speaking and Listening Standard 4.

The students have just finished reading the first chapter. The book club session starts with a summary of the chapter from Hailey, the session leader.

Hailey: This chapter is about Judy and her brother, Stink, drawing designs for a Crazy Strips contest. Stink finishes his right away and Judy does not even have an idea yet. At the end of the chapter she is in a bad mood. Kalynn, you go first.

Kalynn: I put my first sticky note on the first page. I wrote, "My brother does that, too."

Emily: What? You have to tell us about the part of the book you mean.

Kalynn: Hold on…let me see. Oh, so Stink just walks in without knocking. I have a brother, and he does that.

Hailey: Yeah, I made the same note, only for my sister. She is so annoying! One time I was sleeping and she came in and jumped on me.

Kalynn: Oh yeah, Dave just did it yesterday. I was on my laptop and didn't know he was there and I screamed! OK, Riley, you go.

Riley: Judy is playing with a doctor kit. I like to play doctor, too. I've got a fake shot, and my mom hates it when I use it on her. She's afraid of a plastic shot!

Emily: I'm afraid of shots, too.

Riley: [picking the next person to go] Umm…Emily.

Emily: I like to read cereal boxes in the morning. I read all of the sides. Sometimes they have contests on them or games. I'm like Judy and the Crazy Strips box.

Donnida:	Oh yeah—me, too. I just read about a photo contest. You can get on the front of the box.
Hailey:	I wrote a sticky note on that, too. I entered a coloring contest at the library when I was 6 and they hung my picture on the wall.
Riley:	What did you color?
Hailey:	A picture of a turtle reading. I did it with glitter crayons. I think that's why I won.
Donnida:	You are a really good artist. That's probably why you won.
Emily:	Who didn't go yet? OK, Donnida.
Donnida:	I put a sticky note on the part about the squeaky markers, and I drew a face with swirly eyes and a zigzag mouth. I hate that squeaky sound. Ms. Rine sometimes does that with the whiteboard markers, and it gives me the chills.

The students continue their discussion. They each recount several stories as they make connections to the book. At the end of the session, they decide to read Chapter 2 and meet again in two days. They liked making connections and will use the same procedures for the next chapter. Before they move on to their next activity, each group member fills out a self-assessment sheet to show Ms. Rine. They report how well they understood the chapter and rate their contribution to the conversation.

Kindergarten Vignette for Speaking and Listening Standard 6: Speak audibly and express thoughts, feelings, and ideas clearly.

Ms. Hildesham watches her reading group complete their reading journal entries. Each student has drawn an animal and written about where that animal lives. The kindergartners use invented spelling, and this group writes primarily strings of consonants.

Their writing is in response to the text they just finished, *Animals in the Rainforest* (Windsor, 1999). This text features vibrant photographs of rainforest animals.

Now the students are ready to present their writing to their peers. Ms. Hildesham begins by reminding the students of the sharing procedures.

Ms. Hildesham:	Whose turn is it to talk?
Children:	Mine!
Ms. Hildesham:	Should your friends talk?
Children:	No!

Ms. Hildesham:	OK, now what kind of voice do we need when it's our turn?
Renie:	A big voice.
Ms. Hildesham:	Should we shout?
Children:	No!
Ms. Hildesham:	OK, I think we're ready. Billy, you go first.
Billy:	*Dogs are in the house.*
Ms. Hildesham:	Nice big voice, Billy! Did you draw your dog?
Billy:	Yes, this is Bruno. See that spot right there? And he's in my bedroom. I want him to sleep on my bed. Mom says no.
Ms. Hildesham:	Thank you. I like the way Billy read his sentence and told us about things in his picture. Who thinks they can do it in a big voice like Billy?
Lihwa:	[attempting a big voice] It's a kangaroo. He has a baby. [pointing] There. In Australia.
Ms. Hildesham:	Lovely kangaroo, Lihwa. Please read your sentence.
Lihwa:	*A kangaroo's in Australia.*
Ms. Hildesham:	Nicely done. Look, Lihwa remembered a sentence ends with a period. Tristan, tell us about your penguin.
Tristan:	He's cold.
Ms. Hildesham:	Poor guy. Why is he cold?
Tristan:	'Cause he in the South Pole.
Ms. Hildesham:	Oh, of course! What does your sentence say?
Tristan:	*Penguins live at the South Pole and slide on their bellies and do tricks in the water.*
Ms. Hildesham:	Wow! That sentence is great. You had a lot of information about penguins in there! I'm proud of that big voice you found to read that sentence. You should feel good.
Ruben:	Yeah, good job, Tristan!

With prompting, Ms. Hildesham's students were able to speak clearly and coherently. They will continue to develop appropriate speaking voices with many more opportunities throughout the year.

Putting the Language Standards Into Practice

The kindergarten through grade 2 Common Core State Standards for Language are divided into three categories. The first category is Conventions of Standard English, the second is Knowledge of Language, and the third is Vocabulary Acquisition and Use.

The first set of Vocabulary Acquisition and Use Standards focuses on children's understandings of the connections and relationships in word meanings. They are called the Conventions of Standard English.

When we speak conventionally, we can be understood. Although ideas are the most important part of communication, without knowing and using the conventions of language, others may have a difficult time understanding what we say. In addition, aside from one's physical appearance, the next impression of ourselves is how we speak. When the conventions of language are not used, it makes it difficult to gain access to careers or college education. When a person doesn't speak in complete sentences or pronounces words incorrectly, it may give the impression that he or she does not have the skills to go to college or carry out a job in the manner we expect.

The conventions of language are difficult to learn for young children. Students' backgrounds are diverse, and although we must respect the different dialects and social or cultural influences on language development, children must learn the conventions of Standard English (Delpit, 1995). Teachers need to discuss how everyone must learn to speak different types of English depending on where they are and what they are doing. They must also learn that vernacular expressions are perfectly acceptable in more casual contexts with friends, siblings, or peers but that they need to know how to switch between formal and informal English to be successful in school and, later, with colleagues and employers.

Knowledge of Language deals with students' understanding of how language functions in different contexts in order to make effective choices for meaning or style, and to comprehend fully when reading, writing, listening, or speaking.

Vocabulary Acquisition and Use is another section in the Language Standards. According to these standards, children can learn words independently if they (a) use contextual information from the general topic of the conversation or text; (b) use information about parts of words such as prefixes, suffixes, and roots; and (c) use resources such as the dictionary, glossary, and various technologies. Helping children to learn the meanings of words on their own, or becoming word conscious (Stahl & Nagy, 2006), is important because it is impossible for teachers to teach the meanings of all words children need to know.

In the sections that follow, we provide types of experiences young students should have in early childhood to achieve CCSS in Language under these three specific categories (NGA Center & CCSSO, 2010, p. 26). We discuss the Standard and then provide classroom vignettes that describe experiences demonstrating the mastery of the Standard.

Conventions of Standard English and Knowledge of Language

Because children in grade 2 are capable of switching from formal to informal language and back again, educators teaching second grade need to engage children in explicit discussions and explorations of differences between formal and informal language through reading or being read to and listening to others. These discussions will help children to understand the different language registers and that "correctness" of language depends on a variety of factors such as communication context, audience, purpose, and desired impact on the listener or reader.

Second-Grade Vignette for Language Standards 2 and 3: Demonstrate command of the conventions of standard English capitalization, punctuation, and spelling when writing. Use knowledge of language and its conventions when writing, speaking, reading, or listening and to compare formal and informal uses of English. When Ms. Howard read Language Standard 3 for the first time, she immediately thought of the Caldecott Honor book *Yo! Yes?* (Raschka, 1993). This book gives examples of informal language, which is appropriate in a conversation between two friends. After securing a copy, she wrote a plan to include it in an introductory lesson to explicitly teach that people use different language conventions depending on whom they are addressing. The week the class read the story, they greeted each other by saying, "Yo!" and giving a high five.

To help with this standard, the students will Skype with a person from the State Department of Environmental Protection. This event is a part of an Earth unit that puts students in charge of identifying a local environmental issue and enacting a solution. So far the class has spent a considerable amount of time researching local recycling rules and surveying residents about their ability to understand and follow these rules as well as engage in other healthy Earth practices (e.g., reducing waste and conserving energy). Based on the data they collected, the students are beginning to form plans to solve an identified problem. A list of problems hangs on the wall from a previous lesson:

1. Some people do not know the recycling rules, and others do not understand them.
2. Some people only recycle and do not know other healthy-Earth practices.
3. Some people know the rules but don't follow them.

In today's lesson, the students are preparing questions for their Skype session, which should help them begin to form solutions to these problems. Ms. Howard begins the lesson by referring to her initial lesson that used the book *Yo! Yes?* (Raschka, 1993).

Ms. Howard:	Do you remember when we read *Yo! Yes?* What was the purpose of that lesson?
Samson:	That we can talk to different people different ways.
Ms. Howard:	Right. And when we talk to Mr. Lityule from the DEP, what do you think is appropriate?
Maeve:	We won't be like, "Yo! Wassup!"
Ms. Howard:	Yes. So we should use formal English. Let's remember that as we write down some questions for Mr. Lityule. Take a look at the poster and see what other information you might want to know based on our problems. Let's do an example together before you write down some questions on your own: Problem number one talks about not knowing or understanding the recycling rules. We don't need to ask Mr. Lityule what the rules are because we already found that information on our town's website. What we might want to ask him is who makes up the rules or how we can change them. Who can turn that into a question? Remember we need to use formal English.
Layna:	Who makes the recycling rules? Can we help change our town's rules?
Ms. Howard:	Good, Layna. Write that down for us.

The children break off in pairs and write down questions for the Skype session. After about 12 minutes, Ms. Howard calls them back together to review the questions they have come up with. Ms. Howard calls on Jeremy to read his questions. While he reads, the other students listen to see if they have the same questions and also if his questions are properly phrased following conventions of formal English.

Jeremy: [reading down his list] *How can we conserve energy? How does giving away your clothes help make less trash 'cause they're gonna be chucked anyway? Do you know any interesting facts that might get people to care?*

Hands shoot up when Jeremy reads his second question. Several students have noticed the informal language he has used.

Misty: You can't say *gonna*. You have to say *going to*.

J'lina: Not *chucked*. Say, *throwed out*.

Zaida: No, *throwed out* isn't a word. It's *threw out*.

Ms. Howard: *Threw out* is correct if you're saying, *They threw out the clothes*, but in this sentence it should be *they are going to be thrown out anyway*. There's actually one more word to change in Jeremy's question. This is a really common one. You might not even realize it doesn't follow formal language rules. The word you want isn't *'cause* even though *cause* is a word. What word does Jeremy want?

Monique: *Because.*

Ms. Howard: So now we have, *How does giving away your clothes help make less trash because they're going to be thrown out anyway?* Can I change the word *anyway* to *eventually*? It means that it's not going to happen now, but it is definitely going to happen in the future. That's the perfect word for what you're asking.

Jeremy: Yes, that's good.

The class continues to read and rewrite their questions. When they are finished, the students are prepared to use language that is appropriate for a discussion with an environmental expert.

Vocabulary Acquisition and Use

Second-Grade Vignette for Language Standard 4: Determine or clarify the meaning of unknown and multiple-meaning words and phrases based on grade 2 reading and content, choosing flexibly from an array of strategies. The following is a vignette illustrating classroom practices that demonstrate second graders determining or clarifying the meaning of unknown and multiple-meaning words and phrases independently.

Each month the second graders study a poem from the poetry collection *Snow Toward Evening: A Year in a River Valley/Nature Poems* (Loots, 1990). This very special collection of poems is illustrated by Thomas Locker, an artist who creates stunning landscape paintings. Authors represented in this collection range from the very well-known (e.g., John Updike, Langston Hughes, William Wordsworth) to lesser known poets. The combination of expert paintings and well-crafted poetry makes this book an excellent tool for teaching about the "magic" of good writing—that is, writing in which the words can make a picture come alive.

It is time to introduce the September poem to the class. Ms. Prinsea begins by asking the students what makes poetry different from other writing, like storybooks and magazines. They decide together that a poem is an artistic way to tell what someone feels or thinks and may or may not rhyme. Ms. Prinsea shares that poetry often takes something very simple in nature, just one small thing, and describes it in detail so that the reader can feel what the author feels and see what the author sees.

A copy of "Mountain Wind" (Loots, 1990) is accessed on the interactive whiteboard. Ms. Prinsea shares that this might be her favorite poem of all time. Before they read it, they preview some of the vocabulary.

Ms. Prinsea: Have you ever read something and realized you didn't understand what the author wrote because you didn't really know what some of the words meant?

Class: Yes.

Ms. Prinsea: That's why I want to start by going over the hard words. It will help us understand. We know that good readers don't just say all of the words correctly; they understand what they read—that's the most important part of being a good reader.

Ms. Prinsea highlights several of the words in the poem. They use a variety of strategies to identify the meanings of those words one at a time, as Language Standard 4 suggests.

Ms. Prinsea: [pointing to *timber*] Who can read this word?

[a student reads]

Ms. Prinsea: Good, now how have you heard that word used before?

Jorge:	TIMBER! Like when a tree is chopped down.
Ms. Prinsea:	Exactly. So we know that timber has to do with trees. How about the next word? What does that say?
Ravi:	*Chutes.*
Ms. Prinsea:	Has anyone heard that word before? Do you know what a chute is?
Irina:	Is it, like, when you shoot someone?
Ms. Prinsea:	No, that word is spelled s-h-o-o-t. *Shoot* and *chute* have different meanings, but sound the same. That's called a homophone, by the way. I've got a board game with the word *chute* in the title. Has anyone played Chutes and Ladders before?
Elizabeth:	Oh, yeah! The chute is the slide!
Ms. Prinsea:	That's right. So we know that *timber* has to do with trees and a *chute* is a slide. The first line is, "Windrush down the timber chutes." It's like saying the wind rushes down the tree slides. I have a picture in my mind that the wind is using the branches of the trees as a slide. Did anyone else get that picture? Yeah? Good!
Ms. Prinsea:	OK. The next one's a little harder. If you look at each word part, you can probably read it.
Class:	[looking at a part of the word at a time] *Reck-less-ness.*
Ms. Prinsea:	OK, so we can read it, but do we know what it means? No? Ah-ha! See that's why understanding is more important than just reading the words correctly! How about if we take the ending off? Does anyone know the word *reckless*?
Wyatt:	It's when you're a crazy driver.
Ms. Prinsea:	It can be used to describe a driver. How about if we look at the words around it? The line says, "a recklessness of branches." What could that phrase mean?
Wyatt:	It's like the branches are going crazy…crashing into each other and going, "crack, crack, crack!"
Ms. Prinsea:	Oh yes, Wyatt. Very good. You put a picture into my mind! Do you all have a picture of "a recklessness of branches?" Great!

The class listens as Ms. Prinsea reads with great expression, altering the volume of her voice to reflect the swelling wind and using her body to move with the poem. The kids like it so much that they clap at her performance. Ms. Prinsea invites them to read with her and the class choral reads the poem for the second reading.

Next, Ms. Prinsea brings out the book that the poem came from, *Snow Toward Evening* (Loots, 1990) to show her students the picture that goes with it. She reads it one more time so that they can see if the words make the painting come alive, like a movie. Of course, several students are able to share that they could see the trees shaking, the air swirling around, and the water flowing in the picture.

To wrap up this lesson, Ms. Prinsea adds the vocabulary words to a wipe-off poster titled "Words We Love" as the students write them into their spelling dictionaries for later use.

The class will read this poem several more times throughout the month. They will engage in activities connected to the poem, such as mixing up the lines and putting them back together. At the end of the month, they will make a recording for their class radio show using musical instruments like rain sticks, sandpaper blocks, and wooden rhythm sticks to represent the wind and clanging branches.

Listening, Speaking, and Language Development Throughout the Day

Listening, speaking, and language development can be enhanced with the integration of the language arts in content areas with themes that bring new words into the discussion. When a theme is embedded into art, music, play, science, and social studies, the language becomes richer. For example, if a theme is about the five senses, there will be words about tasting, smelling, touching, hearing, and seeing. All these sensory words will require description. If baking a cake, children will discuss the recipe, the utensils needed, and the cooking activities, such as kneading and mixing. As the cake is baking, talk about the wonderful aroma coming from the oven. When the baking is done, a description of how it looks and how it changed from batter to a well-formed cake can be discussed. The icing will generate a great deal of discussion, as well as any decorations that will go on top. Eating the cake will of course bring up words about how the cake looks, smells, and tastes; the texture of the cake when it is touched and eaten can be addressed also. Without the content areas, we would have a much more difficult time expanding our vocabulary.

The CCSS are asking us to address this area of language arts very specifically. In the classroom, we may have conversations that deal with some of these standards but not in an intentional way. We need to carry out research to see what is happening in classrooms to strengthen children's listening, speaking and language abilities. The integration of language arts when learning about things that are relevant is the best way to achieve success.

TRY THIS!

- After reading Arnold Lobel's *Frog and Toad Together*, have students retell the story by acting it out. By acting out the text, students can demonstrate their understanding of a critical message or lesson from the story.

- After reading Wendy Pfeffer's *From Seed to Pumpkin*, divide your whiteboard (or chalkboard) into five to eight sections (depending on how many sections you want students to explore). Then, randomly assign one of the sections to a group of students. Have the students illustrate the pumpkin's growth at the point in time of their assigned section. Next, have students write in their own words what happens during this time of growth. To complete the illustrations and text, students will refer to Pfeffer's textual details and illustrations. This integration of language arts during content learning is the best way to achieve success.

DISCUSSION QUESTIONS

1. Morrow and Kramer discuss in depth the two categories of the CCSS for kindergarten through grade 2: (a) Comprehension and Collaboration and (b) Presentation of Knowledge and Ideas. How do Morrow and Kramer illustrate these categories in each of the vignettes? How do Morrow and Kramer's examples apply to your classroom?

2. Language Standard 4 addresses unknown multiple-meaning words and phrases. Teachers are encouraged to use an array of strategies. Using Morrow and Kramer's vignette, explain and discuss at least three strategies available to classroom teachers that help students make meaning from unfamiliar words.

3. Morrow and Kramer discuss code switching, which is the ability to change one's language based on social situations. Using this concept,

discuss the importance of learning and using Standard English. What social situations warrant use of Standard English and which do not?

REFERENCES

Delpit, L. (1995). *Other people's children: Cultural conflict in the classroom*. New York: New Press.

Dickinson, D.K., & Tabors, P.O. (Eds.). (2001). *Beginning literacy with language: Young children learning at home and school*. Baltimore: Paul H. Brookes.

Gillam, S., & Reutzel, D.R. (2013). Common Core State Standards (CCSS): New directions for enhancing young children's oral language development. In L.M. Morrow, T. Shanahan, & K. Wixson (Eds.), *Common Core State Standards: Impact on literacy instruction* (pp. 107–127). New York: Guilford.

National Governors Association Center for Best Practices & Council of Chief State School Officers. (2010). *Common Core State Standards for English language arts and literacy in history/social studies, science, and technical subjects*. Washington, DC: Authors. Retrieved from www.core standards.org/assets/CCSSI_ELA%20 Standards.pdf

Roskos, K., Tabors, P.O., & Lenhart, L.A. (2009). *Oral language and early literacy in preschool: Talking, reading, and writing*. Newark, DE: International Reading Association.

Stahl, S.A., & Nagy, W.E. (2006). *Teaching word meanings*. Mahwah, NJ: Erlbaum.

LITERATURE CITED

Loots, B.K. (1990). Mountain wind. In J. Frank (Ed.), *Snow toward evening: A year in a river valley/nature poems*. New York: Dial.

McDonald, M. (2002). *Judy Moody saves the world*. Cambridge, MA: Candlewick.

Raschka, C. (1993). *Yo! Yes?* New York: Orchard.

Windsor, J. (1999). *Animals of the rainforest*. Austin, TX: Harcourt Achieve.

CHAPTER 4

Informational Text and the Common Core State Standards

Juliet L. Halladay & Nell K. Duke

The development and widespread adoption of the Common Core State Standards (CCSS; National Governors Association Center for Best Practices & Council of Chief State School Officers [NGA Center & CCSSO], 2010) have drawn increased attention to the types of texts used in K–12 classrooms. The CCSS call for opportunities for students to engage with a wide range of complex informational as well as literary texts. In this chapter, we describe the CCSS as they relate to the use of informational texts for classroom instruction. In doing so, we make connections between the CCSS recommendations and research on informational text, and we offer some practical suggestions for implementing the CCSS in K–5 classrooms.

Distribution of Literary and Informational Texts in the CCSS

One common misconception is that the reading standards leave no room for literary texts. The CCSS, in fact, follow the 2009 Reading Framework of the National Assessment of Educational Progress (NAEP; National Assessment Governing Board, 2008) in calling for an equal balance of literary and informational texts in multiple subject areas for the elementary grades, with the percentage of informational texts increasing through middle school and high school. Through grade 4, the standards call for half of all reading time to be devoted to literary text, with the balance shifting to 45% of time on literary text by grade 8. By grade 12, just under one-third of curricular time is to remain focused on literary text (see Table 4.1). And while there are separate standards for informational and literary texts, those standards address parallel content and allow some opportunities for teachers to teach across standards and genres. For example, the

Quality Reading Instruction in the Age of Common Core Standards, edited by Susan B. Neuman and Linda B. Gambrell. © 2013 by the International Reading Association.

Table 4.1. Recommended Distribution of Literary and Informational Texts (NGA Center & CCSSO, 2010, p. 5)

Grade	Literary	Informational
4	50%	50%
8	45%	55%
12	30%	70%

Source. National Assessment Governing Board. (2008). *Reading framework for the 2009 National Assessment of Educational Progress.* Washington, DC: U.S. Government Printing Office.

K–5 reading standards for literary and informational text both include standards that focus on identifying details and dealing with unfamiliar words.

Informational texts are also addressed through the writing standards. As do the reading standards, the writing standards call for a distribution of text types across grade levels, following the NAEP Writing Framework (National Assessment Governing Board, 2011). Again students are expected to engage in considerable interaction with informational text—this is shown in Table 4.2, with writing to persuade and explain generally falling under the informational category, and writing to convey experience generally falling under the literary category. Likewise, as with the reading standards, the writing standards cover a range of text types and purposes, focusing on parallel skills within each genre. For example, while the standards related to informative, explanatory texts address topic development and the precise use of domain-specific language, the standards for literary text address character development and precise use of descriptive language.

Table 4.2. Recommended Distribution of Writing Purposes (NGA Center & CCSSO, 2010, p. 5)

Grade	To Persuade	To Explain	To Convey Experience
4	30%	35%	35%
8	35%	35%	30%
12	40%	40%	20%

Source. National Assessment Governing Board. (2007). *Writing framework for the 2011 National Assessment of Educational Progress, pre-publication edition.* Iowa City, IA: ACT, Inc.

Types of Informational Texts

To effectively implement the standards related to informational text, it is important to understand what kinds of texts the CCSS include within this broad category. The CCSS make specific mention of a range of text types, explaining that the category, for K–5, includes "biographies and autobiographies; books about history, social studies, science, and the arts; technical texts, including directions, forms, and information displayed in graphs, charts, or maps; and digital sources on a range of topics" (NGA Center & CCSSO, 2010, p. 31). The informational text standards for grades 6–12 focus on different types of literary nonfiction, including "exposition, argument, and functional text in the form of personal essays, speeches, opinion pieces, essays about art or literature, biographies, memoirs, journalism, and historical, scientific, technical, or economic accounts (including digital sources) written for a broad audience" (p. 57) as well as science/technical texts and history/social studies texts (pp. 61–62).

While these various text types are similar in that they all convey information to a reader, there are also important differences among them. For example, while biographies are typically written with specific or proper nouns and third-person singular pronouns (e.g., George Washington/ he) and are often organized chronologically, informational books about science topics are typically written with generic nouns and third-person plural pronouns (e.g., mammals/they) and are often organized topically. Students need experience with each type of informational text that we want them to learn to read and write; lots of experience and skill with reading and writing biography, for example, will not alone be enough to render students able to read and write typical informational texts about science topics. Thus, the CCSS not only require that students read and write a lot of informational text but also a lot of different *kinds* of informational text.

Specific Standards for Reading and Writing Informational Texts

A close look at the CCSS for reading informational texts shows that there are 10 standards per grade level, divided into 4 categories: Key Ideas and Details, Craft and Structure, Integration of Knowledge and Ideas, and Range of Reading and Level of Text Complexity. Taken together, the 10 standards describe what students should know and be able to do as they read and comprehend complex informational texts.

The three Key Ideas and Details Standards address identifying and understanding relationships between main points and supporting details. The three Craft and Structure Standards focus on understanding unfamiliar words, using text features, and inferring an author's purpose and perspective. For Integration of Knowledge and Ideas, the three standards address students' ability to interpret, analyze, and apply information from individual and across multiple texts. The one standard in the final category—Range of Reading and Level of Text Complexity— states the expectation that students will independently and proficiently read and comprehend complex informational texts appropriate for the grade level across subject areas. The standards describe text complexity for informational (as well as literary) texts using a three-part model composed of (a) qualitative evaluation of the text, such as an assessment of the knowledge demands posed by the text; (b) quantitative evaluation of the text, as through readability formulae that place text difficulty on a numerical scale; and (c) matching reader to text and task, by considering the particular motivations the reader brings to the text and the difficulty of the reading tasks to be completed.

For writing, the CCSS also contain 10 standards per grade level, again divided into four categories: Text Types and Purposes, Production and Distribution of Writing, Research to Build and Present Knowledge, and Range of Writing. The three Text Types and Purposes Standards each address a different type of writing: opinion pieces, informative/ explanatory texts, and narratives. For each type, the standards expect students to develop and organize their ideas, using precise language and appropriate levels of detail. The three Production and Distribution of Writing Standards (two at grades K–2) require students to produce and revise writing by using technology and considering task, purpose, and audience. The three Research to Build and Present Knowledge Standards (two at grades K–3) address skills needed to gather and synthesize information, and to work collaboratively to build and convey knowledge. The single Range of Writing Standard, which begins at grade 3, expresses the importance of giving students opportunities to write frequently, in a range of genres, and for a range of purposes and audiences.

If we look across the standards for reading and writing informational texts, we can identify some recurring themes. First, there is an emphasis on developing skills with a range of different text types, including digital texts. Second, there is a repeated focus on working with multiple texts, whether by reading across multiple texts or drawing on multiple texts in researching and writing. In addition to understanding individual texts, students are expected to compare and contrast different texts, use multiple texts to build content knowledge, and develop their writing across multiple texts on a topic. Third, as with the standards for reading literary texts, the informational text standards emphasize the importance of understanding how texts work and why authors do what they do. Students are expected to think about the content and features of a text in relation to the author's (or, in writing, their own) purpose, task, and perspective—the author's craft.

Research-Supported Instructional Strategies With Informational Text

Research involving informational text has been conducted at every grade level. A full review of this research is not possible within the confines of this chapter; instead, we will discuss five key studies spanning the elementary grades. These studies suggest research-supported strategies teachers can use to develop students' informational reading and writing skills as required by the CCSS.

Kindergarten

At the kindergarten level, one study examined young children's pretend readings of informational books before and after such books were read aloud to them (Duke & Kays, 1998; see also Pappas, 1993). Pretend reading is when the reader doesn't actually read the words of a text, but rather says what she or he thinks the text might say. Pretend readings can reveal children's language knowledge; in this case they revealed that young children can learn the language of informational books from listening to them read aloud. For example, the following are excerpts from the same child's pretend reading of an unfamiliar informational book about firefighters. The first excerpt is from September; during the intervening three months, informational books as well as narratives were read aloud to the child on a near-daily basis. Compare the first excerpt to the second excerpt, from December (ellipses indicate intonation units, typically involving a pause):

September
tree...house...car...bell...that's the fire when the house burnt up...there he got to squirt the house because...or it's going to burn up...and that's the operator...for the house don't burn up...

December
first people call...the firefighters...and then...the firefighters come...and then sometimes...operators help the firefighters...and firefighters have to learn how...to do this stuff...

(Duke & Kays, 1998, p. 307)

The child, like many others in the study, uses more generic noun phrases in December: instead of talking about a specific firefighter in the picture or treating the firefighter as a character, she talks about firefighters in general. She also uses more timeless verb constructions in December: she isn't talking about a specific point in time but rather what is true across time (for example, that across time *firefighters have to learn how to do this stuff*). This research provides some support for the potential learning opportunities that result from the inclusion of informational text—as well as literary text—during read-aloud time in the classrooms of even young children.

First Grade

At the first-grade level, one study involving informational text tested the impact of a curriculum in which it was included (Santoro, Chard, Howard, & Baker, 2008). The curriculum included 15 units of four lessons each. Two of the lessons in each unit focused on informational text, while two focused on narrative text, and all of those texts were read aloud to the children. The curriculum used a gradual release of responsibility model (e.g., Duke, Pearson, Strachan, & Billman, 2011; Pearson & Gallagher, 1983): the first five units mainly involved teacher demonstration of comprehension processes; the next five units involved more student engagement in comprehension processes, with teachers prompting and supporting as needed; and the final five units required the most student responsibility, with reduced teacher prompting and support. Lessons focused on a range of comprehension processes before, during, and after reading, such as previewing and predicting before reading; discussing text and making textual connections (texts to other texts, texts to a knowledge base, and texts to one's own experiences) during reading; and retelling, reviewing, and extending key vocabulary after reading. Researchers compared student performance for classrooms with and without the intervention, finding that students who received the enhanced read-aloud curriculum showed higher levels of vocabulary knowledge and comprehension. The curriculum did indeed benefit comprehension, suggesting that reading aloud informational text with specific kinds of instruction and discussion can be a valuable vehicle for promoting comprehension in early schooling.

Second and Third Grades

A study at the second- and third-grade levels suggests that the purposes for which students are reading and writing informational text may be important to their literacy development, particularly their ability to comprehend and compose informational texts (Purcell-Gates, Duke, & Martineau, 2007). The study took place during science instruction and involved reading and writing procedural "how-to" documents as well as expository informational texts (e.g., books conveying information about simple machines). The researchers found that teachers who engaged students in reading and writing procedural and expository informational texts more like those found outside of schooling settings and who engaged students in reading and writing for purposes beyond just satisfying school assignments had students with higher rates of growth in comprehension and writing. The students who tended to show higher growth were reading procedural text because they actually wanted or needed to learn how to do something, and they were writing procedural texts to teach someone else how to do something (e.g., to teach the custodian how he or she could use simple machines to make a particular building management task easier). The students with higher growth were reading expository informational text to gain information they genuinely wanted or needed to know, and they were writing expository text to convey information to someone who wanted or needed to know it (e.g., to share information about the Michigan climate with pen pals in Costa Rica). This study suggests that informational genres must be carefully incorporated into classrooms in ways that stay true to the purposes for which these texts are read and written in the world outside of a schooling context.

Fourth Grade

At the fourth-grade level, an example of a study involving informational text comes from Klingner and colleagues (Klingner, Vaughn, Arguelles, Hughes, & Leftwich, 2004) and is one of many that demonstrates the positive effects on reading comprehension of an approach called Collaborative Strategic Reading (CSR). In CSR, students are taught how to read informational text more effectively. Specifically, they are taught to

- Preview text
- "Click and clunk" (i.e., monitor their comprehension—*click* means it makes sense; *clunk* means meaning has broken down)
- Look for the main idea(s) in the text (called "get the gist")
- Review the main ideas(s) in the text after reading (called "wrap up")

Students learn these strategies in part through teacher instruction and modeling but also through working in small groups to apply the strategies to informational text. In the groups, students take specific roles, such as the "gist pro" and the "clunk expert" to aid in the group's construction of meaning. In this study, students in classrooms receiving the CSR intervention made significant gains in reading comprehension compared to students in non-CSR classrooms. The study suggests that teaching students *how* to comprehend informational text is highly effective in increasing students' comprehension.

Fifth Grade

At the fifth-grade level, a recent study (Guthrie et al., 2009) measured the effects of an instructional approach called Concept-Oriented Reading Instruction (CORI). CORI is designed to provide students with hands-on, content-rich learning experiences that foster motivation and achievement in reading and science. While Guthrie and his colleagues have conducted extensive research on CORI over the years, this specific study focused on the types of supports that low-achieving fifth-grade students need to be successful. Students experienced a 12-week thematic CORI unit focused on plant–animal communities. During this unit, students built their conceptual knowledge of science topics by participating in lessons and activities related to ecosystems and plant–animal interactions. They built literacy skills through targeted instruction and by reading both informational and literary texts related to the unit theme. Supports for low-achieving students included explicit instruction; access to appropriate texts; and motivational supports such as choice of texts, concrete and relevant learning opportunities, and daily collaboration with peers. Researchers found that both low- and high-achieving students who participated in the 12-week CORI program outperformed students receiving traditional instruction on a range of measures. This research shows the value of informational text instruction that devotes considerable time and attention to motivation and to development of content knowledge.

Recommendations for Using Informational Texts to Implement the CCSS in the Classroom

Previous sections of this chapter have established the centrality of informational text to the CCSS and described some research-supported practices for teaching informational text reading and writing. We now turn to some additional suggestions for implementing the CCSS and using informational texts in the classroom. We begin by offering some specific recommendations, organized around the major categories of standards that fall under reading and writing of informational text. We then discuss broader strategies for motivating students to engage in the demanding reading and writing work required to meet these rigorous standards.

Reading: Key Ideas and Details

To help students identify topics, supporting details, and connections among ideas, teachers can provide students with graphic organizers to help them visualize the hierarchy of ideas in a text. For example, a chart or web that requires students to align main points with supporting details can help students to build a firmer understanding of relationships among concepts. Teachers can also use read-alouds as avenues for guiding students in strategic discussions of informational texts, helping students identify main points, explain connections among ideas, and draw inferences based on prior knowledge and textual cues.

Reading: Craft and Structure

The Craft and Structure Standards dealing with word meanings can be addressed by instruction that helps students build vocabulary knowledge and gain strategies for unlocking the meaning of new words. For example, as students explore a topic through informational texts, they can use semantic word maps (Rupley, Logan, & Nichols, 1998) to look for connections across words. A semantic map during a study of rain forests could include a range of new words—such as *canopy, jaguar, fern*, and *humidity*—organized into broader categories—such as *plants, animals*, and *climate*. Other aspects of craft and structure can be taught by engaging students in discussions about the author's intent and practices, with questions such as the following:

- Why do you think the author said it this way?
- Why do you think the author put this graphic here?
- What are some features of this text that help you learn the information you want or need?
- What are some ways this text could convey information more effectively?

Through conversations addressing questions such as these, we have seen even young children engage in sophisticated critiques of informational texts. Teachers can help students meet Craft and Structure Standards related to structure by providing guided instruction focused on text features. For example, a lesson about headings and subheadings can help students understand how these text elements signal text topics and key ideas. Instruction on informational text structures, including the use of graphic organizers, has been shown to improve reading comprehension and writing (e.g., Shanahan et al., 2010).

Reading: Integration of Knowledge and Ideas

As previously discussed, the Standards in this category focus on bringing together information from multiple sources. Students are expected to make connections between text and graphics, between different parts of a text, and across multiple texts. To help students make these connections, the most important step is to provide opportunities for students to read across multiple texts, a practice reinforced by the CCSS' inclusion of separate Standards for Range of Reading and Text Complexity. For example, a social studies unit on the U.S. Civil War could include biographies of historical figures, narrative accounts of important battles, exposition about the causes of the war, and primary-source documents, such as the Gettysburg Address. Students can then be prompted to think across texts by using graphic organizers and by participating in high-quality class discussions. Students could use a Venn diagram to compare and contrast the information provided in different texts. They could then follow that activity with a discussion about the ways that the differences among texts might represent differences in the authors' points of view.

Writing: Text Types and Purposes

As mentioned earlier in this chapter, the CCSS for writing require students to create three general types of texts: opinion pieces, informative/ explanatory texts, and narratives. One technique to help students learn to include the specific elements of these types of text is to teach genre-specific revision. Rather than solely looking at characteristics that apply across text types when revising (e.g., capitalization, punctuation, clarity of wording), students can be guided to look for those markers of quality that are associated with specific types of text. For example, a sheet to guide students in revising their writing of an opinion text might ask, among other things, whether they clearly stated their opinion/position, gave reasons for their position, and offered facts and details to support their reasons. Likewise, students writing oral histories by community members as part of a study of local history could use a revision guide with indicators specific to narrative genres, evaluating whether events are recounted in order, transitions are used to indicate sequence, and details are used to describe events.

Writing: Production and Distribution of Writing

In this section of the CCSS, the standards emphasize the importance of working collaboratively and using various tools, including digital tools, to move through stages of a writing process. Students are expected to write in ways that are appropriate to various tasks, purposes, and audiences. To help students meet these standards, teachers should provide opportunities for collaborative writing in multiple media while supporting students through each step of their writing process. Teachers can use graphic organizers and various software programs to help students brainstorm topic ideas and organize information from multiple sources. Students can also use various online platforms to jointly construct drafts, offer peer feedback, and collaborate on revisions. For example, as part of a study of life cycles, students could document their own observations of butterflies in the classroom by creating digital texts that combine voice, written words, and images. Teachers could enhance motivation by providing students with opportunities to share their observations with an outside audience—such as students in another classroom or a different part of the country who are also observing butterfly life cycles—perhaps by posting their texts on a classroom website or blog. Through all of these activities, students can build content knowledge while strengthening writing skills and gaining expertise with technology.

Writing: Research to Build and Present Knowledge

This section of the writing standards outlines the CCSS expectations related to conducting research and producing texts to convey information and ideas. This is an area in which the reading and writing standards are closely linked; students are expected to read outside sources and then transform that information into an original product. In doing so, students often need to learn strategies for locating information sources, evaluating sources for relevance and credibility, and drawing on sources without plagiarizing. They also need opportunities to write across multiple texts, drawing diverse sources together in an organized way. Teachers can provide scaffolded instruction in all of these areas, building students' research and writing skills. For example, they could use the WWWDOT approach, in which students are taught to consider each of the following in evaluating the credibility of an information source (Zhang, Duke, & Jiménez, 2011):

- **W**ho wrote this (and what credentials do they have)?
- **W**hy did they write it?

- **W**hen was it written and updated?
- **D**oes this help meet my needs (and how)?
- **O**rganization of site (you can write or draw).
- **T**o-do list for the future.

Instruction like this can help students develop the critical disposition toward text that is encouraged in the CCSS.

Motivational Scaffolds

The CCSS make barely a mention of motivation or engagement, but the standards are sufficiently challenging—and require sufficiently difficult cognitive and social work that teachers will need to motivate and engage their students in order to meet these rigorous standards. Fortunately, we already know quite a bit about ways to motivate students to take on and persist with reading and writing.

One useful framework for fostering reading and writing motivation is the 6 Cs (Turner & Paris, 1995; subsequent research further validates its components [e.g., Guthrie, McRae, & Klauda, 2007]). This framework posits that six characteristics are associated with more motivating reading and writing tasks:

1. **C**hoice
2. **C**hallenge
3. **C**ontrol
4. **C**ollaboration
5. **C**onstructing meaning
6. **C**onsequences

With informational text, *choice* might involve allowing students to select the topic of informational texts they will read or write. *Challenge* could include such things as ensuring the tasks involve students in learning new information or using new devices to convey information to their audience. *Control* might involve students in determining the range of sources they use in their research or which mentor text(s) they will emulate in their writing. *Collaboration* is especially consistent with the CCSS, which call for collaborative writing beginning in kindergarten. Many of the research-supported instructional strategies discussed in the previous section could facilitate the *constructing meaning* characteristic—with these strategies, students are placed in situations in which gleaning knowledge from text is expected. Students are taught that text should make sense, and they are taught strategies to help make it make sense. Finally, *consequences* with informational text can mean that what students learn from reading and writing informational text matters—not just for a grade or for stickers, but for some larger purpose. Some examples of writing informational text that has a compelling purpose and a real audience and that involve consequences are writing guides for exhibits at the local zoo, writing informational books to send to children in under-resourced schools in Uganda, writing how-to-save-the-earth books to sell at a local home goods store, and developing a website to persuade others to avoid products with habitat-destroying palm oil. For full descriptions of these and many other reading and writing projects involving informational text, see Duke, Caughlan, Juzwik, and Martin (2012).

Concluding Thoughts

Scholars have called for greater attention to informational text in the elementary grades for many years. The CCSS draw that attention to an unprecedented degree. To take greatest advantage of this opportunity, we should look to research-supported instructional techniques and take particular care to provide the motivational and content-rich context that is most likely to inspire students to meet these rigorous standards, both in reading and in writing. In that way, our informational text instruction will be in top form.

TRY THIS!

- Integrate reading and writing by having students conduct research and then produce their own informational texts on the topic. For example, as students work to plant and maintain their school garden, a teacher can have them read a number of texts about the topic, organize their information, and then produce a range of informational texts: how-to books for planting a garden, illustrated field guides with information about the various plants, or cookbooks with recipes using food from the garden. In addition to providing engaging experiences using informational texts for authentic purposes, these activities help students build content knowledge and strengthen skills in reading, writing, and research.

- Consider using a graphic organizer to help students organize their expanding content knowledge and understand connections among new vocabulary words. For example, while reading an informational text about ocean animals, students can work together to complete charts by listing the names of various animals and then, for each animal, placing a check mark in columns listing characteristics that apply (for example: fish, mammal, crustacean, mollusk, herbivore, carnivore). This technique, often called semantic feature analysis (SFA), can help students establish meaningful links between their prior knowledge and words that are conceptually related. It can also help teachers monitor students' understanding of content knowledge and key vocabulary words.

DISCUSSION QUESTIONS

1. As Halladay and Duke suggest, the CCSS do not mention motivating students to read and write about informational texts. However, Halladay and Duke rely on previous research about motivation to read and write to offer suggestions for teachers. What are the six characteristics associated with motivating students to read and write, originally identified by Turner and Paris (1995) and described in this chapter by the authors? How do these factors affect students and classroom teachers as they prepare to address the CCSS for informational text?

2. The CCSS emphasize the importance of working collaboratively during the writing process. How can classroom teachers make collaborative writing work in their classrooms? How can they create tasks that combine collaborative writing with the reading of increasingly complex informational texts?

3. How can the WWWDOT strategy help students evaluate the credibility of an informational source?

REFERENCES

Duke, N.K., Caughlan, S., Juzwik, M.M., & Martin, N.M. (2012). *Reading and writing genre with purpose in K–8 classrooms*. Portsmouth, NH: Heinemann.

Duke, N.K., & Kays, J. (1998). "Can I say 'Once Upon a Time'?": Kindergarten children developing knowledge of information book language. *Early Childhood Research*

Quarterly, 13(2), 295–318. doi:10.1016/S0885-2006(99)80041-6

Duke, N.K., Pearson, P.D., Strachan, S.L., & Billman, A.K. (2011). Essential elements of fostering and teaching reading comprehension. In S.J. Samuels & A.E. Farstrup (Eds.), *What research has to say about reading instruction* (4th ed., pp.

51–93). Newark, DE: International Reading Association.

Guthrie, J.T., McRae, A., Coddington, C.S., Klauda, S.L., Wigfield, A., & Barbosa, P. (2009). Impacts of comprehensive reading instruction on diverse outcomes of low- and high-achieving readers. *Journal of Learning Disabilities, 42*(3), 195–214. doi:10.1177/0022219408331039

Guthrie, J.T., McRae, A., & Klauda, S.L. (2007). Contributions of Concept-Oriented Reading Instruction to knowledge about interventions for motivations in reading. *Educational Psychologist, 42*(4), 237–250. doi:10.1080/00461520701621087

Klingner, J.K., Vaughn, S., Arguelles, M.E., Hughes, M.T., & Leftwich, S.A. (2004). Collaborative strategic reading: "Real-world" lessons from classroom teachers. *Remedial and Special Education, 25*(5), 291–302. doi:10.1177/07419325040250050301

National Assessment Governing Board. (2008). *Reading framework for the 2009 National Assessment of Educational Progress.* Washington, DC: Author.

National Assessment Governing Board. (2011). *Writing framework for the 2011 National Assessment of Educational Progress.* Washington, DC: Author.

National Governors Association Center for Best Practices & Council of Chief State School Officers. (2010). *Common Core State Standards for English language arts and literacy in history/social studies, science, and technical subjects.* Washington, DC: Authors. Retrieved from www.core standards.org/assets/CCSSI_ELA%20 Standards.pdf

Pappas, C. (1993). Is narrative "primary"? Some insights from kindergarteners' pretend readings of stories and information books. *Journal of Literacy Research, 25*(1), 97–129.

Pearson, P.D., & Gallagher, M.C. (1983). The instruction of reading comprehension. *Contemporary Educational Psychology, 8*(3), 317–344. doi:10.1016/0361-476X(83)90019-X

Purcell-Gates, V., Duke, N.K., & Martineau, J.A. (2007). Learning to read and write genre-specific text: Roles of authentic experience and explicit teaching. *Reading Research Quarterly, 42*(1), 8–45. doi:10.1598/ RRQ.42.1.1

Rupley, W.H., Logan, J.W., & Nichols, W.D. (1998). Vocabulary instruction in a balanced reading program. *The Reading Teacher, 52*(4), 336–346.

Santoro, L.E., Chard, D.J., Howard, L., & Baker, S.K. (2008). Making the *very* most of classroom read-alouds to promote comprehension and vocabulary. *The Reading Teacher, 61*(5), 396–408. doi:10.1598/RT.61.5.4

Shanahan, T., Callison, K., Carriere, C., Duke, N.K., Pearson, P.D., Schatschneider, C., & Torgeson, J. (2010). *Improving reading comprehension in kindergarten through 3rd grade: A practice guide* (NCEE 2010–4038). Washington, DC: National Center for Education Evaluation and Regional Assistance, Institute of Education Sciences, U.S. Department of Education. Retrieved from whatworks.ed.gov/publications/ practiceguides.

Turner, J., & Paris, S.G. (1995). How literacy tasks influence children's motivation for literacy. *The Reading Teacher, 48*(8), 662–673.

Zhang, S., Duke, N.K., & Jiménez, L.J. (2011). The WWWDOT approach to improving students' critical evaluation of websites. *The Reading Teacher, 65*(2), 150–158. doi:10.1002/TRTR.01016

Implementation of the Common Core State Standards and the Practitioner: Pitfalls and Possibilities

D. Ray Reutzel

mplementation of the Common Core State Standards (CCSS; National Governors Association Center for Best Practices & Council of Chief State School Officers [NGA Center & CCSSO], 2010a) looms ever larger on the current landscape of educational practice. The rollout of the Standards in districts, schools, and classrooms across the United States is proceeding at light speed. To encourage states and territories that have not yet adopted the Common Core Standards, the U.S. Department of Education has promised waivers of current No Child Left Behind (NCLB) provisions. In this climate of rapid and sweeping educational change, one cannot help but ponder the centrality of the role of the individual educational practitioner— the classroom teacher—in the overall success of this emerging process.

Despite the publication of the meticulously crafted and widely disseminated English Language Arts (ELA) Standards for grades K–12 and the assurance of innovative performance assessments of these standards to follow soon, achieving the goal of ensuring that students are college and career ready by the end of high school as articulated in the Standards (NGA Center & CCSSO, 2010a, p. 3) is fundamentally dependent upon the knowledge and effectiveness of literacy instruction offered by individual educational practitioners in the classroom. In short, the classroom teacher is the lynchpin of success for the implementation of the ELA Standards! Recognizing this fact, in this chapter, I raise several pitfalls and possibilities surrounding the capacity of and support for current educational practitioners to successfully rise to the challenge of preparing students to be college and career ready in literacy.

Quality Reading Instruction in the Age of Common Core Standards, edited by Susan B. Neuman and Linda B. Gambrell. © 2013 by the International Reading Association.

Education Reform in the New Millennium: The Primacy of the Practitioner in Teaching Reading

The primacy of the educational practitioner's influence upon student academic progress and growth in school is well documented (Darling-Hammond, 2006; Hanushek, 2010; Peske & Haycock, 2006; Snow, Griffin, & Burns, 2005; Strickland, Snow, Griffin, Burns, & McNamara, 2002). In a national survey by Haselkorn and Harris (2001), 89% of Americans responded that it is very important to have a well-qualified teacher in every classroom. More recently, U.S. Secretary of Education Arne Duncan (2011) declared again that every student has a right to a highly qualified and effective classroom teacher.

Thus, over the past decade, federal legislation such as NCLB, along with more recent federal and state educational reform initiatives such as the CCSS implementation (NGA Center & CCSSO, 2010a), continue to underscore the urgent need for highly qualified and demonstrably effective teachers in every classroom in the United States, especially in the most needy schools (Hanushek, 2010). Researchers in the social sciences and education continue to amass evidence that classroom teachers add substantial value to their students' learning. As such, teachers are recognized as either the most important or among the most important contributors to students' learning once they reach the years of typical schooling (Darling-Hammond, 2004, 2006; Rowan, Correnti, & Miller, 2002; Sanders & Horn, 1994).

Pearson (2007) reminds members of the teaching profession, "It is the solemn responsibility of any profession to monitor the professional knowledge of its members. This responsibility comprises the essence of the social contract between any profession and society" (p. 2). The empirical claim advanced by the teaching profession itself is fairly straightforward—teachers who know more teach better, and consequently their students learn more. This empirical claim and the attendant social contract between the public and the education establishment cut to the very heart of issues contiguous to teacher quality and effectiveness.

As a group, teachers fare quite well compared with other college graduates on tests of general verbal and reading abilities—teachers perform at levels similar to lawyers, engineers, accountants, and doctors (Bruschi & Coley, 1999). However, in a more recent study of teacher knowledge, Phelps (2009) found that effective reading teachers, as compared to teachers trained in other content areas, hold specialized knowledge about language, text, and reading processes. He also found that the specialized knowledge needed for teaching reading in elementary schools is quite distinct from an individual teacher's general verbal and reading abilities.

The significance of the teacher's specialized knowledge about effective reading instruction must not be underestimated. Research indicates and it is commonly assumed that teachers' content (subject-matter) knowledge has the potential to influence their instructional decisions, such as the extent to which certain concepts are taught and mastered, or which concepts are deemed as irrelevant and are eliminated from the curriculum, as well as which materials are selected for instruction (Kolis & Dunlap, 2004; Valencia, Place, Martin, & Grossman, 2006). However, assuming (as the ELA Standards do) that the typical elementary school teacher is sufficiently well prepared to provide high-quality, effective reading instruction is perhaps not justifiable in view of the evidence. Although all of us want to honor the knowledge, skills, and professionalism of our teachers, we cannot afford to stick our heads into the proverbial sand with respect to how much specialized knowledge typical elementary school teachers have about effective, evidence-based reading instruction.

For example, Strickland and colleagues (2002) report that primary-grade elementary school teachers took an average of 1.3 courses in the teaching of reading in their preservice preparation program, with a recent survey indicating a slight increase to 2.2 courses. These researchers indicate, "Even with the slight increase, the total time spent on preparing to teach reading is entirely inadequate" (p. 21). The situation is no better for inservice teachers. Somewhere between a quarter and a third of inservice teachers are receiving professional development in effective, evidence-based reading instruction in "one-shot" sessions, yet we know that this type of professional development is not highly effective. With the effects of the economic recession beginning in 2007 resulting in massive budget cuts in educational funding across the United States, the amount of professional development in the teaching of reading has fallen excessively for almost all inservice teachers in recent years. All of this is occurring in the face of mounting evidence showing that high-quality professional development improves classroom reading instruction (Morrow, Shanahan, & Wixson, 2012; Rosemary, Roskos, & Landreth, 2007; Strickland & Kamil, 2004; Strickland et al., 2002).

More recently, in the now-popular movie and book *Waiting for "Superman,"* Eric Hanushek (2010) notes that there are very important differences among teachers—some teachers are simply much more knowledgeable, skilled, and effective than others. The magnitude of the differences among teachers in effectiveness is quite simply stunning. In a single academic year, an effective teacher will get 1.5 years of grade-level growth from students while a less effective teacher will get only 0.5 years of grade-level growth (Hanushek, 2010). In fact, the differences among teacher effectiveness *within* schools are much greater than the differences *between* schools.

Furthermore, we have yet to identify a sufficiently well-defined set of teacher-quality inputs so as to be able to predict teacher performance and effectiveness in the classroom. As a consequence, the CCSS place a premium on student outcomes rather than on teacher inputs as the principal indicators of teacher effectiveness. Situate these facts in juxtaposition to the CCSS Initiative and the documented lack of quality professional development support offered to underprepared reading teachers to implement them, and the assumption inherent in these standards—that teachers need no specific guidance on "how to teach"— is questionable at best.

With the current focus squarely on the criticality and the effectiveness of the individual classroom teacher, identifying effective teachers from ineffective teachers has become the holy grail of much of current educational reform (Hanushek, 2010). A recognition of the teacher's crucial role in students' school progress has strengthened and emboldened an already solid culture of accountability in U.S. education. The use of high-stakes testing to determine which teachers effectively increase their students' general and literacy achievement is but one integral feature of this robust culture of accountability (Coburn, Pearson, & Woulfin, 2011; Ravitch, 2010).

A Culture of Accountability in a Standards-Based Era

Having established the centrality of the teacher in relation to the quality and effectiveness of instruction and students' progress, recent educational policies have continued to focus considerable attention on designing standards and coupling this effort with the development of high-stakes accountability systems to assess the achievement of these standards (Coburn et al., 2011; Ravitch, 2010). As accountability continues to permeate the everyday life of the classroom teacher, one might ask about the extant evidence that supports the efficacy of standards and standards-based assessment in promoting the desired outcomes. For example, what evidence is there that publishing standards and carrying out large-scale testing programs assessing these standards leads to improved classroom instruction or higher student test scores in literacy? This is not the first time in the United States that policymakers have attempted to implement national education standards and accountability systems with very mixed and often disappointing results (Ravitch, 2010).

Another concern focuses on reducing the amount of available classroom instructional time to make more time in the school day for assessment. Of course, quality assessment that informs instruction without detracting from the time for instruction would be the ideal. Nevertheless, in an effort to hold teachers and students accountable for achieving the goals of the Standards, too much time devoted to testing may result in lower, not higher, test scores and student growth.

Finally, one must wonder a bit about the wisdom of developing assessments directly from standards rather than from a well-articulated curriculum, a well-understood and defined set of learning progressions from basic to complex, and expertly crafted and classroom-validated lessons (Calkins, 2012; Ravitch, 2010). Even more concerning is the fact that none of the standards-based assessments will be available until *after* the initial implementation of the Standards. As such, teachers are left to imagine the nature and content of the assessments that will be used to evaluate their work and their students' learning.

Establishing and Disseminating an Evidence Base in Literacy Education: Preferred Practices Teachers Should Use

Within documents that accompany the CCSS, the authors repeatedly make the claim that the ELA Standards are evidence and research based (e.g., NGA Center & CCSSO, 2010a, p. 3). However, although a perusal of the bibliography in Appendix A supporting the K–12 ELA Standards (NGA Center & CCSSO, 2010b) reveals a mix of cited original research reports published in journals and nationally published professional books, the Standards' evidence base, as presented in this bibliography, is obviously lacking citations and references to several major national research syntheses that now form the basis of what is widely accepted as the scientific evidence base for teaching reading. The most important question, then, is to what degree are teachers well prepared to teach using evidence-based, preferred practices in their classroom reading instruction? Relatedly, does the use of the ELA Standards require practitioners to know and use evidence-based practices in teaching literacy?

A major evolution (some might say revolution) in teacher education in the past two decades has been a movement away from the long-established and accepted "apprenticeship model," where a practitioner's training was largely guided by the craft knowledge of other practitioners. Instead, teacher education has been steadily moving toward a scientific, evidence-based model of professional knowledge and practice. In this evolution of the profession toward models of evidence-based knowledge and practice, literacy education has led the way.

Prior to the turn of the millennium, literacy education took center stage in the process of evidence-based educational reform. Coming as a direct result of the report of the National Reading Panel (National Institute of Child Health and Human Development, 2000), literacy educators now have a well-defined but limited evidence base that has come to be generally known in the vernacular of the field as the five pillars, essentials, or elements of effective reading instruction: phonemic awareness, phonics, fluency, vocabulary, and comprehension. Although now largely accepted as the scientific basis for effective reading instruction, initial findings and recommendations of the National Reading Panel report were not immediately accepted by all in the literacy education community (Allington, 2002; Coles, 2000; Garan, 2002; Goodman, 1998; Pressley, 2002). Nonetheless, in the years subsequent to the publication of the National Reading Panel report, several other research synthesis reports on evidence-based practices for the teaching of reading have followed and constitute an evolving and robust collection of research evidence (August & Shanahan, 2006; McCardle & Chhabra, 2004; Torgesen et al., 2007).

With the introduction of an evidence-based approach to the teaching of reading came the near Herculean task of disseminating this information to the broad base of educational practitioners in school districts and classrooms across the United States. Under the banner of NCLB, billions of dollars were allocated to a new federal program called Reading First. The purpose of Reading First was to prepare K–3 classroom teachers to implement in their classrooms the evidence-based practices of effective reading instruction as recommended in the National Reading Panel report to help struggling readers attending low-achieving schools in high-poverty areas.

Given the size and scope of the Reading First program's budget and mandate to implement evidence-based reading instruction, it almost immediately became a target of corrupt practices engaged in by unscrupulous individuals and corporate interests as well as the focus of increased scrutiny by those who were less enthused over the methods and findings of the National Reading Panel report. Soon after the initiation of the Reading First program, it was tainted by allegations of corruption in the U.S. Department of Education's application process for states to obtain funding. Later it was found that specific publishing companies and consulting agencies were given preferential treatment by U.S. Department of Education officials overseeing the Reading First program's grant application process (U.S. Department of Education, 2006).

After nearly six years of efforts to inculcate the use of evidence-based practices based upon the report of the National Reading Panel in reading instruction in primary-grade classrooms, the results of a nationally funded evaluation study of Reading First showed no difference between non–Reading First and Reading First schools on a standardized, norm-referenced test of reading comprehension (Gamse, Jacob, Horst, Boulay, & Unlu, 2008). The already tainted program was now not only viewed as corrupt but also ineffective. Consequently, the public press and some individuals within the education community were quick to claim that the "evidence base" in reading instruction was not effective for teaching children to read.

However, the assertion that Reading First failed because of the ineffectiveness of the evidence-based practices was speculative at best. The purpose of the Reading First program (unlike its predecessor, the Reading Excellence Act of 1998) was not to test the evidence base for teaching reading. Rather, it was to determine if the expenditure of billions of federal dollars to provide teachers with professional development in evidence-based reading instruction along with stringent compliance guidelines would sufficiently support and motivate classroom teachers to diligently use these practices to obtain results found in scores of well-controlled studies. Thus, both the purpose of Reading First and the findings about its effectiveness lead one inexorably to questions about practitioner compliance (addressed later in this chapter) and paint a picture of rather restricted access to the knowledge of evidence-based reading instruction practices for the majority of teachers across the nation who had no involvement with the Reading First program and the evidence base that it was charged to disseminate and implement in schools.

Near the end of the first decade of the 21st century, reports began to surface about the accessibility of information about evidence-based practices in reading instruction. In one hotly debated study supported by the National Council on Teacher Quality (Walsh, Glaser, & Wilcox, 2006), the authors determined that few of the then-current teacher preparation institutions were faithfully transmitting the evidence base of the National Reading Panel to preservice teachers. Other studies of teacher knowledge about evidence-based reading practices paint a rather grim picture as well (Bell, Ziegler, & McCallum, 2004; Bos, Mather, Dickson, Podhajski, & Char, 2001; Frahm, 2010; Stotsky, 2009). Bos and colleagues (2001) found that preservice teachers scored 53% and inservice teachers scored 60%

on tests of teachers' knowledge about effective reading instruction. Bell and colleagues (2004) reported similar results with educators who taught adult learners to read. In a recent study of teacher knowledge tests, Stotsky (2009) found that currently used reading instruction knowledge tests were insufficiently assessing the evidence base of effective reading instruction. And finally, Frahm (2010) reported that performance rates of Connecticut preservice teachers on a test of evidence-based reading knowledge and practices ranged from a low score of 60% to a high score of 91% with a mean score of 73% among a smattering of students who voluntarily took the test. These reports raise serious questions about how well disseminated the evidence base of effective reading instruction is among elementary, secondary, and special education teachers, let alone how well or frequently these practices are actually used in classrooms.

In addition to NCLB and Reading First, the tidal wave of educational reform in the United States at the turn of the millennium hit the Office of Educational Research and Improvement in the U.S. Department of Education. This agency was dismantled and renamed the Institute of Education Sciences (IES) with a refocused mission on generating scientific evidence to support instruction and assessment practices to be used in the nation's schools, classrooms, and universities. Within a few short years, IES also established the What Works Clearinghouse (ies.ed.gov/ncee/wwc), which was charged with vetting evidence of effectiveness for numerous proprietary instructional and intervention programs marketed and sold by large educational corporations. This new clearinghouse provided classroom teachers with access to objective, easily retrieved information to sort out the many and often exaggerated claims made by educational product and program vendors.

Practitioner Compliance in Using Standards and Evidence-Based Practices

In education, as in medicine, engineering, law, and other professional fields of practice, the indispensable and crucial role of the individual practitioner is seldom disputed. Another irrefutable point is that the quality and effectiveness of services rendered by professional practitioners are regularly and rigorously judged in contemporary society, and this judgment is composed of at least two major components: (1) the practices, protocols, procedures, or treatments selected for use by the professional and (2) the diligence and skill with which these are implemented. Thus, all professions are obligated as a part of an implied social contract to establish standards of ethical and effective practice, employ evidence-based practices in their work, and follow with fidelity the accepted protocols and procedures generally accepted by the profession for practice. Accordingly, society has an abiding interest in and a right to expect that all professions will construct and ensure that practitioners comply with a rigorous system of generally accepted and evidence-based practices. Failure to do so often results in having a system of generally accepted and evidence-based practices imposed upon a profession by external entities such as legislatures and courts.

Among all the professions, obtaining compliance of practitioners with generally accepted and evidence-based standards of practice is a long-standing issue. This is because the very nature of practicing a profession requires that practitioners use their knowledge to make informed decisions in what are often less than clear-cut situations. Said differently, professionals cannot simply and mechanistically comply with a set of generally accepted or evidence-based practices and at the same time remain thinking, responsible professionals. An historical case from the medical profession may serve to illustrate this point.

In 1847, long before the discovery of germs, Dr. Ignac Semmelweis introduced hand washing with chlorinated lime solutions. The introduction of this practice immediately reduced the incidence of fatal childbed or puerperal fever from 10% to about 1–2%. Now, in the 21st century, many years later, no one disputes the efficacy of hand washing in stopping the spread of infectious disease. In view of the consensus around the efficacy of hand washing as an evidence-based practice, one might reasonably assume that today's medical practitioners in hospitals and clinics would be at near 100% compliance with the scientifically proven practice of hand washing (Centers for Disease Control and Prevention, 2012).

Unfortunately, this is not the case. Dr. Atul Gwande (2007) reports a study of his hospital's infectious disease control team, whose full-time job it was to control the spread of infectious disease in the hospital. The focus of this study was on the practice of hand washing and the failure of the infectious disease control team's efforts to get modern-day medical practitioners to adequately disinfect their hands. They tried everything. They repositioned sinks and had new ones installed. They bought $5,000 "precaution carts" to make washing, gloving, and gowning easy and efficient. They posted admonishing signs and issued hygiene "report cards." They even gave away free movie tickets as an incentive for cleaning up. Nothing worked!

What is the take-away message for educational reform from these historical and contemporary reports of medical practices and practitioners?

First, getting practitioners to diligently apply evidence-based practices and standards in their teaching is a thorny issue—one needing much more research and attention than has been given in relation to the rollout of the Standards. Second, assuring that practitioners have sufficient professional knowledge of applicable standards and the clinical skill to implement standards and evidence-based practices in diverse and often difficult education settings must be an integral part of the overall initial preparation and continuing professional development of the classroom practitioner. Third, having an established set of standards and evidence-based practices is only part of what is needed in total to bring about necessary and important reforms in educational practice and literacy education. So what else is missing in the call for implementation of the CCSS?

Missing Elements for Practitioners to Successfully Implement the Standards

Ravitch (2010) laments the use of standards to drive the construction of accountability systems without first putting into place a carefully developed, coherent, and rich curriculum to support the teaching of the standards. Ravitch writes, "Tests should follow the curriculum. They should be based on the curriculum. They should not replace it or precede it" (p. 16). Ravitch opines,

> We should attend to the quality of the curriculum—that is, what is taught. Every school should have a well-conceived, coherent, sequential curriculum. A curriculum is not a script but a set of general guidelines.... The curriculum is the starting place for other reforms. (p. 231)

Standards are not curriculum! Tests are not curriculum! A curriculum is intended to specify not only what is taught but also the sequence of what is taught along a clearly demarcated pathway of development from simple to complex. For example, such a curriculum answers questions like, What does mastering the skill of getting the main idea look like when progressing from reading easy to complex texts? An understanding of the learning progressions needed to adequately support student learning to achieve the Standards has yet to be composed or evaluated. In the meantime, educational program publishers are reconfiguring program contents in order to tie them to the Standards without having first engaged in the hard and expensive work of developing and evaluating an excellent curriculum that sufficiently specifies learning progressions for the purpose of lesson development.

Other nations to which the United States is often compared have diligently labored to develop excellent curricula that specify what students are supposed to be learning. Japanese educators provide an interesting example of how to design lessons to support a system of articulated learning progressions in literacy. Japanese teachers invest a great deal of teacher time during the normal school day in collaboration with other teachers preparing well-constructed, tried-and-true lessons in a process called "Japanese Lesson Study" to support the teaching of the curriculum (Durbin, 2010). Classroom-tested, validated lessons in education are in many ways the equivalent of treatment protocols in medicine. No serious effort to reform medical practice would leave to chance something as valuable and effective as treatment protocols. Yet in U.S. educational reform efforts, the equivalent of protocols—effective, clinically validated lessons that routinely and effectively employ evidence-based practices—are habitually overlooked, including in the current Standards movement.

Teacher-developed and validated lessons resulting from the "lesson study" of local teachers are of such value in Japan that bookstores routinely stock and sell them to other teachers and the public. Think about how such a process as Japanese Lesson Study builds the capacity of teachers to design effective reading lessons using evidence-based practices, standards, and curriculum, and consider how marketing and selling these lessons in national and local bookstores respects and recognizes in a tangible way the growing expertise of the educational practitioner.

Thus, issues of practitioner compliance with developed curriculum, lessons, assessment, and the Standards threaten to undermine the success of even the best of efforts to improve educational practice. Accountability systems must not be all sticks and no carrots—teachers need support and time to prepare to implement the Standards. They need ongoing professional development, including coaching by experts within the context of a professional learning community fostered by such practices as lesson study, to develop and evaluate curricula, design and test lessons, and study student data obtained from performance assessments to ultimately implement the Standards successfully. An outside-in imposed process for implementing the Standards is likely to meet with much more resistance than an inside-out, buy-in ownership process in terms of obtaining practitioner compliance (Fullan, 1993). Giving meticulous attention as to how to most effectively and most consistently encourage practitioner compliance with the Standards, curriculum, lessons, and evidence-based, effective instructional practices will ultimately be the boon or bane of the Standards movement in our time.

CAUTION: Moving Forward, or Repeating Past Mistakes?

The current Standards implementation across the United States holds the potential to become the impetus for long-lasting and tangible educational reform. Conversely, the current Standards implementation also holds the potential to become the impetus for yet one more round of poorly thought out, sloppily executed, and under-resourced failures in education reform that may ultimately be blamed on classroom teachers. To avoid this outcome, I would like to suggest several cautions for moving forward in implementing the Standards in the years ahead.

First, we should not assume that teachers do not need guidance, support, and resources about how to teach in adherence to the Standards. The fact is that many current teachers and even those now exiting U.S. teacher education institutions are poorly prepared in terms of knowledge and clinical skill at diligently applying evidence-based practices and in designing effective lessons for teaching reading. Specific and sustained professional development will be needed to support all teachers in the successful implementation of the Standards. Strickland and colleagues (2002) describe a study of over 1,000 school districts in the United States. The conclusion was that every dollar spent on more highly qualified teachers resulted in greater improvements in student achievement than did any other use of school resources.

Second, the creation of an "excellent, coherent curriculum" has not preceded nor resulted from the development and dissemination of the ELA Standards. As a result, many of the current so-called Standards-based literacy instructional programs promoted by large national educational corporations will be marketed and sold as a substitute for doing so. It also follows that the lessons published in these nationally marketed reading instructional programs have not been developed in view of such a curriculum. But, perhaps most importantly, nationally marketed Standards-based literacy instruction programs have not been field-tested for effectiveness nor could they be. Because assessments for measuring achievement of the Standards have yet to be developed, field-tested, and disseminated, there is no credible means by which nationally marketed literacy instruction programs could demonstrate their effectiveness. Consequently, educational vendors should temper any claims made about the potential efficacy of literacy instruction programs marketed to educators as "Standards-based." Furthermore, classroom practitioners should remain somewhat suspicious of literacy-instruction programs marketed as "Standards-based" when no evidence exists to support any claims made that such programs do lead to the expected outcomes in the Standards: producing college- and career-ready students in literacy.

Third, the Standards rollout process has occurred in a way that neglects the development of a Standards-based curriculum and the research and development necessary to produce validated lessons to enact the Standards into effective, evidence-based literacy instruction at the classroom level. Even well-trained, highly educated physicians are not expected to locally engage in the de novo creation of treatment protocols, yet the expectation in the ELA Standards places the burden of local de novo creation of the curriculum and lessons on the backs of teachers. With a wink and a nod toward respecting teacher professionalism by those writing the CCSS, it is unfathomable to think that without a significant infusion of resources teachers will have the time, resources, and expertise to engage in a de novo creation of a rich, coherent language arts curriculum and lessons. Yet this is expected of our nation's teachers. It is little wonder then that many teacher educators have recognized the need for teachers to be supported in Standards implementation by authoring a growing list of teacher help books for implementing the ELA Standards in classrooms (Morrow et al., 2012).

In summary, it is clear that teachers play a central role in the future success or failure of the Common Core State Standards. But given only the Standards and the promise of innovative performance assessments for measuring the Standards at some point in the future, teachers are left to do the lion's share of the work. They must learn the evidence base of effective reading instruction and comply with this evidence base without support— including time to learn, to coach, and to seek professional development. They are asked to create de novo a "coherent," Standards-based curriculum and then develop hundreds of accompanying lessons to support the teaching of the curriculum when given an average of 8.3 minutes during the school day of preparation time for every hour they teach (Strickland et al., 2002). They are asked to teach to known standards but have no knowledge of how their work or their students' literacy work will be assessed. In the headlong rush to implement the Common Core ELA Standards, we seem to be setting up this educational reform movement and the teachers who must implement it for one more failure. Playing on the words of the old song by Simon and Garfunkel, we may want to "slow down; you move too fast—you've got to make the curriculum first!"

- After reading Chapter 1, "On Washing Hands," in the book *Better: A Surgeon's Notes on Performance* by Atul Gawande (2007), identify reasons why educational practitioners, like health care practitioners, may fail to diligently apply evidence-based practices in their classrooms and schools. Invite participants to take turns listing the central ideas found in this chapter. Once completed, educators can use the list to write a summary emphasizing issues around complying with evidence and research in practice and how these issues may be effectively addressed in educational settings.

- After studying the ELA Standards, have participants list on a whiteboard or chart paper the strengths, weaknesses, and gaps they have located in the CCSS. After making this listing, give participants an opportunity to have a far-ranging discussion of how the missing elements of the current CCSS rollout that Reutzel notes in this chapter, along with their own listing of gaps and weaknesses in the standards, can be addressed at the local or state level to optimize the potential for the standards to be implemented skillfully, effectively, and successfully in schools and classrooms.

DISCUSSION QUESTIONS

1. Reutzel makes an argument for teachers to monitor the professional knowledge and competent practice of other teachers. What are the ramifications of *not* monitoring professional knowledge and competent practice within the teaching profession, and, specifically, how do professional knowledge and competent practice relate to the hoped-for successful implementation of the CCSS?

2. The CCSS call for teachers to use evidence-based practices in reading instruction, similar to research evidence disseminated by the National Reading Panel report. How will the use of evidence-based practices ultimately affect the success or failure of implementing the CCSS?

3. According to Reutzel, certain elements are missing from the current rollout of the CCSS nationally. Discuss at least two of the missing elements Reutzel identifies, and explain how these missing elements can negatively impact the success of classroom teachers when implementing the CCSS.

REFERENCES

Allington, R.L. (2002). *Big brother and the national reading curriculum: How ideology trumped evidence.* Portsmouth, NH: Heinemann.

August, D., & Shanahan, T. (Eds.). (2006). *Developing literacy in second-language learners: Report of the National Literacy Panel on Language-Minority Children and Youth.* Mahwah, NJ: Erlbaum.

Bell, S.M., Ziegler, M., & McCallum, R.S. (2004). What adult educators know compared with what they say they know about providing research-based reading instruction. *Journal of Adolescent & Adult Literacy, 47*(7), 542–563.

Bos, C., Mather, N., Dickson, S., Podhajski, B., & Char, D. (2001). Perceptions and knowledge of preservice and inservice educators about early reading instruction. *Annals of Dyslexia, 51*(1), 97–120. doi:10.1007/s11881-001-0007-0

Bruschi, B.A., & Coley, R.J. (1999). *How teachers compare: The prose, document, and quantitative skills of America's teachers* (Policy Information Report). Princeton, NJ: Educational Testing Service.

Calkins, L.M. (2012, March 16). *What's this world coming to? Walking fearlessly forward towards new horizons in literacy education.* Keynote address at the 44th Annual Conference on Reading and Writing, New Brunswick, NJ.

Centers for Disease Control and Prevention. (2012). Hand hygiene in healthcare settings. Retrieved November 18, 2012, from www.cdc.gov/handhygiene.

Coburn, C.E., Pearson, P.D., & Woulfin, S. (2011). Reading policy in the era of accountability. In M.L. Kamil, P.D. Pearson, E.B. Moje, & P.P. Afflerbach (Eds.), *Handbook of reading research* (Vol. 4, pp. 561–593). New York: Routledge.

Coles, G. (2000). *Misreading reading: The bad science that hurts children.* Portsmouth, NH: Heinemann.

Darling-Hammond, L. (2004). Inequality and the right to learn: Access to qualified teachers in California's public schools. *Teachers College Record, 106*(10), 1936–1966.

Darling-Hammond, L. (2006). *Powerful teacher education: Lessons from exemplary programs.* San Francisco: Jossey-Bass.

Duncan, A. (2011). *A new approach to teacher education reform and improvement.* Retrieved November 20, 2012, from www.ed.gov/news/speeches/ new-approach-teacher-education-reform-and-improvement

Durbin, J. (2010). American teachers embrace the Japanese art of lesson study. *The Education Digest, 75*(6), 23–29.

Frahm, R.A. (2010, September 9). Reading exam still an obstacle for would-be teachers. *The Connecticut Mirror.* Retrieved November 20, 2012, from www.ctmirror.com/story/7654/ exam-trips-propective-teacher-90810

Fullan, M. (1993). *Change forces: Probing the depths of educational reform.* New York: Falmer.

Gamse, B.C., Jacob, R.T., Horst, M., Boulay, B., & Unlu, F. (2008). *Reading First Impact Study final report* (NCEE 2009–4038). Washington, DC: National Center for Education Evaluation and Regional Assistance, Institute of Education Science, U.S. Department of Education.

Garan, E.M. (2002). Beyond the smoke and mirrors: A critique of the National Reading Panel Report on Phonics. In R.L. Allington (Ed.), *Big brother and the national reading curriculum: How ideology trumped evidence* (pp. 90–111). Portsmouth, NH: Heinemann.

Goodman, K.S. (1998). *In defense of good teaching: What teachers need to know about the "reading wars."* York, ME: Stenhouse.

Gwande, A. (2007). *Better: A surgeon's notes on performance.* New York: Henry Holt.

Hanushek, E. (2010). The difference is great teachers. In K. Weber (Ed.), *Waiting for "Superman": How we can save America's failing public schools* (pp. 81–100). New York: Public Affairs Press.

Haselkorn, D., & Harris, L. (2001). *The essential profession: American education at the crossroads.* Belmont, MA: Recruiting New Teachers.

Kolis, M., & Dunlap, W.P. (2004). The knowledge of teaching: The K3P3 model. *Reading Improvement, 41*(2), 97–107.

McCardle, P., & Chhabra, V. (2004). *The voice of evidence in reading research.* Baltimore: Paul H. Brookes.

Morrow, L.M., Shanahan, T., & Wixson, K.K. (Eds.). (2012). *Teaching with the Common Core Standards for English Language Arts, preK–2.* New York: Guilford.

National Governors Association Center for Best Practices & Council of Chief State School Officers. (2010a). *Common Core State Standards for English language arts and literacy in history/social studies, science, and technical subjects.*

Washington, DC: Authors. Retrieved from www.corestandards.org/assets/CCSSI_ELA%20Standards.pdf

National Governors Association Center for Best Practices & Council of Chief State School Officers. (2010b). *Common Core State Standards for English language arts and literacy in history/social studies, science, and technical subjects: Appendix A: Research supporting key elements of the Standards and glossary of key terms.* Washington, DC: Authors. Retrieved from www.corestandards.org/assets/Appendix_A.pdf

National Institute of Child Health and Human Development. (2000). *Report of the National Reading Panel. Teaching children to read: An evidence-based assessment of the scientific research literature on reading and its implications for reading instruction* (NIH Publication No. 00-4769). Washington, DC: U.S. Government Printing Office.

Pearson, P.D. (2007, November 4). *Teacher knowledge and teaching reading.* Keynote address at the College Reading Association Annual Meeting, Salt Lake City, UT. Retrieved November 17, 2007, from www.scienceandliteracy.org

Peske, H.G., & Haycock, K. (2006). *Teaching inequality: How poor and minority students are shortchanged on teacher quality.* Washington, DC: The Education Trust.

Phelps, G. (2009). Just knowing how to read isn't enough! Assessing knowledge for teaching reading. *Educational Assessment, Evaluation and Accountability, 21*(2), 137–154. doi:10.1007/s11092-009-9070-6

Pressley, M. (2002). *Effective beginning reading instruction: The rest of the story from research.* Washington, DC: National Education Association.

Ravitch, D. (2010). *The death and life of the great American school system: How testing and choice are undermining education.* New York: Basic Books.

Rosemary, C.A., Roskos, K.A., & Landreth, L.K. (2007). *Designing professional development in literacy: A framework for effective instruction.* New York: Guilford.

Rowan, B., Correnti, R., & Miller, R.J. (2002). What large-scale, survey research tells us about teachers effects on student achievement. Insights from the prospects study of elementary schools. *Teachers College Record, 104*(8), 1525–1567. doi:10.1111/1467-9620.00212

Sanders, W.L., & Horn, S.P. (1994). The Tennessee value-added assessment system (TVAAS): Mixed-model methodology in educational assessment. *Journal of Personnel Evaluation in Education, 8*(3), 299–311. doi:10.1007/BF00973726

Snow, C.E., Griffin, P., & Burns, M.S. (Eds.) (2005). *Knowledge to support the teaching of reading: Preparing teachers for a changing world.* San Francisco: Jossey-Bass.

Stotsky, S. (2009). Licensure tests for special education teachers: How well they assess knowledge of reading instruction and mathematics. *Journal of Learning Disabilities, 42*(5), 464–474. doi:10.1177/0022219409338740

Strickland, D.S., & Kamil, M.L. (Eds.). (2004). *Improving reading achievement through professional development.* Norwood, MA: Christopher-Gordon.

Strickland, D.S., Snow, C., Griffin, P., Burns, M.S., & McNamara, P. (2002). *Preparing our teachers: Opportunities for better reading instruction.* Washington, DC: Joseph Henry.

Torgesen, J.K., Houston, D.D., Rissman, L.M., Decker, S.M., Roberts, G., Vaughn, S., et al. (2007). *Academic literacy instruction for adolescents: A guidance document from the Center on Instruction.* Portsmouth, NH: RMC Research Corporation, Center on Instruction.

U.S. Department of Education. (2006). *The Reading First program's grant application process: Final inspection report* (ED-OIG/I13–F0017). Washington, DC: Office of the Inspector General.

Valencia, S.W., Place, N.A., Martin, S.D., & Grossman, P.L. (2006). Curriculum materials for elementary reading: Shackles and scaffolds for four beginning teachers. *The Elementary School Journal, 107*(1), 93–120. doi:10.1086/509528

Walsh, K., Glaser, D., & Wilcox, D.D. (2006). *What education schools aren't teaching about reading and what elementary teachers aren't learning.* Washington, DC: National Council on Teacher Quality.

CHAPTER 6

Common Core State Standards: Structuring and Protecting Equitable Pathways for African American Boys

Alfred W. Tatum

n July 2012, President Barack Obama issued Executive Order 13621—
White House Initiative on Educational Excellence for African Americans,
in which he called for the need

> to restore the country to its role as the global leader in education, to
> strengthen the Nation by improving educational outcomes for African
> Americans of all ages, and to help ensure that all African Americans
> receive an education that properly prepares them for college, productive
> careers, and satisfying lives.... (p. 45471)

This Executive Order is premised on the idea that significantly improving
the educational outcomes of African Americans will provide substantial
benefits for the United States by, among other things, increasing college
completion rates, productivity, employment rates, and the number of
African American teachers. Enhanced educational outcomes lead to more
productive careers, improved economic opportunity, and greater social
well-being for all Americans. This Executive Order comes on the heels
of implementation of the Common Core State Standards (CCSS; National
Governors Association Center for Best Practices & Council of Chief
State School Officers [NGA Center & CCSSO], 2010) in school districts
throughout the United States.

In this chapter, I discuss the promise and potential shortcomings of
the CCSS for protecting the rights of African American males in grades
K–12 to quality reading and writing instruction. Will the CCSS provide
the type of in-classroom sanctuary needed for these young males to
achieve academic excellence? Or will African American males be defaulted
by another failed educational approach? In other words, will the CCSS

Quality Reading Instruction in the Age of Common Core Standards, edited by Susan B. Neuman and
Linda B. Gambrell. © 2013 by the International Reading Association.

become another metaphorical noose that hangs these young males from data sheets and statistics until the next "best" idea is offered for the nation's children? I ground my discussion and analysis in a sociohistorical perspective before offering recommendations for implementing the Standards in K–12 classrooms in ways that protect African American males' rights to excellent reading and writing instruction, particularly those students attending schools in high-poverty communities.

A Sociohistorical View of Literacy for African American Males

In July 1827, William Hamilton, the first President of the New York African Marine Society, offered specific suggestions for the education of African American youth. In his address delivered in the African Zion Church in commemoration of the abolition of domestic slavery in the state of New York, he stated,

> Next, I would invite you to the study of the sciences. Here lies an open field of pleasure, that is increased at every step you take therein.... It has been the policy of white men to give you a high opinion of your advancement, when you have made but smattering attainments. They know that a little education is necessary for the better accomplishing the menial services you are in the habit of performing for them. They do not wish you to be equal with them—much less superior. Therefore, in all advancements they assist in (I speak of them generally) they will take care that you do not rise above mediocrity.
>
> My young friends, it is a laudable ambition that prompts us to the highest standing in literature.... Why look up to others, when we may obtain the highest standing ourselves? There is a height of knowledge which you may easily attain to, that when arrived at, you will look down at amazement, at the depth of ignorance you have risen from.... Therefore, my young friends, I look to you, and pray you, by all proper pride you feel in being men, that you show yourselves such, by performing acts of worth equal with other men. Why not form yourselves into literary companies for the study of the sciences. (Porter, 1995, p. 103)

Studying the sciences and literature as a pathway to social and economic parity and as a pathway to manhood was the resounding call almost 200 years ago. Yet in the year 2012, there still was a need for the issuance of a Presidential Executive Order focused on the educational excellence of African American youth. When combined, the two statements that span close to two centuries call for advancement in the sciences, the highest standing in literature, preparation for college and careers, and development of African American men to live satisfying lives.

The call to place nonfiction and fiction texts at the center of the literacy development of African American males has a long-standing tradition in the United States. A clear demarcation between reading fiction and nonfiction did not exist. Instead, the focus on reading was driven by reading the best texts available, texts that stimulated intellectual development and shaped pathways for progress and human liberty.

The existing educational, sociological, and psychological literatures point to vulnerable conditions and circumstances that can interrupt students' reading and writing achievement. I am often confronted with a particular imagination and description of African American males when I am invited by school and district leaders to help improve the reading achievement, and writing achievement to a lesser degree, of African American boys. The narrative is the same throughout the country:

> We have these boys who come from these homes who are not making the progress we had hoped for. They continue to lag behind our white students. [This is always followed by colorful charts with bar graphs and percentages.] Many of these boys come from homes with little support. Is it possible for our teachers, many of whom are white, to improve these boys' reading achievement? How do we get these boys to care about reading? And how do we pay attention to the needs of these boys without ignoring other students? Why do we have to make the instruction relevant? Should they read what everyone else is reading? We have to do something because these boys are dropping out, being suspended, or going to prison at disproportionate rates. [This is always followed by more charts of statistics.] Can you give me some skills or very practical strategies to get us started? Is the Common Core realistic for black boys?

Missing the Mark and the Narrative of Reform

I have heard the previous narrative more than a hundred times over the past 10 years in the contexts of several different reforms and initiatives. In short, the narrative indicates that we continue to miss the mark with African American males (as indicated by standardized reading assessments) despite literacy reform efforts, initiatives, and policies informed by empirical reading research, significant allocation of funds, and the formation of panels and commissions during the past decade (e.g., No Child Left Behind, Reading First, Reading Next, National Reading Panel). A great deal of promise and energy were associated with these efforts at the national, state, and local levels. However, reversing the widespread reading and writing underperformance of African American males who live in some of the nation's most underprivileged communities has not occurred.

The failure to advance the literacy development of African American males in grades K–12 can be attributed to, among many things, a narrow lens of literacy instruction taken by educators that fails to address the depth of needs of these young males. The failure can also be attributed to a poor conceptualization of the roles of literacy instruction authorized by district administrators and principals. There has been an open focus on meeting minimum standards or simply meeting national norms, the low-hanging fruit of literacy reform efforts. Each aligns with the academic needs of students without regard to the broader contexts that inform their lives. This is why I have called for a more comprehensive model of literacy instruction for African American males in grades K–12 that brings attention to curriculum orientations; roles of literacy instruction; and the ways to teach text to nurture reading, writing, and human development (Tatum, 2012; Tatum & Gue, 2010, 2012). The primary argument is that we should not focus on one while neglecting the others.

We must place the CCSS in the larger reform narrative, examining both the promises and potential shortcomings. Many large-scale reforms have failed, yielded lukewarm success, or dissipated. Still, I am cautiously optimistic as one who favors the CCSS. However, I want to offer two points:

1. The absence of sanctioned standards is not the root cause of the reading and writing outcomes for African American males.

2. The implementation of the CCSS will not be at the epicenter of the academic success for African American males.

The CCSS are merely a proposed lever for addressing the uneven academic performance of students and addressing the dissatisfaction that state governors expressed about the academic preparedness of graduating high school seniors entering the workplace or colleges. We need a Common Core Plus (+). Teachers who figure this out will place themselves well ahead of the curve while others are focusing on key staples of CCSS—close reading, complex text, and the balance between fiction and nonfiction—things that fit neatly into a checklist and can be assessed. The CCSS represent a point on a continuum, and the Standards are not the endpoint of the continuum for African American males. However, the CCSS align well with the historical pathway taken to advance their literacy development (see Table 6.1).

A close look at Table 6.1 reveals synergy between the historical orientations of literacy development for African American males and the emerging CCSS. There is more similarity than differences with curriculum and texts, writing, and language. With regard to curriculum and texts, there is a common call for a wide range of texts, and writing has been

Table 6.1. Conceptual Framing for Literacy and African American Males

Historical Orientations of Literacy for African American Males	Orientation of the Common Core State Standards	Agreement*
	Literacy/Reading	
• Reading and writing, debating, critiquing, and being able to make meaning of one's identity • Securing freedom and becoming self-determined • Establishing platforms to secure civil, economic, educational, political, and social rights • Building agendas to improve and enhance the condition of the African American community	• Providing appropriate benchmarks for all students, regardless of where they live • Defining the knowledge and skills students should have within their K–12 education careers so that they will graduate high school able to succeed in entry-level, credit-bearing academic college courses and in workforce training programs • Including rigorous content and application of knowledge through high-order skills • Preparing students to succeed in our global economy and society • Increasing complexity in what students must be able to read so that all students are ready for the demands of college- and career-level reading no later than the end of high school • Requiring the progressive development of reading comprehension so that students advancing through the grades are able to gain more from whatever they read • Ensuring that teachers across disciplines focus on reading and writing to build knowledge within their subject areas	Low
	Curriculum and Texts	
• Reading texts that included classics from English writers, laws of the land, national and international news, letters, sermons, speeches, poetry, narratives, essays, biographies, broadsides, and short stories	• Reading a diverse array of classic and contemporary literature as well as challenging informational texts in a range of subjects to broaden students' perspectives • Mandating certain critical types of content for all students, including classic myths and stories from around the world, foundational U.S. documents, seminal works of American literature, and the writings of Shakespeare	High

(continued)

Table 6.1. Conceptual Framing for Literacy and African American Males (continued)

Historical Orientations of Literacy for African American Males	Orientation of the Common Core State Standards	Agreement*
Curriculum and Texts		
• Reading across multiple subject areas as common practice; prominently reading literature, science, humanities, and history texts	• Focusing on complex texts outside of literature to ensure that these standards are helping African American males to prepare to read, write, and research across the curriculum, including history and science	
Writing		
• Producing texts that defined their lives and defined their times	• Writing logical arguments based on substantive claims, sound reasoning, and relevant evidence	Moderate to high
Language		
• Using language to (re)claim authority and counter oppressive and harsh circumstances (Tatum, 2009) • Sharing knowledge, promoting ideas, and cultivating a scholarly and literate way of life (Belt-Beyan, 2004) • Cultivating speakers and thinkers	• Growing students' vocabularies through a mix of conversations, direct instruction, and reading • Expanding students' repertoire of words and phrases • Preparing students for real-life experience at college and in 21st-century careers • Using formal English in writing and speaking and making skillful choices among the many ways to express themselves through language • Gaining, evaluating, and presenting increasingly complex information, ideas, and evidence through listening and speaking as well as through media • Having academic discussions and being able to deliver formal presentations in a variety of contexts • Collaborating to answer questions, build understanding, and solve problems	Moderate to high

* Low = 0 to 1 connections, moderate = 2 to 3 connections, high = 3 or more connections.

central to the advancement of African American males. However, there is a radical difference between the conceptual frames and literacy in African American males.

The historical orientations of literacy instruction for African Americans were people- or humanity-centered—literacy involved making meaning of one's identity, becoming self-determined, establishing platforms to secure a range of rights, and building agendas to improve and enhance the conditions of the African American community. The CCSS are economy centered—providing benchmarks, defining knowledge and skills for entry-level into colleges and careers, and preparing students to succeed in a global economy and society. These are without regard to some of the people- and humanity-centered orientations. In other words, there is no expressed interest or intentionality toward African American males in CCSS, but there is an expressed interest in the economy and other structures. There must be reconciliation between the two.

I share a conversation I had with a colleague about exemplar texts to further explain this point of reconciling the two conceptual frames. The colleague expressed that students need to read *The Adventures of Tom Sawyer* by Mark Twain because this is the type of text that students will receive in their regular English classrooms. I raised a concern because the metric for selection was being able to say our students read a wide range of texts. My litmus test for text selection, although still focused on a wide range of texts, is the potential of the text to serve as a rich model for writing and language development and to advance intellectual development, human liberty, and equality. I am less concerned about the exemplar text checklist. I asked my colleague, "Can we take the knowledge of *Tom Sawyer* and begin to soldier the cross for progress in our community and nation? If we can answer 'yes' without equivocation, then *Tom Sawyer* fits. If not, I raise cautions." My colleague's comments were grounded in using text as some form of literary nostalgia to preserve the integrity of the literary canon. They were not focused on rebuilding students' relationship with texts so that reading becomes a marker of progress in the larger sociopolitical landscape in which many young African American males are confronted with immediate assaults, such as violence, classism, poor schooling, or other conditions, that cause many of them to feel dehumanized and devalued.

A misinterpretation of CCSS can lead teachers to focus on complex texts (see the CCSS conceptual frame in Table 6.1) while ignoring the complexity of students' lives and their need for more (see the column "Historical Orientation of Literacy Development for African American Males"). For African American males, these texts contribute to a healthy psyche/identity; provide a roadmap for being, doing, and acting; and provide modern awareness of the real world (Tatum, 2007, 2008, 2009). Also grounding narrative and expository writing in four purposes—defining self, nurturing resilience, engaging others, and building capacity—is useful for stimulating their writing (Tatum, 2012; Tatum & Gue, 2012). Thus, my call for Common Core Plus (+) for African American males.

Common Core Plus (+) as a Pathway of Protection for African American Males

I hope the other chapter authors in this volume have grounded their discussions in reading research in ways that carve a clearer pathway for moving forward with CCSS. I decided to take a different approach. It is important to contextualize the CCSS in a sociohistorical narrative that is often ignored. Understanding the historical narrative is important for taking a critical view of literacy aims and practices, including CCSS, and their potential for safeguarding the academic and personal welfare of African American male youth.

This chapter is not a call for a "different" type of literacy instruction for African American males under the CCSS but rather a call for a better, more responsive type of literacy instruction. Literacy instruction cannot be conceived as an in-school phenomenon related to standards and test scores alone. We've gone down that path before. This has led to African American males being underserved in schools during the past five decades. Thus, I offer six recommendations as teachers move forward with implementing the CCSS:

1. Do not reject the CCSS based on perceived notions of the ability or capacity of African American males to handle complex text across a wide range of subjects. Many of them will fail to handle complex texts, but so will many other students. The failure will not be based on race. Be patient and steadfast.

2. Increase African American males' exposure to rare words and language in grades K–12. Use rich language while speaking. Select texts for read-alouds that are language rich. Share examples of your own writing that models how you use rich language.

3. Focus on the intersection of reading, writing, and intellectual development. Require students to demonstrate their comprehension through reading and writing. Develop a writing template that requires students to demonstrate their new understandings that emerge from the texts.

4. Move beyond texts during instruction that are "cultural feel-goods" in favor of texts that advance students' cognitive and social development.

5. Become better arbiters of the texts you use with students or change how you plan to use the texts. Establish a litmus test for your text selections that moves beyond mandated materials.

6. Conceptualize reading, writing, and language as tools of protection for African American males and refuse to be circumscribed by the ongoing crisis narrative.

These six recommendations require taking a more comprehensive approach to literacy teaching while implementing the CCSS. To illustrate this comprehensive approach, I provide components from a lesson that I taught to a group of fourth-grade African American boys who struggled with reading as part of a pilot study aimed to have these boys read three years above grade level on their state's standardized reading test. The lesson is based on a seven-step multidimensional reading model (see Figure 6.1) that requires students to read across multiple texts, at least one fiction and nonfiction, and write across the texts during a one-hour lesson. This lesson also provides an example of several of the recommendations in action.

Figure 6.1. Multidimensional Reading Model

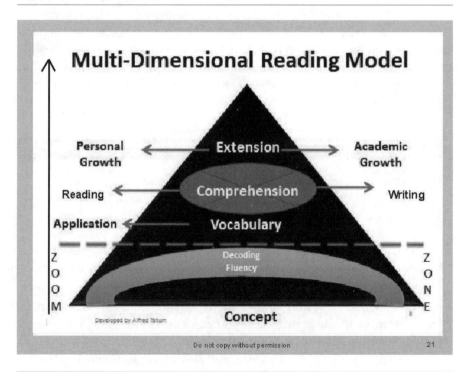

The multidimensional reading model and lesson were developed based on the historical orientation of the literacy development of African American males. It also aligns with the emerging Common Core Standards. The boys were reading and writing across multiple texts to learn about juvenile justice. The lesson focuses on the intersection of reading, writing, and intellectual development. The following seven components are part of each lesson that involves multiple texts:

1. Anticipation guide and vocabulary (see the example in Figure 6.2)
2. Decoding exercise—list of 6 to 10 words (see Figure 6.3)
3. Fluency practice piece (see Figure 6.4)
4. Companion text (see Figure 6.5)
5. Line sets (see Figure 6.6)
6. Thinking Across Texts writing template (see Figure 6.7)
7. Information sheet (see Figure 6.8)

Conclusion

Structuring equitable academic pathways for African American males and protecting them will not be easy. Some administrators will simply require the bare minimum and will doubt teachers' capacity to move beyond a Common Core checklist. This is the bureaucratic nature of schools that gives me skepticism. Implementing the CCSS Plus (+) that reconciles historical orientations of literacy for African American males and the emerging CCSS requires a revolutionary act of sorts if we are serious about changing the literacy practices and literacy outcomes for African American males.

TRY THIS!

- Have students read historical informational texts about Frederick Douglass and W.E.B. Du Bois. Once students have finished reading the selections, divide students into two groups. One group will advocate education to grow the economy, similar to Douglass's position. The other group will argue for a wider view of education, citing reasons given by Du Bois. During the debate, students must refer to and cite information within the texts to support their arguments.

- Have students read competing views by African American economists who examine the intersection of economics and race (e.g., Roland Fryer, Thomas Sowell). Once finished, have students list similarities and differences between the views and fashion an argument to accept, reject, or craft a new view on economics and race. Finally, have groups of students write and "deliver" their views and suggest a platform for action.

Figure 6.2. Sample Anticipation Guide With Lesson Vocabulary

Name: _____ Date: _____

New knowledge: juvenile justice

Reading skills: decoding/reading fluently/reading and writing across texts

Should laws be made to help or punish juveniles who break the law?

1. A 10-year-old homeless boy steals food to eat. *Punish him / do not punish him*
2. An 11-year-old girl is forced to carry a knife by a 16-year-old boy and gets caught. *Punish her / do not punish her*
3. A 15-year-old plays a joke on a kid that leads to the kid's death. *Punish him / do not punish him*

When should the laws punish juveniles, and when should the laws help juveniles?

Directions: Read the following poems to help you think about juvenile justice. Underline one line in each poem that connects the poem to the concept of juvenile justice.

Poem 1 (text 1)

Hurt My Sister
by Dr. A. Tatum

He hurt my sister
Made me mad
I hurt him
Made me glad

The police came
Took me away
To stop me
From hurting another day

The judge said, "Lock him away for eight
 years."
My sister and my momma were in tears
I told the judge, "I am only ten."
He said, "We need to make sure you never
 hurt anyone again"

Do you agree with the judge?

Poem 2 (text 2)

I Was Tricked
by Dr. A. Tatum

No food at home, no bed
"Big Joe" had an idea
To get me fed
He was nineteen
I was only ten
Come on little man, he said
Three minutes later
Lil' Johnny was dead

I heard the sirens
Started to run

Hey, Lil boy
Drop that gun

Big Joe told me to do it
He told me it was a trick

Think about that for the next nine years
As you hear the cell door, CLICK

Can you help me, judge?
I was in pain trying to find my way on my own?

Too late for that, boy
Another kid's gone.

Do you agree with the judge?

Figure 6.3. Sample Decoding Exercise

A, E, I, O, U   1, 2

Split consonant between vowels.
    bal / lad

Move one consonant between vowels to the next syllable.
    te / na / cious

Split neighboring vowels.
    jo / vi / al

Do not separate blends or word groupings that need each other.
    ous, qu, bl, cl, dr

Examples: so / ci / e / ty

Row 1:   j u v e n i l e   p r o t e c t   p u n i s h

Row 2:   c o m m i t   v i o l e n t   c r e a t e

Figure 6.4. Sample Fluency Practice Piece

Juvenile Justice

What are your rights as a juvenile (person under 18 years old)? Some people believe laws should protect juveniles. They believe juveniles and adults should not be placed in the same prison because juveniles would learn more bad behaviors from adults. Do you agree or disagree? Other people believe laws should punish juveniles like adults and place them in the same prison if they commit a violent crime. A rise in crime in the 1980s and 1990s led some people to create laws to "get tough on crime." Juvenile crimes were treated like adult crimes. Instead of helping kids, some laws were made to punish kids. Which is right?

Figure 6.5. Sample Companion Text

Nonfiction Text (Text 3)

Juvenile Justice

What are your rights as a juvenile (person under 18 years old)? Some people believe laws should protect juveniles. They believe juveniles and adults should not be placed in the same prison because juveniles would learn more bad behaviors from adults. Do you agree or disagree? Other people believe laws should punish juveniles like adults and place them in the same prison if they commit a violent crime. A rise in crime in the 1980s and 1990s led some people to create laws to "get tough on crime." Juvenile crimes were treated like adult crimes. Instead of helping kids, some laws were made to punish kids. Which is right?

The treatment of juveniles has caused a great deal of debate. Some people believe that juveniles who live under poor conditions with little support from parents should receive help and support, not jail time. Others believe that juveniles know right from wrong, and it is foolish to blame criminal behaviors on not having support from parents. Kids should be wise enough to take care of themselves or seek help they need from other adults.

Figure 6.6. Sample Line Sets

Circle the line set that best explains the paragraphs in the companion text (close reading).

Line Set 1:
- Others believe that juveniles know right from wrong, and it is foolish to blame criminal behavior on not having support from parents.
- Other people believe laws should punish juveniles like adults and place them in the same prison if they commit a violent crime.
- Kids should be wise enough to take care of themselves or seek help they need from other adults.

Line Set 2:
- Some people believe laws should protect juveniles.
- A rise in crime in the 1980s and 1990s led some people to create laws to "get tough on crime."
- The treatment of juveniles has caused a great deal of debate.

Figure 6.7. Sample Thinking Across Texts Writing Template

Concept: juvenile justice—laws for kids 18 years old and younger

• Should laws be made to help or punish juveniles who break the law?

• How do you think the judges in the poems would answer this question? Give lines to support your answer.

    I believe the judge in poem 1 would say help / punish (circle one) because. . .

    I believe the judge in poem 2 would say help / punish (circle one) because. . .

• We read about juvenile justice today. What do you think about juvenile justice following our readings and discussions?

Figure 6.8. Sample Information Sheet

Here are some juvenile rights:

• Can a juvenile receive life in prison? *Yes and No*

• Can a juvenile's mother or father allow other people to search his or her property? *No*

• Can teachers and principals search my locker or book bag? *Yes*

• Can teachers and principals force me to provide a written statement about my behavior? *No*

• Do juveniles have to talk to the police if they are questioned? *Yes and No—They have to provide their names if asked. But they do not have to give information about anything else. They can ask for a parent or lawyer to be present. It is a good idea to be respectful.*

• Can I leave when being questioned by the police? *Yes and No—You should ask if it is okay to leave.*

• Do juveniles have the right to make phone calls if they feel they are being mistreated by the police? *Yes—They have the right to make two phone calls.*

DISCUSSION QUESTIONS

1. Much of Tatum's argument hinges on the social, historical, and political elements in literacy traditions of African American males. As a teacher, how are the goals of literacy for African American males unique?

2. Tatum refers to a "narrow lens of literacy instruction" and argues that this view, at least in part, is responsible for a failure to advance the literacy development of African American males in grades K–12. How

can we, as classroom teachers, expand our views of literacy instruction to help *all* students?

3. For Tatum, the CCSS focus on economy, which shortchanges people- and humanity-centered orientations. Given this fact, how will a singular focus on economy potentially impact African American males?

REFERENCES

Belt-Beyan, P.M. (2004). *The emergence of African American literacy traditions: Family and community efforts in the nineteenth century.* Westport, CT: Praeger.

Exec. Order No. 13621, 77 Fed. Reg. 148 (July 26, 2012). Retrieved from www.gpo.gov/fdsys/pkg/FR-2012-08-01/pdf/2012-18868.pdf

National Governors Association Center for Best Practices & Council of Chief State School Officers. (2010). *Common Core State Standards for English language arts and literacy in history/social studies, science, and technical subjects.* Washington, DC: Authors. Retrieved from www.corestandards.org/assets/CCSSI_ELA%20Standards.pdf

Porter, D. (1995). *Early Negro writing, 1760–1837.* Baltimore: Black Classic Press.

Tatum, A.W. (2007). Building the textual lineages of African American male adolescents. In K. Beers, R.E. Probst, & L. Rief (Eds.), *Adolescent literacy: Turning promise into practice* (pp. 81–85). Portsmouth, NH: Heinemann.

Tatum, A.W. (2008). Toward a more anatomically complete model of literacy instruction: A focus on African American male adolescents and texts. *Harvard Educational Review, 78*(1), 155–180.

Tatum, A.W. (2009). *Reading for their life: (Re) building the textual lineages of African American adolescent males.* Portsmouth, NH: Heinemann.

Tatum, A.W. (2012). Nurturing resiliency among African American adolescent males: A focus on writing. In J. Moore & C. Lewis (Eds.), *Urban school contexts for African American students: Crisis and prospects for improvement* (pp. 53–74). New York: Peter Lang.

Tatum, A.W., & Gue, V. (2010). Adolescents and texts: Raw writing—A critical support for adolescents. *English Journal, 99*(4), 90–93.

Tatum, A.W., & Gue, V. (2012). The sociocultural benefits of writing for African American adolescent males. *Reading & Writing Quarterly, 28*(2), 123–142. doi:10.1080/10573569.2012.651075

Opportunities and Oversights Within the Common Core State Standards for English Learners' Language and Literacy Achievement

Theresa A. Roberts

This chapter will focus on the Common Core State Standards (CCSS; National Governors Association Center for Best Practices & Council of Chief State School Officers [NGA Center & CCSSO], 2010) for English Language Arts (ELA) for grades K–5 and their potential impact on English learners' language and literacy achievement. I acknowledge and applaud that the CCSS, as noted by many practitioners and scholars, establish the same high expectations for ELA achievement for all students, including English learners. Achievement in the English language arts remains at the heart of the group achievement gap between English learners and students who begin school speaking English as their first language (Goldenberg, 2011). The extent to which CCSS may pave the road for ensuring that English learners are career and college ready— or present obstacles that are simply insurmountable for many—will be influenced by schools, students, and their families embracing and sharing the responsibility for achieving the Standards. This chapter focuses on schools' responsibilities for creating the needed balance.

In this chapter, I discuss four opportunities that can contribute to shifting the conceptualization of English learners from being considered "at risk" to being considered "at promise." I move on to identify five oversights within the CCSS. Throughout these sections, I make recommendations for teaching and school practices to increase the likelihood that these opportunities are fulfilled and the oversights are rectified.

Quality Reading Instruction in the Age of Common Core Standards, edited by Susan B. Neuman and Linda B. Gambrell. © 2013 by the International Reading Association.

Opportunities for English Learners Within the CCSS

Focus on Learning Outcomes

In the minds of many educators, an understood postscript to the No Child Left Behind Act of 2001 is an association among standards, high-stakes testing, and punitive consequences for individual students and schools for failure to make adequate progress in achieving specified standards at individual or aggregate levels. While the CCSS also explicitly specify grade-level standards for expected levels of ELA achievement, achievement of them is not linked to fiscal or other punitive consequences. Therefore, enacting the CCSS may present a fresh opportunity for a forward-looking, student-focused orientation to learning for each English learner. To this end, thinking of standards as student-learning outcomes seems useful as a proactive strategy to (a) distribute attention between incremental progress and endpoint achievement and (b) maintain attention on the quality of learning opportunities for achieving the CCSS. These two foci are especially apt for English learners who typically have developmental trajectories for ELA achievement that may be different from that of English proficient students.

Extensive Attention to the Importance of Language Production

The field of second-language acquisition has been dominated for the last 30 years by input theories. Input theories emphasize the importance of exposing English learners to a great deal of language that is "comprehensible" (e.g., Krashen, 1985). Comprehensible input that contains structures just beyond a student's current level of language proficiency is believed to maximally drive second-language acquisition. A corollary of the input hypothesis is that speaking does not need to be taught or practiced directly, and in the strongest form, speaking should not be taught at all, as it is believed to emerge as the acquirer gains proficiency. Input theories have contributed to notions that silent, pre-production or receptive periods in second-language acquisition are natural or perhaps even desirable.

There is no doubt that the amount and quality of language input influences acquisition of a first or second language (Hoff & Shatz, 2007). However, second-language input theories have not attended sufficiently to how output, or language production, contributes to language acquisition (Izumi, 2003; Swain, 2005). Thus, there is reason to be somewhat optimistic that the robust expectations for oral language competencies contained within the CCSS ELA categories of Reading, Speaking and Listening, and the subcategory Conventions of Standard English within the Language category may direct extensive and focused attention to English language development (ELD) in general and the importance of output within it. To the extent that implementation of the Standards is associated with effective output learning experiences within ELD and language and literacy instruction, English learners' proficiency in English is likely to benefit (Ellis, 2005).

The emphasis on oral-language production contained within the K–5 Standards for Reading, Speaking and Listening, and Conventions of Standard English at each grade level adds a welcome and needed balance to the historical emphasis on input for achieving English proficiency. Details within output theories identify that language production may be especially beneficial for acquiring language structure—key components of language structure include accurate pronunciation (phonology), correct word order and use of rules governing how desired relationships among ideas may be effectively constructed (syntax), and conventions for modifying words for present and past tense or singular and plural forms (morphology). Achieving a command of English language structure is particularly challenging for English learners and is a roadblock for achieving advanced levels of English proficiency (August & Shanahan, 2008; Genesee, Lindholm-Leary, Saunders, & Christian, 2006).

Expecting students to talk is an important foundation for programs that balance input with output. However, all talk is not equal. Talk that is motivated by a conceptualization of a meaning to be communicated followed by assembling appropriate language structures to express the meaning (Ellis, 2005) is most important. Therefore, effective teaching of language structure does not imply only the simple completion and repetition of oral exercises, such as students repeating, "The deer is jumping. The deer jumped," to learn past tense. A more effective practice because it integrates text, instruction in language structure and student communication of text-related meanings would be to orally read an informational history selection on Susan B. Anthony, review words from that text that could be formed into regular past tense (such as *want, vote, assert,* and *march*), instruct students in the use of *-ed* for past tense, and then ask students to "tell your partner" two things that women did to secure the right to vote. Other features of instruction to bear in mind are as follows (Genesee et al., 2006; Izumi, 2003):

- Learning activities that are focused on task completion without structuring interaction may lead to a "just do it" student response.

- Heterogeneous language grouping is useful, but students must be trained in how to elicit and support the engagement of their peer English learners.
- Activities that require the contribution of all students may increase English learners' participation.
- Beginning and intermediate English learners need more support to effectively participate in classroom interactions.

Instruction and learning experiences crafted to ensure that the type, amount, and quality of language production needed for learning language structure and for promoting academic-oriented communication are necessary.

Recommendations
- Ensure that teachers have extensive and current knowledge of how first and second languages develop.
- Ensure that teachers have knowledge and skills for implementing classroom language output practices that begin with student conceptualization of meanings followed by output into language structures.
- Provide peer collaboration and interaction carefully structured to promote output of specific features of language within tasks that are motivating and require communication among students.

Clear Recognition of the Importance of Language Structure

The CCSS contain double the number of learning outcomes for language structure compared with the average in state standards (Porter, McMaken, Hwang, & Yang, 2011). Language structure refers to semantics (vocabulary), phonology, syntax, and morphology (as discussed previously in this chapter). The competencies specified in the Conventions of Standard English subcategory in the Language Standards of the CCSS refer primarily to specific skills in syntax and morphology and other more complex components of language structure.

Many teachers believe that because they model and teach language all day, children will implicitly learn sufficient language structure in this manner. Indeed, when teacher language models scaffold, request clarification, and use correct structures, English proficiency can grow. However, research increasingly shows that intentional and explicit teaching of English language structure is an added benefit to students'

English proficiency (Ellis, 2005). A recent study found that only 6% of the time allocated for English language development instruction was devoted to language structure (Saunders, Foorman, & Carlson, 2006) and that achievement of English learners who regularly participated in a separate ELD block of time was higher than those students who did not participate in a separate ELD block.

The K–5 CCSS foreground using language for academic purposes in interaction and collaboration with peers. The related learning outcomes are housed primarily in the Reading and Speaking and Listening categories. Standards associated with interaction and collaboration as well as academic language may benefit English learners because properly designed collaboration and interaction can enhance their learning, and English learners may benefit from extensive opportunities to master academic language (August & Shanahan 2008; Genesee et al., 2006). Using language for academic learning requires competence with language structure. Thus, the Reading, Speaking and Listening, and Conventions of Standard English Standards logically have the potential to work together in supporting English learners' speaking, acquisition of language structure, and academic language competence, although research would be needed to confirm this possibility.

The academic communication referenced in these categories of the Standards includes argumentation, reasoning, questioning, and presentation related to grade-level topics and texts. Less proficient English learners will find these academic language expectations very challenging because of limited English proficiency in spite of the fact that they are capable of executing the specified thinking skills (e.g., argumentation) to the same level as similar English proficient students. Explicit teaching of language structure combined with meaningful and motivational opportunities to produce language can be expected to support English learners' achievement of the CCSS.

Recommendations

- Ensure that teachers have extensive knowledge of language structure, including semantics, phonology, syntax, and morphology.
- Provide a specific block of time for daily ELD.
- Use scaffolding, requests for clarification, and feedback practices that model correct language structure while maintaining a stance as a collaborative language partner.
- Implement instruction that explicitly teaches English learners the structure of the English language (semantics, phonology, syntax, morphology, and pragmatics).

- Ensure that teachers have curricula and instructional resources for teaching language structure.

Specific Attention to Teaching Vocabulary

One of the three subcategories within the Language category of the CCSS is Vocabulary Acquisition and Use. Achieving sufficient English vocabulary knowledge is a well-established challenge for English learners, particularly beyond grade 3 and within content area reading (August & Shanahan, 2008; Genesee et al., 2006). Fortunately, evidence suggests that English learners' vocabularies can be enhanced with a variety of explicit and implicit teaching practices. Direct explanation, visual supports, and structured opportunities for usage of new vocabulary are examples of these strategies. The strong emphasis on vocabulary acquisition and use if effectively implemented may be an important opportunity for increasing English learners' school achievement.

The Vocabulary Acquisition and Use section of the CCSS also includes a standard for the ability to clarify and determine word meaning (NGA Center & CCSSO, 2010, p. 25). These two abilities are essentially word-learning strategies. There has been recent conjecture about the value of teaching word-learning strategies to all students, but there is as yet insufficient evidence to conclude that it is possible to effectively teach word-learning strategies to English learners. Therefore, the effect of this part of the standard on English learners cannot be gauged at this time.

The importance of vocabulary instruction for overall school achievement has been trumpeted for the past 20 years, yet studies of classroom practice reveal that limited vocabulary instruction takes place and the instruction often does not include research-based methods. Recent evidence documents this same finding for instruction of English learners, even during specific ELD instruction (Saunders et al., 2006). Vocabulary development garnered only 3–7% of instructional time. In grades K–5 general education, words to be taught are typically selected from reading texts but often without an articulated word-selection framework or planned sequence from year-to-year, and without sufficient attention to instruction of other important categories of vocabulary needed by English learners. These learners need vocabulary development that (a) fosters communicative language ability, (b) provides understanding of words used in instruction, (c) promotes access to content area learning, and (d) supports reading comprehension.

Recommendations

- Ensure that teachers understand each of the preceding four categories.
- Ensure that English learners receive vocabulary instruction in each of the preceding four categories.
- Select and align instructional resources into a multiyear vocabulary instruction program that identifies words to teach in each of the preceding four categories.

Oversights

First Language as a Language Arts Resource

The CCSS append the descriptor "language arts" with "English," an addition not made for mathematics. The introduction to the CCSS states that the Standards represent those competencies that are "most essential" for career and college readiness (NGA Center & CCSSO, 2010, p. 3); not all valuable competencies are included. This labeling and qualification serves to indirectly but firmly close discussion of cultivating language resources other than English because only *English* language arts is addressed and because the expected inference is that bilingualism is not one of *most essential* competencies for career and college readiness.

An alternative perspective to help maximize the career and college readiness of English learners can be suggested. This perspective is based on evidence supporting the view that bilingualism is one of the most essential competencies for incipient bilinguals (and is, in fact, valuable for *all* students). Other countries have adopted this view. The ELA Standards could be labeled "Language Arts," and each Standard could be appended with the phrase "in English or English plus first language." For example, a kindergarten Listening and Speaking Standard could read "Speak audibly and express thoughts, feelings, and ideas clearly in English or English plus a first language." These simple revisions would recognize and create opportunities for using the existing language arts strengths of English learners.

The recommendation that English learners' potential for bilingualism be viewed as one of the most essential language arts competencies is very defensible on the basis of research conducted over the past 35 years. Bilingualism confers cognitive and other advantages to English learners. Bilingualism benefits planning and reflection—called executive functioning, cognitive flexibility, and language awareness. All of these cognitive abilities can be applied in second-language, school-based learning (Bialystok & Craik, 2010). Benefits of bilingualism seem to fit in very well with the increased emphasis on text-based analysis, argumentation, and reasoning within the CCSS compared with existing state standards (Porter et al., 2011). Benefits of bilingualism extend beyond school achievement. One interesting example of this far-reaching benefit is that being bilingual is associated with an average delay of four years in the onset of dementia (Bialystok, Craik, & Freedman, 2007).

Classroom use of students' first language supports English achievement and contributes to bilingualism. In spite of a long history of contentious debate and more recent formal roadblocks enacted by state laws or educational policies regarding using students' first language in school-based language arts development, an overarching fact emerges from the research. This fact is that some use of students' first language for reading instruction leads to higher English reading achievement than do programs that do not include any first language. Four separate meta-analyses have reached this conclusion (Greene, 1997; Rolstad, Mahoney, & Glass, 2005; Slavin & Cheung, 2005; Willig, 1985). Moreover, recent studies support using first languages in preschool (Barnett, Yarosz, Thomas, Jung, & Blanco, 2007; Farver, Lonigan, & Eppe, 2009; Roberts, 2008).

The advantage in reading scores for programs that included first-language reading instruction is about 12–15% (Goldenberg, 2008). This is an advantage greater than that found for class-size reduction (Goldenberg, 2008), a popular and strongly supported initiative. Further, an important finding of the Slavin and Cheung (2005) review was that reading programs including instruction in both the first and second language in the same year yielded positive effects for English reading achievement. Enacting programs that teach English learners to read in their first language and English at the same time—for example at different times within the same day—is one strategic means for strengthening English learners' second-language reading achievement and supporting their bilingual development. This plan may simultaneously finesse current restrictions on providing first-language instruction because there is no delay to English instruction, and first-language instruction can legitimately be positioned as a support for English learning, allowable in most classroom settings. Refraining from promoting bilingualism and from providing first-language reading instruction detracts from potential levels of language arts and other academic achievement and diminishes opportunity for potential cognition and other benefits for English learners.

Important caveats should be noted. First, almost all of the studies on first-language reading instruction are of Spanish. Second, there is very limited understanding of the relationships among subtleties of first-language reading instruction, individual differences among English learners, and differences among languages and learning. Third, the reviews do not evaluate whether or not there may be some benefit of using first language in writing or speaking and listening.

Recommendations

- Append the CCSS with a broader standard for promoting language arts resources.
- Promote bilingualism.
- Teach children to read in English and the first language at the same time.
- Articulate a rationale for first-language reading instruction as a support for English reading achievement.

Recognition for English Learners' Time Needed to Achieve Grade-Level Expectations

Language from the CCSS presents educators with a very big conundrum for determining how to practically apply the Standards to English learners:

> The National Governors Association Center for Best Practices and the Council of Chief State School Officers strongly believe that all students should be held to the same high expectations outlined in the Common Core State Standards. This includes students who are English language learners (ELLs). However, these students may require additional time, appropriate instructional support, and aligned assessments as they acquire both English language proficiency and content area knowledge…. Teachers should recognize that it is possible to achieve the standards for reading and literature, writing and research, language development and speaking and listening without manifesting native-like control of conventions and vocabulary. (NGA Center & CCSSO, 2012a, p. 1)

One can reasonably be very confused about what this language means for educational practice and particularly for determining if standards have been met. Undoubtedly, educators must grapple with these issues. They must also put into place specific grading, progress-monitoring, assessment, evaluation, reporting to families, and other practices that respond to them.

The first part of the quote stipulates that English learners are to be held to the same high expectations—expressed within the CSSS as yearly grade-level standards—as all other students. Yet it simultaneously stipulates that English learners may take longer to meet them. The second part of the quote states that English learners may meet the standards for

Reading, Language, and Speaking and Listening without demonstrating "native-like" control of conventions and vocabulary. And yet one of the three categories of Language Standards is labeled Conventions of Standard English. To illustrate concretely this difficulty, a selection of the kindergarten Conventions of Standard English follows:

- Use frequently occurring nouns and verbs.
- Form regular plural nouns orally by adding /s/ or /es/ (e.g., *dog, dogs; wish, wishes*).
- Understand and use question words (interrogatives) (e.g., *who, what, where, when, why, how*).
- Use the most frequently occurring prepositions (e.g., *to, from, in, out, on, off, for, of, by, with*).
- Produce and expand complete sentences in shared-language activities. (NGA Center & CCSSO, 2010, p. 26)

The statement that English learners need more time to achieve the Standards may not be very troublesome if it were likely that English learners might be given additional time within a year and achieve the Standards by the end of each year. However, this is unlikely to be the case because the best estimates are that it takes between four and seven years to develop English proficiency depending on whether the target level of proficiency is oral/communicative language or academic language (Hakuta, Butler, & Witt, 2000). It is very probable that a large proportion of K–5 English learners, who characteristically have limited levels of English proficiency at kindergarten entry, will not meet all of the Speaking and Listening, Conventions of Standard English, or Reading Standards, which are heavily dependent on language proficiency at each grade level, because these standards have been calibrated as grade appropriate for English proficient students.

Unfortunately, there is no clear evidence to guide educators on this deeply important question of how to maintain high standards while simultaneously adjusting for English learners' developing English proficiency. What might make sense in these circumstances? One idea is to link levels of proficiency (rather than grade) to expected levels of achievement on CCSS across a multiyear (K–5) framework (which conveniently aligns with the time needed to acquire English proficiency). English learners could be expected to achieve the K–5 ELA Standards by the end of a six-year period, with progress expected in ELD and aligned English Language Arts CCSS every year, supported by high-quality instruction and learning experiences providing access to their grade-appropriate content. This possibility simultaneously draws attention to English proficiency level and Standards achievement and, in so doing, accurately portrays the interactive relationship among them (Genesee et al., 2006).

This approach could bolster attention to students' progress in English proficiency, support the implementation of robust ELD instruction, and foster alignment between ELD and CCSS because of overlap among speaking and listening, knowledge and use of language structure, and vocabulary acquisition. This alignment may support curricular focus and efficient use of precious instructional minutes for ELD and ELA by preventing redundancy and by building effective sequences of learning between them.

Finally, coupling the level of English proficiency with expected Standards achievement over a six-year period has the potential to apply the CCSS to individual English learners in a manner consistent with individual trajectories of ELD while simultaneously avoiding unreasonable judgments of inadequacy when English learners do not meet standards due to limitations in English proficiency—judgments that are troubling to both teachers and families.

Recommendations

- Study and formally clarify the relationship of levels of English proficiency (which vary among states) and achievement of the CCSS.
- Consider linking levels of proficiency to expected levels of achievement in CCSS across a multiyear (K–5) framework.
- Consider implications for grading, evaluation, and reporting to parents aligned with this approach.

The Importance of Preschool

There are no CCSS for preschool. This oversight of including preschool in the CCSS may matter for English learners. There is a great deal of evidence documenting that preschool children's language abilities, prereading skills, and competencies in other areas of ELA affect students' progress in learning to read and other areas of school achievement for many years (Scarborough, 2002). However, there is robust evidence that preschool experience has not consistently led to the gains in language development and prereading skills that can be expected in the highest quality programs. Appropriately extending the CCSS to preschool may boost the language and literacy learning of English learners in preschool by supporting high-quality language and literacy instruction and learning opportunities at that level.

Another reason why an expansion of CCSS to include preschool may benefit English learners is because it could potentially add an additional year of language and literacy learning based on a well-reasoned progression of preschool language arts. Expanding the time period for achieving language proficiency and literacy achievement has the potential to benefit English learners for all of the reasons already discussed. The exclusion of preschool from CCSS has also contributed to what may be developmental missteps in the kindergarten standards. To illustrate, the current kindergarten CCSS stipulate the ability to identify syllables and to name letters of the alphabet as learning outcomes, competencies that are well within the learning capabilities and interests of most typically developing four-year-olds and many three-year-olds. Having these skills at kindergarten entry is likely to be a support for English learners with limited English skills because it would ease the cognitive and linguistic demands of kindergarten instruction.

Finally, most states have adopted learning guidelines, foundations, or standards for public preschool programs (Neuman & Roskos, 2005). Preschool educators, particularly those whose programs are housed within school districts, are left to struggle with how to align those existing state and national preschool standards with the CCSS. The time, resources, and expertise to do so are not readily available in many programs.

Recommendations

- Advocate to expand the CCSS to preschool.
- Work with preschool programs to determine how the categories within the CCSS may be appropriately extended to preschool.
- Integrate preschool and elementary programs into a multiyear, comprehensive language development program.

The Importance of Motivation and Engagement for ELA Achievement

The CCSS do not identify positive motivation and related behaviors as ELA learning outcomes. English learners are among those who find academic achievement most challenging because of their typically limited English proficiency. Therefore, instruction and learning opportunities that incorporate practices to foster and sustain motivation and engagement during ELA instruction are very important for English learners.

Classroom motivation studies identify practices that can enhance or thwart motivation and engagement. Opportunities for challenge, autonomy, self-regulation, and feedback emphasizing effort and providing specific information are a few of the classroom practices known to influence ELA motivation. Learner-regulated collaborations and interactions with others identified in the literacy and language CCSS can be expected to support English learners' motivation and engagement (August & Shanahan, 2008; Ellis, 2005). Classroom instruction and learning experiences need to be designed to create speaking experiences that motivate English learners and provide positive social support (Genesee et al., 2006; Hoff & Shatz, 2007).

Recommendations

- Ensure that teachers understand conditions and practices that support language arts motivation and engagement.
- Plan and implement lessons designed to promote motivation and engagement as well as learning outcomes.

The Importance of Research on Effective Teaching Practices

Throughout this chapter, the sensitivity of learning outcomes specified in the CCSS to instructional variation and quality has been identified. Commentary accompanying the CCSS unambiguously states that teacher knowledge of what works is the best guide for instructional practice. The discussion of myths and facts on the CCSS website (www.corestandards.org/about-the-standards/myths-vs-facts) includes this information:

Myth: The Standards tell teachers how to teach.

Fact: The best understanding of what works in the classroom comes from the teachers who are in them. That's why these standards will establish *what* students need to learn, but they will not dictate *how* teachers should teach. Instead, schools and teachers will decide how best to help students reach the standards. (NGA Center & CCSSO, 2012b, n.p.)

This explanation and the lack of attention to teaching within the Standards belies the significant scientific evidence identifying effective (and less effective) teaching practices for ELA and may draw attention away from the importance of relying on available research to guide instruction for English learners (Gersten & Baker, 2000). English learners who are developing English proficiency are more sensitive to instructional quality than are peers whose native language is English.

Furthermore, practices that may appear logical or that grow out of well-intentioned teacher reflection and assessment of student learning may not always be consistent with the research. As one example, it seems logical to think that the amount of English instruction would be directly related to English acquisition. But the evidence shows that stronger English achievement occurs when there is less English and more first-language instruction. The position taken in the CCSS for selecting teaching practices may, in part, be reaction to what many believe has been overly proscriptive and rigid adherence to reading curriculum and programs in recent years.

Recommendations

- Provide continuing professional development promoting instructional quality and practices that have an evidence base.
- Establish clear expectations to use instructional practices and materials that are evidence based and in alignment with achieving the CCSS.
- Balance teacher autonomy in determining classroom instruction with research on effective instruction.
- Establish instructional planning that requires addressing the question, What is the evidence base for this practice?

Final Words

Standards alone will not determine the academic achievement or underachievement of English learners. They are but one piece of a very complex mosaic of schooling influences on English learners' achievement. These effects include the response of schools to students' cultural, linguistic, and socioeconomic circumstances; the emotional experiences imparted through daily classroom interactions with teachers and peers; the richness of the curriculum; the quality of the instruction; the effectiveness of English language development programs; the degree to which learning opportunities foster engagement, motivation, and self-regulation; the degree to which standards support learning; the decisions made on the basis of progress monitoring; and the practices for meaningful and positive collaborations among educators and families, among others. The aggregate of the day-to-day, lived experience of each English learner during school will tell the tale.

There is much that is unknown about second-language and literacy development and practices to increase it. Collaboration among educators and researchers to conduct high-quality research on these topics would benefit English learners. Enactment of the CCSS will be effortful, particularly if ideas for multiyear planning for achieving learning outcomes and vocabulary instruction programs suggested in this chapter are explored. Planning early and within a multiyear framework, proceeding carefully using student learning data, thinking complexly, and maintaining optimism and forward thinking regarding the potential for English learners to achieve rigorous learning outcomes in the ELA will help to steer the course.

TRY THIS!

- How do teaching manuals for your grade level and the overall reading program in your school address vocabulary instruction? What is the basis for how words are selected in the program? How many minutes per day or how big a portion of the lessons are allocated to vocabulary instruction? How much guidance are you given in how to teach those words?

- Think of two English learners with different levels of English proficiency. Look at the CCSS for Speaking and Listening Standards and the Language Standards for Conventions of Standard English for the grade you teach and consider how each student might do on each Standard. Identify a specific practice you could use to help them achieve those standards you believe will be the most challenging for them.

DISCUSSION QUESTIONS

1. Roberts suggests that teachers have "extensive and current knowledge of how first and second languages develop." What knowledge about language development can most help you effectively teach English learners in your classroom? How can classrooms teachers who have limited knowledge of first- and second-language acquisition increase their knowledge base to meet the demands of ever increasing numbers of English learners?

2. According to Roberts, the CCSS call for more language structure (e.g., semantics, phonology, syntax, morphology) outcomes than do many state standards. How can studying language structure and enhancing

English learners' communication abilities when using the English language be integrated?

3. Roberts asserts that the CCSS need to include preschool standards and argues that an additional year of language and literacy learning can be an added benefit to English learners. Do you agree, or do you think the CCSS should not address preschool standards for English learners (or any other preschool students)?

REFERENCES

August, D., & Shanahan, T. (2008). *Developing reading and writing in second-language learners: Lessons from the report of the National Literacy Panel on language-minority children and youth.* New York: Routledge; Washington, DC: Center for Applied Linguistics; Newark, DE: International Reading Association.

Barnett, W.S., Yarosz, D.J., Thomas, J., Jung, K., & Blanco, D. (2007). Two-way and monolingual English immersion in preschool education: An experimental comparison. *Early Childhood Research Quarterly, 22*(3), 277–293. doi:10.1016/j.ecresq.2007.03.003

Bialystok, E., & Craik, F.I.M. (2010). Cognitive and linguistic processing in the bilingual mind. *Current Directions in Psychological Science, 19*(1), 19–23. doi:10.1177/0963721409358571

Bialystok, E., Craik, F.I.M., & Freedman, M. (2007). Bilingualism as a protection against the onset of symptoms of dementia. *Neuropsychologia, 45*(2), 459–464. doi:10.1016/j.neuropsychologia.2006.10.009

Ellis, R. (2005). Principles of instructed language learning. *System, 33*(2), 209–224. doi:10.1016/j.system.2004.12.006

Farver, J.M., Lonigan, C.J., & Eppe, S. (2009). Effective early literacy skill development for young Spanish-speaking English language learners: An experimental study of two methods. *Child Development, 80*(3), 703–719. doi:10.1111/j.1467-8624.2009.01292.x

Genesee, F., Lindholm-Leary, K., Saunders, W.M., & Christian, D. (2006). *Educating English language learners: A synthesis of research evidence.* New York: Cambridge.

Gersten, R., & Baker, S. (2000). The professional knowledge base on instructional practices that support cognitive growth for English-language learners. In R. Gersten, E.P. Schiller, & S.R. Vaughn (Eds.), *Contemporary special education research: Syntheses of the knowledge base on critical instructional issues* (pp. 31–79). Mahwah, NJ: Erlbaum.

Goldenberg, C. (2008). Teaching English language learners. What the research does—and does not—say. *American Educator, 32*(3) 8–44.

Goldenberg, C. (2011). Reading instruction for English language learners. In M.L. Kamil, P.D. Pearson, E.B. Moje, & P.P. Afflerbach (Eds.), *Handbook of reading research* (Vol. 4, pp. 684–710). New York: Routledge.

Greene, J.P. (1997). A meta-analysis of the Rossell and Baker review of bilingual education research. *Bilingual Research Journal, 21*(3), 103–122.

Hakuta, K., Butler, Y.G., & Witt, D. (2000). *How long does it take English learners to attain proficiency?* (Policy Report No. 2000–1). Santa Barbara: University of California Linguistic Minority Research Institute.

Hoff, E., & Shatz, M. (Eds.). (2007). *Blackwell handbook of language development.* Malden, MA: Blackwell. doi:10.1002/9780470757833

Izumi, S. (2003). Comprehension and production processes in second language learning: In search of the psycholinguistic rationale of the output hypothesis. *Applied Linguistics, 24*(2), 168–196. doi:10.1093/applin/24.2.168

Krashen, S.D. (1985). *The input hypothesis: Issues and implications.* New York: Longman.

National Governors Association Center for Best Practices & Council of Chief State School Officers. (2010). *Common Core State Standards for English language arts and literacy in history/social studies, science, and technical subjects.* Washington, DC: Authors. Retrieved from www.corestandards.org/assets/CCSSI_ELA%20Standards.pdf

National Governors Association Center for Best Practices & Council of Chief State

School Officers. (2012a). *Application of Common Core State Standards for English language learners.* Washington, DC: Authors. Retrieved November 26, 2012, from www.corestandards.org/assets/application-for-english-learners.pdf

National Governors Association Center for Best Practices & Council of Chief State School Officers. (2012b). *Myths vs. facts.* Washington, DC: Authors. Retrieved November 21, 2012, from www.core standards.org/about-the-standards/myths-vs-facts

Neuman, S.B., & Roskos, K. (2005). The state of state pre-kindergarten standards. *Early Childhood Research Quarterly, 20*(2), 125–145. doi:10.1016/j.ecresq.2005.04.010

Porter, A., McMaken, J., Hwang, J., & Yang, R. (2011). Common Core Standards: The new U.S. intended curriculum. *Educational Researcher, 40*(3), 103–116. doi:10.3102/0013189X11405038

Roberts, T.A. (2008). Home storybook reading in primary or second language with preschool children: Evidence of equal effectiveness for second-language vocabulary acquisition. *Reading Research Quarterly, 43*(2), 103–130. doi:10.1598/RRQ.43.2.1

Rolstad, K., Mahoney, K., & Glass, G.V. (2005). The big picture: A meta-analysis of program effectiveness research on English language learners. *Educational Policy, 19*(4), 572–594. doi:10.1177/0895904805278067

Saunders, W.M., Foorman, B.R., & Carlson, C.D. (2006). Is a separate block of time for oral English language development in programs for English learners needed? *The Elementary School Journal, 107*(2), 181–198. doi:10.1086/510654

Scarborough, H.S. (2002). Connecting early language and literacy to later reading (dis) abilities: Evidence, theory, and practice. In S.B. Neuman & D.K. Dickinson (Eds.), *Handbook of early literacy research* (Vol. 1, pp. 97–110). New York: Guilford.

Slavin, R.E., & Cheung, A. (2005). A synthesis of research on language of reading instruction for English language learners. *Review of Educational Research, 75*(2), 247–284. doi:10.3102/00346543075002247

Swain, M. (2005). The output hypothesis: Theory and research. In E. Hinkel (Ed.), *Handbook of research in second language teaching and learning* (pp. 471–483). Mahwah, NJ: Erlbaum.

Willig, A.C. (1985). A meta-analysis of selected studies on the effectiveness of bilingual education. *Review of Educational Research, 55*(3), 269–317.

CHAPTER 8

RTI and the Common Core

Anne McGill-Franzen & Kandy Smith

Response to Intervention (RTI) is a multifaceted approach full of promise that requires special and regular education teachers to cross professional disciplinary boundaries, "collect and analyze student data, make data-based decisions, and apply appropriate instructional interventions based on individual student needs" (Hoover, Baca, Wexler-Love, & Saenz, 2008, p. 3). Most students who are and have been identified with learning disabilities are so classified because they have fallen far behind their peers in reading. RTI, however, is about preventing failure, not identifying and labeling those who fail. It may become the preferred approach to addressing problems of underachievement in reading, taking precedence over what is known as the IQ discrepancy formula for classifying students with learning disabilities. At the present time, most states support RTI as an option for meeting federal regulations, and six states identify themselves as RTI *only* states (Colorado, Connecticut, Delaware, Hawaii, Illinois, and Rhode Island; see state.rti4success.org). The majority of school districts report implementing a version of RTI (Fuchs & Fuchs, 2006), but it is questionable whether this broad and diffuse implementation adheres to the intent of RTI—that is, to prevent severe reading difficulties by providing high-quality classroom instruction to all students and targeted early intervention to those most at risk (Johnston, 2011).

RTI is not a packaged program. Like the Common Core State Standards (CCSS; National Governors Association Center for Best Practices & Council of Chief State School Officers [NGA Center & CCSSO], 2010a), RTI requires teachers' expertise—deep knowledge of content, pedagogy, and insight into students' thinking. As Johnston (2011) astutely observes, "Teachers who do not understand the students they are teaching are more likely to decide that the child has a learning disability" (p. 521).

The CCSS will support the effectiveness of RTI. In this chapter, we demonstrate this by discussing RTI's lineage in Title I interventions, describing what RTI is and what it is not, and illustrating the relationships between RTI and the CCSS.

Quality Reading Instruction in the Age of Common Core Standards, edited by Susan B. Neuman and Linda B. Gambrell. © 2013 by the International Reading Association.

RTI Is Rooted in Title I Interventions

When RTI is configured not as a packaged program but as a coherent curriculum with responsive teaching, the CCSS can support its successful implementation. As we know, the CCSS are not grounded in constrained or foundational skills, as was Reading First, but in mastery of challenging content. Likewise, RTI is not grounded in constrained or basic skills, but rather in the range of activities and instruction that are appropriate for learners to achieve grade-level standards. Many educators and researchers have forgotten that the idea of supplemental instruction, such as RTI, did not emerge from Individuals with Disabilities Education Act (IDEA) legislation but, instead, was rooted in Title I of the 1965 Elementary and Secondary Education Act (ESEA) and has been part of most district policies since that time. Challenging curricula is the holy grail of the CCSS, but every national evaluation of Title I since 1992 also has demonstrated that all children—but especially struggling children—need high-quality instruction that includes academically challenging materials (Crawford, 1989), more content area reading, and opportunities to participate in discussion (Puma & Drury, 2000)—all recommendations of the CCSS. To underscore this point, we quote Puma and Drury (2000) from their summary of the findings of previous Title I studies: "instruction for disadvantaged children that emphasizes reasoning and problem solving is more effective at teaching advanced skills, at least as effective at teaching basic skills, and better at engaging students in learning" (p. 12). Students who are eligible for Title I, that is, students from low-income families who struggle, are those most likely to be targeted for RTI. We believe that it is important at the outset of this chapter to note that RTI as supplemental instruction for struggling readers is not a new idea, only newly funded under the auspice of the 2004 reauthorization of IDEA, and that challenging and coherent curricula are not anathema to successful intervention, but essential to it, as previous studies have demonstrated.

Educators are rightly confused about what RTI is, what RTI can and should be, and what RTI most definitely is *not*, let alone how RTI might relate to the CCSS. Contrary to what many publishers might have educators believe, RTI is not a packaged program, and most definitely, RTI is not *one* packaged program layered onto another packaged program in "tiers."

RTI Is Not a Plethora of Packaged Programs

In a study of RTI implementation in two school districts, Harn, Chard, Biancarosa, and Kame'enui (2011) discovered that students who are most at risk, that is, those targeted for early intervention to prevent reading difficulties, participated in up to five different pull-out packaged RTI reading programs—some daily, some twice weekly, some once a week—and these programs differed substantially in instructional approach. Yet at-risk students are least likely to be able to generalize reading strategies across these incongruent approaches, a situation described recently in this study by Harn and colleagues (2011) and also much earlier in reading research (Johnston, Allington, & Afflerbach, 1985; McGill-Franzen & Allington, 1990), and these students most likely missed core reading instruction in the regular classroom literacy block to participate in what appeared to be randomly assigned interventions. Unfortunately, the students who needed the most instructional time and the most focused teaching were shortchanged considerably by the implementation of RTI in these districts.

The U.S. Department of Education's What Works Clearinghouse website (ies.ed.gov/ncee/wwc) routinely reviews the latest findings from experimental studies on the effectiveness of commercial programs that purport to be "research-based" interventions appropriate for RTI initiatives. Very few commercial programs meet the federal government's standard for research-based evidence of effectiveness in any area of reading, and of those that do, none meet that standard for all students at every grade level and in every component of reading. The Clearinghouse clearly indicates which programs have demonstrated effectiveness for alphabetics, fluency, comprehension, and general reading achievement, and for which student groups. Although there may be evidence to suggest that particular interventions have been effective with particular groups of students, there is not a single commercial intervention that is appropriate for all students.

RTI Requires Curricular Alignment

Besides the plethora of packaged programs, a second area of concern identified by Harn and colleagues (2011) and earlier by Johnston and colleagues (1985) and McGill-Franzen and Allington (1990) is the lack of coordination across instructional settings, an inconsistency that inhibits not only the generalization of reading strategies on the part of struggling students, but also limits teachers' understandings of the students' encounters with various materials, previous instructional experiences, and mastery of skills in different contexts. To rectify the situation that Harn and colleagues (2011) found in the districts under study, they revised the RTI instruction so that it aligned with the core reading program (in this case, Open Court). Their RTI model of coordination was most effective for the most at-risk students, but less so with students who evidenced higher initial levels of reading. There were no significant differences on the Passage Comprehensions tests of the Woodcock Reading Mastery Test–Revised between students who participated in RTI aligned with Open Court and those from the previous year (historical peers) who did not. In the aligned RTI model, the researchers emphasized fidelity to "explicit and consistent teacher wording," immediate corrective feedback, re-teaching of skills from the Open Court core program, and student engagement, defined as "many opportunities to respond as a group and individually with feedback" (p. 344). However, RTI interventions that have been found effective across a broader range of learners than that of the study by Harn and colleagues have supported the autonomy of individual teachers to make appropriate instructional decisions rather than rely on strict fidelity to script or pacing.

RTI Requires Teacher Autonomy and Collaboration

An intervention study by Wonder-McDowell, Reutzel, and Smith (2011) tested the efficacy of a commercial scripted program (Read Well) versus a homegrown reading specialist intervention that was aligned with the core program. The commercial Read Well program differed substantially from the core program in pace, scope, and sequence. Reading specialists serving second-grade struggling students across 12 schools participated in extensive professional development to learn to deliver either the Read Well program with fidelity or to align the supplemental instruction with the core program, matching it in content, method of instruction, pace, scope, and sequence. For example, blending was taught by writing using whiteboards—the same phonics patterns, vocabulary, and thematic content from the core program were developed, and the supplemental instruction addressed the same elements each day—phonics, rereading of previously read texts, comprehension, and vocabulary. It is important to note that this homegrown intervention differed substantially from that of Harn and colleagues' (2011) model of coordination in the degree of autonomy and decision making granted to those who taught the supplemental instruction to struggling readers. Contrary to the tightly controlled language and pace of Harn and colleagues' model, Wonder-McDowell and colleagues' model (2011) encouraged teachers to adapt these elements according to the needs of the learners:

> While there was little flexibility provided in what to teach because all supplementary instruction was designed to practice skills, concepts, and

strategies aligned with the scope and sequence of classroom core reading instruction, reading specialists used their knowledge and expertise from reading endorsement courses and district professional development to adjust specific teaching activities to the needs of the students so long as fidelity to the scope and sequence of classroom core reading instruction was maintained. (p. 269)

Thus, RTI need not and *should not* be a standard treatment or packaged program for struggling students, and it is not necessarily delivered in tiers or pullout interventions. In fact, pullout interventions may not be the most effective way to support below-level readers' achievement of the CCSS, even foundational ones. Kennedy (2010), whose award-winning study improved the literacy achievement of at-risk first graders, identified several critical components of effective intervention, chief among them challenge and coherence in curriculum and opportunities for collaboration and "push-in" classroom support to achieve those standards. In this successful intervention, administrators "honored" teacher autonomy so that they were able to design the curriculum and respond in unique and personal ways to the needs of students.

The critical element of RTI is differentiation according to need—first in the classroom by the classroom teacher. Contrary to the RTI implementation observed by Harn and colleagues (2011), where teachers believed "differentiation to be when students were actually pulled from Tier I [the classroom] to receive intervention" (p. 349), support for small-group and side-by-side teaching in the classroom has been associated with higher student achievement across grade levels in many national research studies (for example, Taylor, Peterson, Pearson, & Rodrigues, 2002). Conversely, whole-class instruction has been associated with diminished achievement. Universal design, consistent with the CCSS, and championed by disability advocates, offers many opportunities for differentiation within the classroom so that all students might participate effectively in challenging grade-level curricula.

In our recent study of 14 successful "beating the odds" elementary schools across Tennessee, participants responded to the question, "To what do you attribute your school's success?" (Smith, Bell, Benner, & McGill-Franzen, 2010). These educators (administrators, general education teachers, and special education teachers), without knowing the empirical research concerning successful schools or RTI, identified elements that were common not only across the widely diverse schools in the study but also across successful schools in other states. Most surprising was that these schools subscribed to full inclusion of special education students in the regular classroom; provided universal access to the core curriculum; expressed shared accountability for the academic performance of all students; and collaborated across disciplinary boundaries to analyze student work, organize assessment data, and plan instruction. Although few used the term *Response to Intervention*, these educators, in fact, described practices that align completely with International Reading Association principles (IRA, 2010) for responsive teaching and differentiation as well as systematic and comprehensive approaches to curriculum and evaluation. And because these schools met the state's highest standards for achievement, value-added assessment, and Adequate Yearly Progress, and they did so by including the most struggling learners and by crossing professional disciplinary borders to offer push-in classroom support, we hold out hope for compatibility between RTI and CCSS.

CCSS Provide Focus and Coherence

Embedded within the CCSS is a curricular focus and consistency in that the same 10 Reading Standards apply across grade levels, differing only in the level of text complexity in Standard 10. Theoretically, the focus and consistency of the CCSS and the expression of a developmental continuum across the grades should make implementation and alignment of RTI with classroom instruction easier. Most notably, the Standards provide an emphasis on the interconnectedness and reciprocity of reading, writing, language, and content knowledge.

Nonetheless, the writers of the CCSS did not specify the pedagogy appropriate for achieving the Standards, leaving decisions of teaching strategies up to teachers. As researchers struggle with the particulars of the Standards and their implications (for example, the admonition to make "full use of text"), it is an opportunity to revisit RTI in a way that could provide access to a core curriculum for all students—like Universal Design for Learning materials that are educative for a wide range of student levels, and instruction flexible enough to accommodate diversity. To master the Standards, all students need to develop the ability to make inferences within and across complex texts and to read and write in different genres, and all teachers need to support students and scaffold instruction in a way that does not diminish the need to actually read the text. Let's be clear—to enable the neediest students to meet the challenges of the CCSS will take resources and incentives—research that takes into account our history of remedial interventions and moves us forward instead of backward; investment in teacher expertise that builds on what we know about teacher efficacy and motivation; and assessments that actually inform the work of teachers, not simply tell teachers what they already know: that some students need extra support.

Meeting the Challenge Requires Investment in Teachers

It is a truism to say that teachers matter. They do, and they matter most for the neediest students. Teacher education that builds deep knowledge of content and pedagogy, that develops diagnostic insight into the thinking of students and the ethical disposition of commitment to and responsibility for their learning, is an investment in our future. Whether that education is delivered by universities or schools or nurtured in professional learning communities matters not.

Several exploratory studies have documented that teachers can and do learn the content and pedagogy needed to improve the achievement of students who struggle. A one-to-one interactive strategies intervention developed by Gelzheiser, Scanlon, Vellutino, Hallgren-Flynn, and Schatschneider (2011) was effectively implemented by classroom teachers with older struggling students. Our own research (McGill-Franzen, Payne, & Dennis, 2010) with teachers of young, at-risk students also supported teacher development as an alternative to packaged interventions. The model in that study was similar to a clinical practicum that reading specialists typically conduct to earn licensure. Classroom teachers identified and instructed daily a small group of their most struggling students, and at the same time, participated in a professional development community. Through observation and analysis of students' reading and writing work, they determined what students were able to do. Then, through reflection, collaboration, and knowledge-building talk with their colleagues, they determined ways to adjust their teaching to accommodate the needs of individual students and accelerate their development. As in the research of Gelzheiser and colleagues, students who participated in the intervention made significant progress over matched peers who did not. Further, in both studies, investing in teachers' expertise not only helped struggling students make substantive gains during the time of the intervention but that expertise was also available to all students in the participating teachers' classes, year after year.

Effective professional development can be summarized as that which is "multi-faceted" and "customized rather than prepackaged, takes place over an extended period of time and uses a range of research-based practices" (Kennedy, 2010; p. 386). Further, to sustain teachers' commitment to the difficult work of teaching in challenging contexts, it is important to build teachers' sense of efficacy with early demonstrations of student success. We examine next the puzzling results of several other intervention studies to underscore the importance that teacher expertise holds for RTI and, by extension, for implementation of CCSS.

Even though many of the early regulations on RTI (cf. iris.peabody. vanderbilt.edu/rti01_overview/rti01_05.html) adhered to what has been known as a standard treatment protocol, wherein all students deemed "below benchmark" participated in the same intervention delivered by an educator with fidelity to a script and pacing guide, such standard treatment or "one size fits all" approaches are not or should not be appropriate interpretations of the intent of the IDEA legislation. A standard treatment protocol means standardizing what teachers do and say. A standard treatment protocol emphasizes fidelity of implementation; it requires teachers to follow a set of procedures rather than "moment by moment" decision making.

Studies conducted by researchers (Justice & Ezell, 2002; Wanzek & Vaughn, 2008) and district accountability departments have demonstrated that with minimal training teachers can implement most well-sequenced programs with almost perfect fidelity of implementation yet have no discernable effect on the achievement of children, or in some cases, negative effects on children's development. As a case in point, 35% of the students in the Wanzek and Vaughn study (2008), for example, demonstrated diminished performance in the targeted skill when the researchers amped up the intensity of the treatment (more time). In another study (Knox County Schools Office of Accountability, 2012), an evaluation of a two-year language intervention with 8,000 secondary students, researchers found only negative results on the state tests, norm-referenced standardized reading assessments, attendance, ACTs, and individual student GPAs after participation in the project, and the negative effect accelerated over time. Having examined these data every way—students compared with historical peers, students compared with their own gain score trajectories, and reading grade levels for project completers—the perplexed evaluators concluded, "One unexpected positive outcome of the implementation of the program in 6th grade has been a greater growth trajectory for students not in the program" (p. 64), and this result was with seven coaches hired to monitor fidelity of implementation among district teachers!

Clearly, and these studies left no doubt—it is not the use of materials or procedures per se that constitutes quality interaction (Henry & Pianta, 2011). It is the way teachers respond to children's cues and adjust teaching, a form of on-the run evaluation "conducted in the flow of the instructional process" (Roskos & Neuman, 2012, p. 534). It is the way teachers themselves use language to model for students the thinking behind their actions. It is the way that teachers use language to clarify the dimensions of text or words or sounds under study and the way that teachers embed instruction in authentic and purposeful activity (Justice, Mashburn, Hamre, & Pianta, 2008). RTI requires that teachers mediate students' understandings of how reading and writing work and model for them meaning making from text—these are the same kinds of quality interactions that effective implementation of the CCSS requires.

Diagnostic Assessment Makes Diagnostic Insight and Responsive Teaching Possible

In order for teachers to be able to notice patterns in the reading and writing behaviors of students, they themselves need, first of all, deep content knowledge of the ways these reciprocal language processes are expressed over time. Next, they need diagnostic tools—not fluency probes (Samuels, 2007)—to determine where on the continuum of literacy development—from emergent to proficient—each student falls, and what kinds of support might accelerate that individual's progress. Even at the kindergarten level, students present different profiles of development, from those who cannot recognize their name in print, to those who can read conventional text accurately and with fluency (McGill-Franzen, 2006; McGill-Franzen, Payne, & Dennis, 2010). The metaphor of a "roadmap" has been used to great effect by Spear-Swerling and Sternberg (1996) to help educators visualize "stages" of reading development, not as invariant developmental sequences, but rather as strategic markers along the path to proficiency that develop within the linguistic contexts of students' experiences with oral language and exposure to print. Students who struggle are said to go "off track," and the signposts that mark the path to proficiency—visual cues, phonetic cues, controlled work recognition, automatic word recognition, and strategic and proficient reading— provide a useful framework for teachers to notice patterns, particularly patterns in the acquisition of word knowledge, and may suggest the direction of instruction.

Too often, students who fail standardized assessments are assumed to be a homogeneous group with deficits in basic or foundational skills, and these assumptions hold even among teachers of older struggling readers. In a deeper analysis of the performance of fourth graders who failed the Washington Assessment of Student Learning, for example, Buly and Valencia (2002) found that few failing students actually had difficulty decoding (9%), whereas automatic word recognition and fluent text reading appeared to contribute more of the variance to students' below-average performance. Both nonnative speakers of English and students from low-income families appeared to struggle the most with vocabulary but presented different profiles of abilities in other areas. In a replication of the Washington State study in Tennessee with middle-schoolers using a different diagnostic instrument (Qualitative Reading Inventory, Words Their Way), Dennis (2009) found that students who failed the Tennessee Comprehensive Achievement Test also presented disparate profiles of abilities, rendering a one-size-fits-all packaged intervention singularly ineffective. Hargis (2006) also reported wide variation in the reading levels of adolescents as measured by the Peabody Individual Achievement Test, finding, for example, between 5th- and 10th-grade levels among 7th graders, although most students were able to read text accurately.

Finally—and this is an important parallel between RTI and the CCSS—both demand that teachers accelerate students' ability to read increasingly more complex texts. As the previously cited assessment research suggests, we need evaluation tools that afford insight into students' thinking and help teachers construct individual diagnostic profiles. Whether dealing with RTI or advanced placement students, at grade levels from kindergarten through 12th grade, the CCSS require that they hone the ability to analyze text (Calkins, Ehrenworth, & Lehman, 2012). Calkins and her colleagues at Teachers College asked teachers—in this case, New York City teachers—to approach a familiar text as a student would, say, E.B. White's *Charlotte's Web*, doing what the Standards require of students—identify the central ideas of the text or trace the development of a theme across the text—tasks that turn out to be harder than they appear. Teachers typically have little experience performing these kinds of literacy analyses, but by walking in the student's shoes, so to speak, teachers acquire an understanding of the processes of text analysis, and in doing so, are better able to articulate for students how higher levels of comprehension are accomplished.

The Common Core and RTI—What Will Become of These Initiatives?

A singular problem of any new policy initiative is that new policies do not land "in a vacuum," as Milbrey McLaughlin (1991) once noted. They land on top of other policies. RTI was listed as a "very hot" topic in the 2012 *Reading Today* "What's Hot, What's Not" literacy survey (Cassidy & Loveless, 2011) but fell from that perch in the 2013 survey (Cassidy & Grote-Garcia, 2012) because, as respondents suggested, there was not a strong research base for many of the models that were being implemented. We concur wholeheartedly with that sentiment. Not all "very hot" topics are necessarily new topics in the world of literacy research; RTI is one of those—an old wine in new bottles. RTI may seem new to some, especially teachers who are trying to understand it as both an intervention to prevent reading failures and a referral process to place failing students in special education, but RTI is, in fact, not new. Personalizing instruction has been recognized for decades as the way to improve student achievement.

Initiatives can fade into oblivion. When the RTI process centers on only the procedural markers of screening, fluency probes, and assigning students to tiers (standard treatment protocol), it is not rooted in the essential work of the school—teaching and learning. In that case, if another initiative comes along (see Schmoker, 2011), the weak RTI process may become even weaker, fading into only enough compliance to support the legal requirements of IDEA identification. To illustrate, the state of Tennessee was barely getting RTI underway when it secured Race to the Top (RTTT) funding. Participant observation research conducted at one district site (Smith, 2011) documented that district and building-level administrators found themselves so immersed in the paperwork and legalities of the RTTT initiative that a very fragile RTI process was all but forgotten.

McLaughlin's (1991) admonition about layered policies notwithstanding, we believe that implementation of RTI and the Common Core can be mutually supportive, each initiative helping to accomplish and sustain the goal of accelerated progress for all students. The Common Core provides curriculum focus and coherence. RTI provides a framework for supporting individual learners. Rather than mired in inconsistent language or goals, the CCSS and RTI both seek to prevent failure and accelerate literacy development along a clearly defined trajectory of increasing competence and complexity.

TRY THIS!

- As an intervention strategy, try using K-W-L (Ogle, 1986) before reading. For example, before reading the text *What Do You Do With a Tail Like This?* by Steve Jenkins and Robin Page (listed in NGA Center & CCSSO, 2010b, p. 33, as a K-1 Read-Aloud Informational Text), ask students to list (or tell you as you list) what they know (*K* column) about animals' tails. Then ask students what they want (*W* column) to know about animals' tails. Finally, as students listen to the informational text, have them write or listen for answers to their questions and make notes or offer suggestions as you make notes about new ideas and information in the *L* column.

- Use a point-of-view guide (POVG) to encourage student connections between reading and writing. The POVG connects writing to reading by allowing students to be creative. For example, during reading on a unit about penguins, you could offer students this situation and question:

  Situation: You are about to be interviewed as if you are a baby penguin living in Antarctica.

  Question: As a baby penguin, what is your typical day like?

Before writing their responses on index cards, students read the text and take notes. When answering the question, students write in first person.

DISCUSSION QUESTIONS

1. According to Johnston, what is the intent of RTI? What does RTI look like in your school? What changes need to be made to accomplish the intent of RTI?

2. McGill-Franzen and Smith discuss teacher development as an alternative option to prepackaged reading and literacy programs. Why would involving expert teachers in CCSS instructional decisions offer different (and perhaps better) alternatives to these prepackaged programs?

3. Discuss the differences between diagnostic and fluency probes. Why do educators need more diagnostic probes?

REFERENCES

Buly, M.R., & Valencia, S.W. (2002). Below the bar: Profiles of students who fail state reading assessments. *Educational Evaluation and Policy Analysis, 24*(3), 219–239. doi:10.3102/0162373702400321 9

Calkins, L., Ehrenworth, M., & Lehman, C. (2012). *Pathways to the Common Core*. Portsmouth, NH: Heinemann.

Cassidy, J., & Grote-Garcia, S. (2012). Defining the literacy agenda: Results of the 2013 what's hot and what's not literacy survey. *Reading Today, 30*(1), 9.

Cassidy, J., & Loveless, D. (2011). Taking our pulse in a time of uncertainty: Results of the 2012 what's hot and what's not literacy survey. *Reading Today, 29*(2), 16–21.

Crawford, J. (1989). Instructional activities related to achievement gains in Chapter 1 classes. In R.E. Slavin, N.L. Karweit, & N.A. Madden (Eds.), *Effective programs for students at risk* (pp. 264–290). Boston: Allyn & Bacon.

Dennis, D.V. (2009). "I'm not stupid": How assessment drives (in)appropriate reading instruction. *Journal of Adolescent & Adult Literacy, 53*(4), 283–290. doi:10.1598/JAAL.53.4.2

Fuchs, D., & Fuchs, L.S. (2006). Introduction to Response to Intervention: What, why, and how valid is it? *Reading Research Quarterly, 41*(1), 93–99. doi:10.1598/RRQ.41.1.4

Gelzheiser, L.M., Scanlon, D., Vellutino, F., Hallgren-Flynn, L., & Schatschneider, C. (2011). Effects of the interactive strategies approach-extended: A responsive and comprehensive intervention for intermediate-grade struggling readers. *The Elementary School Journal, 112*(2), 280–306. doi:10.1086/661525

Hargis, C.H. (2006). Setting standards: An exercise in futility? *Phi Delta Kappan, 87*(5), 393–395.

Harn, B.A., Chard, D.J., Biancarosa, G., & Kame'enui, E.J. (2011). Coordinating instructional supports to accelerate at-risk first-grade readers' performance. *The Elementary School Journal, 112*(2), 332–355. doi:10.1086/661997

Henry, A.E., & Pianta, R.C. (2011). Effective teacher–child interactions and children's literacy: Evidence for scalable, aligned approaches to professional development. In S.B. Neuman & D.K. Dickinson (Eds.), *Handbook of early literacy research* (Vol. 3, pp. 308–321). New York: Guilford.

Hoover, J.J., Baca, L., Wexler-Love, E., & Saenz, L. (2008). *National implementation of Response to Intervention (RTI): Research summary.* Boulder, CO: University of Colorado Special Education Leadership and Quality Teacher Initiative, BUENO Center School of Education. Retrieved from www.esc1.net/cms/lib/TX21000366/Centricity/Domain/86/NationalImplementationofRTI-ResearchSummary.pdf.

International Reading Association. (2010). *Response to Intervention: Guiding principles for educators from the International Reading Association.* Newark, DE: Author. Retrieved from www.reading.org/Libraries/Resources/RTI_brochure_web.pdf.

Johnston, P.H. (2011). Response to Intervention in literacy: Problems and possibilities. *The Elementary School Journal, 111*(4), 511–534. doi:10.1086/659030

Johnston, P.H., Allington, R.L., & Afflerbach, P. (1985). The congruence of classroom and remedial reading programs. *The Elementary School Journal, 85*(4), 465–477. doi:10.1086/461414

Justice, L.M., & Ezell, H.K. (2002). Use of storybook reading to increase print awareness in at-risk children. *American Journal of Speech-Language Pathology, 11*(1), 17–29. doi:10.1044/1058-0360(2002/003)

Justice, L.M., Mashburn, A.J., Hamre, B.K., & Pianta, R.C. (2008). Quality of language and literacy instruction in preschool classrooms serving at-risk pupils. *Early Childhood Research Quarterly, 23*(1), 51–68. doi:10.1016/j.ecresq.2007.09.004

Kennedy, E. (2010). Improving literacy achievement in a high-poverty school: Empowering classroom teachers through professional development. *Reading Research Quarterly, 45*(4), 384–387. doi:10.1598/RRQ.45.4.1

Knox County Schools Office of Accountability. (2012, March 9). *Return on investment report: The Knox County Schools.* Retrieved September 17, 2012, from www.knoxvillechamber.com/pdf/ReturnonInvestmentReportFinal2PDF09March2012.pdf

McGill-Franzen, A. (2006). *Kindergarten literacy: Matching assessment and instruction in kindergarten.* New York: Scholastic.

McGill-Franzen, A., & Allington, R.L. (1990). Comprehension and coherence: Neglected elements of literacy instruction in remedial and resource room services. *Journal of Reading, Writing, and Learning Disabilities, 6*(2), 149–181. doi:10.1080/0748763900060206

McGill-Franzen, A., Payne, R.L., & Dennis, D.V. (2010). Responsive intervention: What is the role of appropriate assessment? In P.H. Johnston (Ed.), *RTI in literacy—Responsive and comprehensive* (pp. 115–132). Newark, DE: International Reading Association.

McLaughlin, M.W. (1991). The Rand change agent study: 10 years later. In A.R. Odden (Ed.), *Educational policy implementation* (pp. 143–156). Albany, NY: SUNY Press.

National Governors Association Center for Best Practices & Council of Chief State School Officers. (2010a). *Common Core State Standards for English language arts and literacy in history/social studies, science, and technical subjects.* Washington, DC: Authors. Retrieved from www.corestandards.org/assets/CCSSI_ELA%20Standards.pdf

National Governors Association Center for Best Practices & Council of Chief State School Officers. (2010b). *Common Core State Standards for English language arts and literacy in history/social studies, science, and technical subjects: Appendix B: Text exemplars and sample performance tasks.* Washington, DC: Authors. Retrieved from www.corestandards.org/assets/Appendix_B.pdf

Ogle, D. (1986). K-W-L: A teaching model that develops active reading of expository text. *The Reading Teacher, 39*(6), 564–570.

Puma, M.J., & Drury, D.W. (2000). *Exploring new directions: Title I in the year 2000.* Alexandria, VA: National School Boards Association.

Roskos, K., & Neuman, S.B. (2012). Formative assessments: Simply, no additives. *The Reading Teacher, 65*(8), 534–538. doi:10.1002/TRTR.01079

Samuels, S.J. (2007). The DIBELS tests: Is speed of barking at print what we mean by reading fluency? *Reading Research Quarterly, 42*(4), 563–566.

Schmoker, M. (2011). *Focus: Elevating the essentials to radically improve student learning.* Alexandria, VA: ASCD.

Smith, K. (2011). *RTI policy: Implemented, interpreted, and interrupted.* Paper presented at the annual meeting of the Literacy Research Association, Jacksonville, FL.

Smith, K., Bell, S., Benner, S., & McGill-Franzen, A. (2010, February). *Stories from successful elementary schools serving economically distressed communities and implications for teacher preparation.* Paper presented at the annual meeting of the American Association of Colleges for Teacher Education, Atlanta, GA.

Spear-Swerling, L., & Sternberg, R.J. (1996). *Off track: When poor readers become "learning disabled".* Boulder, CO: Westview.

Taylor, B.M., Peterson, D.S., Pearson, P.D., & Rodrigues, M.C. (2002). Looking inside classrooms: Reflecting on the "how" as well as the "what" in effective reading instruction. *The Reading Teacher, 56*(3), 270–279.

Wanzek, J., & Vaughn, S. (2008). Response to varying amounts of time in reading intervention for students with low response to intervention. *Journal of Learning Disabilities, 41*(2), 126–142. doi:10.1177/0022219407313426

Wonder-McDowell, C ., Reutzel, D.R., & Smith, J.A. (2011). Does instructional alignment matter? Effects on struggling second graders' reading achievement. *The Elementary School Journal, 112*(2), 259–279. doi:10.1086/661524

Vocabulary and Comprehension Instruction for ELs in the Era of Common Core State Standards

Rebecca Silverman & Brie Doyle

Understanding words and making meaning of text are essential skills for college and career readiness. Thus, it is no surprise that vocabulary and comprehension are highlighted prominently in the Common Core State Standards (CCSS; National Governors Association Center for Best Practices & Council of Chief State School Officers [NGA Center & CCSSO], 2010). For example, the College and Career Readiness Anchor Standards for Reading state that students should be able to "read closely to determine what the text says explicitly and to make logical inferences from it" (Standard 1) and "interpret words and phrases as they are used in a text" (Standard 4; p. 10). In fact, several standards across the CCSS domains of Reading, Writing, Speaking and Listening, and Language reference vocabulary and comprehension skills. In light of the focus on vocabulary and comprehension in the CCSS, one group of students that is of particular concern is the English learner (EL) group. Most ELs (i.e., children who speak a language other than English at home) learn to speak conversationally and recognize common words with relative ease, but many ELs struggle to understand and learn from text due to limited knowledge of vocabulary, underdeveloped linguistic awareness, insufficient concept or background knowledge, and inadequate proficiency using comprehension strategies (Lesaux & Geva, 2006).

ELs are the most rapidly growing population in U.S. schools (Calderón, Slavin, & Sánchez, 2011). In fact, by 2025, one out of every four students in the U.S. public schools will be identified as an EL (Van Roekel, 2008). ELs in the United States represent a diverse group of students, speaking over 400 languages nationwide (McKeon, 2005), with the majority speaking Spanish (Fry, 2007). ELs vary considerably in their level of proficiency in English and their home language (National Council of Teachers of

English, 2008). Using the definition set forth here and elsewhere (Gersten et al., 2007) that ELs are students who speak a language other than or in addition to English in the home, *bilingual* students—who are proficient in both English and their home language—would be identified as EL. Some bilingual students may have an advantage over monolinguals in learning to read due to heightened linguistic awareness resulting from using more than one language flexibly (Geva, 2006). However, other bilingual students, despite proficiency in both languages, may still be at a disadvantage if their cultural background does not match that of the school they attend (Goldenberg, Rueda, & August, 2006).

While educators are concerned about the achievement of bilingual students, they are typically even more concerned about students who are not proficient in English, sometimes referred to as limited English proficient (LEP) students. ELs who are proficient in their home language but not in English may be able to transfer some home-language skills to English, though many of these ELs will not do so naturally; therefore, they must be taught how to transfer skills across languages, and some skills, such as vocabulary knowledge, may not transfer as well as others, such as phonological awareness (Proctor, Carlo, August, & Snow, 2005). Of most concern to educators are ELs who are not proficient in their home language *and* are not proficient in English. These students are the most at risk for difficulty in reading because they do not have adequate resources to draw on to build their linguistic proficiency in English (Snow, Burns, & Griffin, 1998).

While the number of ELs in U.S. schools is rapidly increasing, school-based resources to support ELs often have not increased with the same rapidity (Viadero, 2009). Many students do not receive the supplemental English language instruction they need (Calderón et al., 2011). Most ELs spend the majority of their time in school in general education classrooms with teachers who are unprepared to support them (Calderón et al., 2011). While 40% of teachers report teaching ELs on a daily basis, only 12.5% of teachers report having more than eight hours of training to support ELs (National Center for Education Statistics, 2002). However, research suggests that classroom teachers who have more knowledge about addressing the needs of ELs in their classrooms and have a positive attitude about providing instruction to ELs in an inclusive setting have students with stronger vocabulary and comprehension skills (Gray, 2012).

The CCSS provide guidance to educators on what students should be expected to be able to do to achieve academic success, but they do not recommend how to teach students so that they can meet these expectations. In addition, the CCSS do not suggest specific instructional practices to support ELs. However, the CCSS state that *all* students, including ELs, "should be held to the same high expectations" noted in the Standards, though some ELs "may require additional time, appropriate instructional support, and aligned assessments as they acquire both English language proficiency and content area knowledge" (NGA Center & CCSSO, 2012, p. 1). Considering that many ELs may have to reach farther than their non-EL peers in order to meet the Standards, and given that the CCSS emphasize vocabulary and comprehension in particular, the purpose of the present chapter is to describe research-based instructional practices to support the vocabulary and comprehension of ELs in the era of CCSS. First, we provide background information about the vocabulary and comprehension development of ELs. Next, we discuss general principles of research-based vocabulary and comprehension instruction for ELs. Finally, we recommend specific practices for supporting the vocabulary and comprehension of ELs so they can meet the rigorous standards set for all students in the CCSS.

Vocabulary and Comprehension Development in ELs

Upon entry to preschool and kindergarten, many ELs are already far behind their peers in word learning (Leung, Silverman, Nandakumar, Qian, & Hines, 2011). As ELs progress through school, the vocabulary gap between monolingual English speakers and ELs increases (Lesaux, & Geva, 2006). Thus, ELs need to accelerate their word learning beyond that of their monolingual English-speaking peers just to catch up. Perhaps because of or in addition to their limited vocabulary knowledge and comprehension skills, many ELs have less linguistic awareness than their monolingual English-speaking peers (Proctor, Silverman, Harring, & Montecillo, 2011). Linguistic awareness skills—such as semantic, morphological, and syntactic awareness—have all been shown to be important in understanding words and text (Silverman, Proctor, Harring, Doyle, Meyer, & Mitchell, in submission). Students who can use their awareness of conceptual relations among words and concepts to understand text (semantics), who can apply their knowledge of how words are derived from roots via affixation to figure out the meaning of new words (morphology), and who can understand the meaning of words as they are applied in grammatically complex sentences (syntax) are poised to comprehend text more easily than students without these skills. Finally, many ELs have less comprehension strategy and text structure knowledge than their monolingual English-speaking peers (Lesaux,

Koda, Siegel, & Shanahan, 2006). It may be that having less language with which to access and comprehend text constrains the opportunities ELs have to acquire conceptual and background knowledge and strategy knowledge.

Principles of Research-Based Vocabulary and Comprehension Instruction for ELs

Becker (1977) and Durkin (1978/1979) pointed out decades ago that vocabulary and comprehension instruction were not often seen in elementary school classrooms. However, in the last few years, research has shown that there is a greater amount of vocabulary and comprehension instruction than has been seen in the past (Ness, 2011; Silverman et al., 2012). This is likely due to a focus on vocabulary and comprehension in the National Reading Panel report (National Institute of Child Health and Human Development, 2000) and the Reading First legislation under the No Child Left Behind Act of 2001 that focused attention on not only phonemic awareness, phonics, and fluency, but also on vocabulary development and reading comprehension strategies. However, while recent research suggests that the quantity of vocabulary and comprehension instruction has increased, this research also suggests that instructional quality in vocabulary and comprehension may be limited. Observation studies show that teachers give definitions and contextualize words without providing instructional support, such as acting out and illustrating words and guiding students in analyzing word meanings (Silverman & Crandell, 2010). Furthermore, there is little attention to supporting other linguistic skills required for comprehension, such as semantic, syntactic, and morphological awareness (Silverman et al., 2012). Additionally, the comprehension strategies taught are most often previewing/predicting and questioning (Ness, 2011), which do not provide students with the repertoire of strategies (e.g., monitoring, inferencing, and summarizing) needed for comprehending text. Finally, despite research suggesting that native-language supports are beneficial to ELs in acquiring vocabulary and comprehension skills, very little native-language support is seen in general education classrooms (Silverman et al., 2012).

From intervention research, we know that there are general principles of effective vocabulary and comprehension instruction to support ELs. The Institute of Education Sciences (IES) practice guide for *Effective Literacy and English Language Instruction for English Learners in the Elementary*

Grades lists the following recommendations based on a review of the research in the field (Gersten et al., 2007):

- Assess the reading skills of ELs and use data from assessments to identify and monitor ELs who need supplemental instruction.
- Provide small-group intervention using explicit instruction to address the core reading skills, including vocabulary and comprehension, for students who need supplemental instruction.
- Implement high-quality vocabulary instruction on individual words and phrases and expressions.
- Support ELs in developing academic English skills to comprehend text across the curriculum.
- Provide opportunities for ELs to work collaboratively with peers at different ability and proficiency levels.

In addition, research suggests that multimedia support to provide students with multiple points of reference with which to comprehend verbal information has been shown to be effective for ELs (Silverman & Hines, 2009). Furthermore, teaching students to make connections between English and their home language through cognates and translation has also been shown to support vocabulary and comprehension for ELs (Proctor, Dalton, & Grisham, 2007).

The CCSS Vocabulary Acquisition and Use Standard 4 specifies that students should be able to "determine or clarify the meaning of unknown or multiple-meaning words and phrases" in a text (NGA Center & CCSSO, 2010, p. 25). This requires that students have familiarity with many general academic and domain-specific words, awareness of how words are connected and used across contexts (i.e., linguistic awareness), and knowledge of strategies to figure out unknown words on their own. ELs, in particular, may have limited knowledge of specific words, and they may need explicit instruction in strategies for identifying the meaning of unknown words as they read. A recent synthesis of vocabulary interventions by the National Reading Technical Assistance Center (Butler, Urrutia, Buenger, Hunt, & Gonzalez, 2010) suggests that high-quality vocabulary instruction includes repeated exposure to vocabulary words, explicit instruction of vocabulary words, and questioning and discussion to promote vocabulary knowledge. Explicit vocabulary instruction includes defining words using student-friendly language, contextualizing words in meaningful examples for students, acting out or illustrating words to support students' understanding of word meaning, analyzing words so students see how words are related, and attending to the sound and spelling of words so students recognize them in speech or print (Silverman & Crandell, 2010). Additionally, researchers have shown that attention to linguistic awareness skills, such as morphological awareness, and support for students to acquire independent word-learning strategies, such as using context clues to figure out words, are also important for students (Baumann et al., 2003).

The CCSS note that students should be able to "ask and answer questions" about text, "identify the main [idea or] topic" of a text, and "compare and contrast" within and between texts (e.g., see Key Ideas and Details as well as Craft and Structure Standards within Reading Standards for Literature K–5). Due to the language demands of conceptually rich texts, many ELs may have difficulty with questioning, inferencing, and summarizing. Thus, explicit instruction about navigating text using specific strategies may be particularly helpful to ELs. According to an IES practice guide on *Improving Reading Comprehension in Kindergarten Through 3rd Grade* (Shanahan et al., 2010), high-quality comprehension instruction should (a) provide explicit instruction on using comprehension strategies, (b) teach students to use text structure to comprehend text, (c) support students in discussing texts with others, (d) use rich and appropriate text, and (e) support students' engagement and motivation in reading. Explicit comprehension instruction includes modeling, guided practice, and independent practice of specific comprehension strategies, such as predicting, questioning, monitoring, inferencing, visualizing, and summarizing. Using graphic organizers and teaching students how to use text structure have been shown to support students in comprehending text (Williams et al., 2005, 2007, 2009). Additionally, discussions that engage students in debating and analyzing important concepts in text have been shown to support text comprehension. Recent research also suggests that attention to linguistic awareness skills, such as semantic, morphological, and syntactic awareness, may support students' text comprehension (Silverman, Proctor, et al., 2012).

Recommended Instructional Practices for Vocabulary and Comprehension for ELs

The first author of this chapter has implemented several observation and intervention studies with ELs over the past decade and has identified several instructional strategies that embody principles of research-based instruction and seem particularly promising to support ELs in meeting the CCSS related to vocabulary and comprehension. These include (a) explicit instruction of vocabulary words, comprehension strategies, and linguistic awareness skills, (b) the use of collaborative learning to engage students in discussion of words and text, and (c) the use of multimedia to support instruction.

Explicit Instruction

Explicit instruction is "systematic, direct, engaging, and success oriented" (Archer & Hughes, 2011). This kind of instruction is helpful for non-ELs, but it is particularly important for ELs who may not be able to intuit word meanings, the structures of language, and the strategies they need to comprehend text. Explicit instruction includes modeling, guided practice, and independent practice (Duke & Pearson, 2002).

Vocabulary. An intervention study conducted by the first author with non-ELs and ELs in kindergarten in which explicit vocabulary instruction was included through read-alouds showed that while non-ELs and ELs alike benefitted from instruction, ELs grew faster in vocabulary and learned more words over the course of the intervention such that they began catching up with their non-EL peers by the end of the study (Silverman, 2007). In the intervention, teachers told children the meanings of words and explained the words in rich contexts; they showed pictures from the book in which the word appeared as well as real pictures downloaded from the Internet to illustrate the words; they asked questions that encouraged students to think critically about what the word means; and they asked students to act out the words themselves as they said the words so they could form a clear association between the target word and its referent. For example, as Mrs. A read the book *Chugga Chugga Choo Choo* by Kevin Lewis, in which the train climbs a steep mountain, she defined the word *steep* in simple terms: "Something that is steep goes up high and is hard to climb." After showing pictures of mountains and valleys, she asked students to decide which one is steep and explain how they knew it is steep. Finally, she had students use their arms to show what a steep mountain would look like versus a low valley. This kind of explicit vocabulary instruction is needed to ensure that EL students meet standards that require them to "acquire and use accurately a range of general academic and domain-specific words and phrases sufficient for reading, writing, speaking, and listening at the college and career readiness level" (NGA Center & CCSSO, 2010, p. 25).

Comprehension. In a recent intervention study conducted by Silverman, Martin-Beltran, and Peercy (2011) in fourth grade, we taught ELs to use a strategy based on the Question–Answer Relationship (Raphael, 1986) model in which students were taught to evaluate whether comprehension questions were "in the book," "just me," or "book and me" questions. Students were taught to think about what kind of question they had been asked and where they could find the answer. This strategy might help EL students meet CCSS Anchor Standard 1 for Reading, which states that students should be able to "read closely to determine what the text says explicitly and to make logical inferences from it; cite specific textual evidence when writing or speaking to support conclusions drawn from the text" (NGA Center & CCSSO, 2010, p. 10). For example, in the intervention, students were asked how Martha, in the book *Martha Speaks* by Susan Meddaugh, felt when her family told her to "shut up." The answer was not directly in the book. Teachers had previously taught students explicitly about the different question types and had given multiple examples of each type of question. Teachers explained that the question was a "book and me" question. Students had to first think about what was happening in the book and then think about how they might feel in a similar situation (e.g., if their mom or dad told them to "shut up") to infer how Martha was feeling in the book. In other lessons, students were asked to decide for themselves what kind of question they had been asked and where they found the evidence to answer it. For students who may not easily discover how to answer questions about text, this kind of instruction might provide ELs with strategies they need to comprehend the texts they encounter in school.

Linguistic Awareness. In addition to explicit instruction in specific vocabulary words and comprehension strategies, EL students may need explicit instruction in linguistic awareness to be able to access the complex language of academic texts. Teaching students how to use word parts to understand new words (i.e., morphology), to think about how words are related in text (i.e., semantics), and to identify the meaning of words in different types of sentence structures (i.e., syntax) may be needed to support students' vocabulary and comprehension skills (Silverman et al., 2012). In a recent small-group, supplemental intervention on "Caring for our Environment" targeting fourth-grade ELs, we focused one set of lessons on the concept of *extinction*. We highlighted the word *disappear* as an important word students could use across content areas to comprehend text. One day, we guided students to think about the prefix *dis-* (not) and the root word *appear* (to become visible or to come into being), and we led students to consider other words with the prefix *dis-* such as *distrust* and *disorganized*. On another day, we supported students in creating a semantic map showing how words and phrases, such as *disappear, extinct, vanish, gone,* and *wiped out,* which were all found in the text students were reading about extinction, and other words, such as *appear* and the Spanish word *desaparecer,* are related. On a third day, we modeled writing sentences with the word *disappear* and asked students to do the same, considering how the word might need to be changed if it was a noun (*disappearance*) or past tense (*disappeared*). Supporting EL students in thinking about aspects of language that affect meaning may help them achieve standards that ask students to be able to "apply knowledge of language to understand how language functions in different contexts, to make effective choices for meaning or style, and to comprehend more fully when reading or listening" (NGA Center & CCSSO, 2010, p. 25).

Collaborative Learning

The CCSS expect students to be able to "prepare for and participate effectively in a range of conversations and collaborations with diverse partners, building on others' ideas and expressing their own clearly and persuasively" (NGA Center & CCSSO, 2010, p. 22). Working with peers may be especially beneficial for ELs because language learning is an inherently socially mediated process (Peregoy & Boyle, 2008). Through the negotiation of meaning that occurs in interaction, ELs not only gain access to comprehensible input but also extend their productive capabilities (Ellis, 1985; Swain, 1995).

Reading Buddies. One method of using collaborative learning to support ELs in vocabulary and comprehension is peer tutoring. Peer tutoring can be implemented using same-age peers (e.g., McMaster, Fuchs, & Fuchs, 2007) or cross-age peers (e.g., Klingner, & Vaughn, 1996). Silverman, Peercy, and Martin-Beltran (2011) are currently developing an intervention that pairs kindergarten (little buddies) and fourth-grade (big buddies) ELs and focuses on vocabulary and comprehension. In the intervention, big buddies prepare beforehand to read to their little buddies, ask questions of their little buddies, and play games related to the text they read with their little buddies. Teachers instruct big buddies on how to use gestures, home-language supports, and clear explanations of words and texts to help their little buddies learn new vocabulary words and academic concepts such as "rights and responsibilities." We implemented the program in a few classrooms recently. In one interaction in a reading buddies classroom, the big buddy explained the word *vote* to her little buddy saying, "When you vote you choose one thing or another thing. *Voto.* You decide. *Decidir.*" The big buddy then gave examples: "Like what would you vote to have for snack? Apples or chips? Would you decide to have apples or chips for snack in your classroom?" When the little buddy didn't seem to get it, the big buddy gestured with her hands to show choosing one or the other and used pictures of apples and chips to help the little buddy decide. By having to explain the words *vote* and *decide*, the big buddy deepened her knowledge of the words, and by having a one-on-one discussion about the words, the little buddy was supported in learning the words for the first time.

Collaborative Reasoning. In a study by Silverman and colleagues (2012), fourth-grade ELs engaged in a form of collaborative learning called Collaborative Reasoning (CR; e.g., Chinn, Anderson, & Waggoner, 2001). The goal of CR is to motivate children, though discourse with one another and facilitation by the teacher, to take a critical stance on a given text (Chinn, Anderson, & Waggoner, 2001). Working in small groups, students were provided a "big question" (Dong, Anderson, Kim, & Li, 2008), typically presented in a yes/no format, on which they were expected to take a position (e.g., make claims and provide text-based evidence for why they are taking such a position; see Clark et al., 2003). For example, after reading a text on environmentalism called *What's the Point of Being Green* by Jacqui Bailey, teachers asked students whether they thought it was easy to "go green." Students had to use examples from the book to show whether they thought going green was easy or hard to do. ELs, who may have limited language abilities, may particularly benefit from talking through words and text with others in such a way so they can co-construct meaning and learn from each other.

Multimedia Support

The CCSS specify that students should be able to "integrate and evaluate information presented in diverse media and formats, including visually, quantitatively, and orally" (NGA Center & CCSSO, 2010, p. 22). While this is an important skill for all students to develop, it may be particularly beneficial for ELs because supporting their understanding of verbal information presented in text with verbal and nonverbal information found in pictures and videos and on the computer may help ELs develop their English language skills (Kamil, Intrator, & Kim, 2000; Neuman, 1997; Paivio, 1986; Proctor, Dalton, & Grisham, 2007). In a study conducted by Silverman and Hines (2009), multimedia supports benefitted the vocabulary learning of ELs, but they did not add to the vocabulary growth of non-ELs in kindergarten through second grade. In this study, teachers focused on the theme of habitats and read books about rainforests, savannas, deserts, and coral reefs to students. They taught students words such as *climate, predator, prey,* and *camouflage.* Teachers provided students with definitions of the words, asked children to say the words, and played word games with them, such as "Finish My Sentence" (e.g., "A place where an animal lives and is in charge is its…territory.") and "Match That Word" (e.g., "Which goes with tropical: ice-cold or very warm?"). Then, teachers in the multimedia condition showed a video of the habitat under study and discussed the target words in relation to scenes in the video. Seeing the words come to life in the video likely made the words more salient to the EL students who may have less language background with which to comprehend the teachers' text reading and verbal instruction.

Other multimedia tools of interest for teachers of ELs include digital learning environments (DLEs). DLEs are computer-based programs that provide students with multimedia support as they read texts. In a study by Proctor, Dalton, and Grisham (2007), fourth-grade EL students who participated in a study using DLEs gained vocabulary and comprehension. DLEs contain such features as hypertext that allows students to click on words to hear a definition, pictures and videos that students can use to support word learning and text comprehension, and English- and Spanish-language audio that students can use to support their text reading. Providing students with options that they can access on their own when they need support enables students to be active learners as they encounter new words and navigate complex texts. Additionally, using computer-based tools such as DLEs encourages students' motivation and engagement for learning. Leveraging new technologies that enable individualized, independent learning with multimedia support is a promising way to foster vocabulary and comprehension for ELs at varying levels of language proficiency.

Summary

To prepare EL students to meet the rigorous college- and career-readiness standards related to vocabulary and comprehension set forth in the CCSS, teachers will need to draw on research-based practices that promote the word learning and critical thinking necessary to meet the Standards. The present chapter provides an overview of principles for research-based instruction for ELs in these domains and describes a few specific instructional approaches that embody these principles. Teachers should consider using these approaches in their classrooms to support ELs in meeting the CCSS related to vocabulary and comprehension.

- Identify related words or concepts for explicit instruction that are relevant across academic areas (e.g., *gain, lose, reduce, expand, increase, decrease, minimize, maximize, multiply, divide*). Model and provide opportunities for students to practice identifying how words are related using a semantic map. Prompt students to identify meaningful word parts (e.g., *min-* and *max-*) and call attention to native-language cognates when applicable (e.g., *reducir, minimizer,* and *divider* in Spanish). Finally, guide students to use related words in their own writing so students can practice applying their word knowledge across syntactic contexts.

- When introducing new words or content, support instruction with the use of multimedia. For instance, in a social studies or science unit on "Protecting the Environment," look for educational television episodes or streaming videos to support complex concepts such as pollution or recycling. After interacting with multimedia, give students the opportunity to discuss new words meaningfully with their peers.

DISCUSSION QUESTIONS

1. Silverman and Doyle provide background information about ELs' vocabulary and comprehension development. What are some vocabulary and comprehension challenges that ELs might encounter as they progress through school? How can teachers support ELs across grade levels to achieve the high standards for college and career readiness of the CCSS?

2. Silverman and Doyle highlight the importance of support for the vocabulary and comprehension development of ELs. How are vocabulary and comprehension interrelated, especially for ELs? How do the instructional suggestions provided by the authors support both vocabulary and comprehension for ELs in particular?

3. In addition to vocabulary and comprehension for ELs, Silverman and Doyle discuss linguistic awareness as integral for students to be able to access and comprehend the complex language of academic texts. Identify the components of linguistic awareness and discuss how having a command of linguistic awareness can help ELs access the increasing complexity of academic texts endorsed by the CCSS. Finally, discuss how teachers can support linguistic awareness in their classrooms.

REFERENCES

Archer, A.L., & Hughes, C.A. (2011). *Explicit instruction: Effective and efficient teaching.* New York: Guilford.

Baumann, J.F., Edwards, E.C., Bolan, E.M., Olejnik, S., & Kame'enui, E.J. (2003). Vocabulary tricks: Effects on instruction in morphology and context on fifth-grade students' ability to derive and infer word meanings. *American Educational Research Journal, 40*(2), 447–494. doi:10.3102/00028312040002447

Becker, W.C. (1977). Teaching reading and language to the disadvantaged—what we have learned from field research. *Harvard Educational Review, 47*(4), 518–543.

Butler, S., Urrutia, K., Buenger, A., Hunt, M., & Gonzalez, N. (2010). *A review of the current research on comprehension instruction: A research synthesis.* Washington, DC: U.S. Department of Education National Reading Technical Assistance Center. Retrieved from alex.state.al.us/ari/ari_files/A%20Review%20of%20the%20Current%20Research%20on%20Comprehension%20Instruction.pdf

Calderón, M., Slavin, R., & Sánchez, M. (2011). Effective instruction for English learners. *The Future of Children, 21*(1), 103–127. doi:10.1353/foc.2011.0007

Chinn, C.A., Anderson, R.C., & Waggoner, M.A. (2001). Patterns of discourse in two kinds of literature discussion. *Reading Research Quarterly, 36*(4), 378–411. doi:10.1598/RRQ.36.4.3

Clark, A., Anderson, R.C., Kuo, L., Kim, I., Archodidou, A., & Nguyen-Jahiel, K. (2003). Collaborative reasoning: Expanding ways for children to talk and think in school. *Educational Psychology Review, 15*(2), 181–198. doi:10.1023/A:1023429215151

Dong, T., Anderson, R.C., Kim, I.-H., & Li, Y. (2008). Collaborative reasoning in China and Korea. *Reading Research Quarterly, 43*(4), 400–424. doi:10.1598/RRQ.43.4.5

Duke, N.K., & Pearson, P.D. (2002). Effective practices for developing reading comprehension. In A.E. Farstrup & S.J. Samuels (Eds.), *What research has to say about reading instruction* (3rd ed., pp. 205–242). Newark, DE: International Reading Association.

Durkin, D. (1978/1979). What classroom observations reveal about reading comprehension instruction. *Reading Research Quarterly, 14*(4), 481–533. doi:10.1598/RRQ.14.4.2

Ellis, R. (1985). *Understanding second language acquisition.* Oxford, England:Oxford University Press.

Fry, R. (2007). *How far behind in math and reading are English language learners?* Washington, DC: Pew Hispanic Center.

Gersten, R., Baker, S.K., Collins, P., Linan-Thompson, S., Scarcella, R., & Shanahan, T. (2007). *Effective literacy and English language instruction for English learners in the elementary grades: A practice guide* (NCEE 2007–4011). Washington, DC: National Center for Education Evaluation and Regional Assistance, Institute of Education Sciences, U.S. Department of Education. Retrieved from ies.ed.gov/ncee/wwc/PracticeGuide.aspx?sid=6

Geva, E. (2006). Second-language oral proficiency and second-language literacy. In D. August & T. Shanahan (Eds.), *Developing literacy in second-language learners: Report of the National Literacy Panel on Language-Minority Children and Youth* (pp. 123–139). Mahwah, NJ: Erlbaum.

Goldenberg, C., Rueda, R.S., & August, D. (2006). Sociocultural influences on the literacy attainment of language-minority children and youth. In D. August & T. Shanahan (Eds.), *Developing literacy in second-language learners: Report of the National Literacy Panel on Language-Minority Children and Youth* (pp. 269–318). Mahwah, NJ: Erlbaum.

Gray, J.L. (2012). *The relationships between teacher variables and outcomes for language minority learners in grades 3–5 on measures of vocabulary knowledge and reading comprehension.* Unpublished doctoral dissertation, University of Maryland, College Park.

Kamil, M.L., Intrator, S.M., & Kim, H.S. (2000). The effects of other technologies on literacy and literacy learning. In M.L. Kamil, P.B. Mosenthal, P.D. Pearson, & R. Barr (Eds.), *Handbook of reading research* (Vol. 3, pp. 771–788). Mahwah, NJ: Erlbaum.

Klingner, J.K., & Vaughn, S. (1996). Reciprocal teaching of reading comprehension strategies for students with learning disabilities who use English as a second language. *The Elementary School Journal, 96*(3), 275–293. doi:10.1086/461828

Lesaux, N.K., & Geva, E. (2006). Synthesis: Development of literacy in language-minority students. In D.L. August & T. Shanahan (Eds.), *Developing literacy in second-language learners: Report of the National Literacy Panel on*

Language-Minority Children and Youth (pp. 53–74). Mahwah, NJ: Erlbaum.

Lesaux, N.K., Koda, K., Siegel, L.S., & Shanahan, T. (2006). Development of literacy of language minority learners. In D.L. August & T. Shanahan (Eds.), Developing literacy in second-language learners: Report of the National Literacy Panel on Language-Minority Children and Youth (pp. 75–122). Mahwah, NJ: Erlbaum.

Leung, C.B., Silverman, R., Nandakumar, R., Qian, X., & Hines, S. (2011). A comparison of difficulty levels of vocabulary in first grade basal readers for preschool dual language learners and monolingual English learners. American Educational Research Journal, 48(2), 421–461. doi:10.3102/0002831210382890

McKeon, D. (2005). Research talking points on English language learners. Retrieved November 19, 2012, from www.nea.org/home/13598.htm.

McMaster, K.L., Fuchs, D., & Fuchs, L.S. (2007). Promises and limitations of peer-assisted learning strategies in reading. Learning Disabilities, 5(2), 97–112.

National Center for Education Statistics. (2002). Schools and staffing survey, 1999–2000. Overview of the data for public, private, public charter, and Bureau of Indian Affairs elementary and secondary schools. Washington, DC: U.S. Department of Education Office of Educational Research and Improvement.

National Council of Teachers of English. (2008). English language learners: A policy research brief produced by the National Council of Teachers of English. Urbana, IL: Author. Retrieved from www.ncte.org/library/NCTEFiles/Resources/PolicyResearch/ELLResearchBrief.pdf

National Governors Association Center for Best Practices & Council of Chief State School Officers. (2010). Common Core State Standards for English language arts and literacy in history/social studies, science, and technical subjects. Washington, DC: Authors. Retrieved from www.corestandards.org/assets/CCSSI_ELA%20Standards.pdf

National Governors Association Center for Best Practices & Council of Chief State School Officers. (2012). Application of Common Core State Standards for English language learners. Retrieved November 26, 2012, from www.corestandards.org/assets/application-for-english-learners.pdf

National Institute of Child Health and Human Development. (2000). Report of the National Reading Panel. Teaching children to read: An evidence-based assessment of the scientific research literature on reading and its implications for reading instruction: Reports of the subgroups (NIH Publication No. 00–4769). Washington, DC: U.S. Government Printing Office.

Ness, M. (2011). Explicit reading comprehension instruction in elementary classrooms: Teacher use of reading comprehension strategies. Journal of Research in Childhood Education, 25(1), 98–117. doi:10.1080/02568543.2010.531076

Neuman, S.B. (1997). Television as a learning environment: A theory of synergy. In J. Flood, S. Brice Heath, & D. Lapp (Eds.), Handbook of research on teaching literacy through the communicative and visual arts (pp. 15–30). Mahwah, NJ: Erlbaum.

Paivio, A. (1986). Mental representation: A dual coding approach. Oxford, England: Oxford University Press.

Peregoy, S.F., & Boyle, O.F. (2008). Reading, writing and learning in ESL: A resource book for teaching K-12 English learners (5th ed.). Boston: Pearson.

Proctor, C.P., Carlo, M., August, D., & Snow, C. (2005). Native Spanish-speaking children reading in English: Toward a model of comprehension. Journal of Educational Psychology, 97(2), 246–256. doi:10.1037/0022-0663.97.2.246

Proctor, C.P., Dalton, B., & Grisham, D.L. (2007). Scaffolding English language learners and struggling readers in a universal literacy environment with embedded strategy instruction and vocabulary support. Journal of Literacy Research, 39(1), 71–93.

Proctor, C.P., Silverman, R.D., Harring, J.R., Meyer, A., & Montecillo, C. (in submission). The contribution of linguistic awareness to reading comprehension for English monolingual and Spanish-English bilingual children in second through fifth grade.

Proctor, C.P., Silverman, R.D., Harring, J.R., & Montecillo, C. (2011). The role of vocabulary depth in predicting reading comprehension among English monolingual and Spanish-English bilingual children in elementary school. Reading and Writing: An Interdisciplinary Journal, 25(7), 517–544. doi:10.1007/s11145-011-9336-5

Raphael, T.E. (1986). Teaching question answer relationships, revisted. The Reading Teacher, 39(6), 516–522.

Shanahan, T., Callison, K., Carriere, C., Duke, N.K., Pearson, P.D., Schatschneider, C.,

& Torgesen, J. (2010). *Improving reading comprehension in kindergarten through 3rd grade: A practice guide* (NCEE 2010–4038). Washington, DC: National Center for Education Evaluation and Regional Assistance, Institute of Education Sciences, U.S. Department of Education. Retrieved from whatworks.ed.gov/publications/practiceguides

Silverman, R.D. (2007). Vocabulary development of English-language and English-only learners in kindergarten. *The Elementary School Journal, 107*(4), 365–383. doi:10.1086/516669

Silverman, R.D., & Crandell, J.D. (2010). Vocabulary practices in prekindergarten and kindergarten classrooms. *Reading Research Quarterly, 45*(3), 318–340. doi:10.1598/RRQ.45.3.3

Silverman, R., & Hines, S. (2009). The effects of multimedia-enhanced instruction on the vocabulary of English-language learners and non-English-language learners in pre-kindergarten through second grade. *Journal of Educational Psychology, 101*(2), 305–314. doi:10.1037/a0014217

Silverman, R., Martin-Beltran, M., & Peercy, M. (2011). *Reinventing reading buddies: Developing a cross-age peer-tutoring program to promote the vocabulary and comprehension of English learners.* Unpublished study, U.S. Department of Education, Institute of Educational Sciences.

Silverman, R., Proctor, P., Harring, J., Doyle, B., Meyer, A.G., & Mitchell, M.A. (2012, November). *Comprehension and vocabulary instruction in linguistically diverse grade 3–5 classrooms.* Paper presented at the annual meeting of the Literacy Research Association, San Diego, CA.

Snow, C.E., Burns, M.S., & Griffin, P. (1998). *Preventing reading difficulties in young children.* Washington, DC: National Academy Press.

Swain, M. (1995). Three functions of output in second language learning. In G. Cook & B. Seidlhofer (Eds.), *Principle and practice in applied linguistics* (pp. 125–144). Oxford, England: Oxford University Press.

Van Roekel, D. (2008). *English language learners face unique challenges* (policy brief). Washington, DC: National Education Association. Retrieved from www.nea.org/assets/docs/mf_PB05_ELL.pdf

Viadero, D. (2009). Delving deep: Research hones focus on ELLs. *Education Week, 28*(17), 3–5. Retrieved from www.cal.org/qualitycounts/quality_counts_cal.pdf

Williams, J.P., Hall, K.M., Lauer, K.D., Stafford, K.B., DeSisto, L.A., & deCani, J.S. (2005). Expository text comprehension in the primary grade classroom. *Journal of Educational Psychology, 97*(4), 538–550. doi:10.1037/0022-0663.97.4.538

Williams, J.P., Nubla-King, A.M., Pollini, S., Stafford, K.B., Garcia, A., & Snyder, A.E. (2007). Teaching cause–effect text structure through social studies content to at-risk second graders. *Journal of Learning Disabilities, 40*(2), 111–120. doi:10.1177/00222194070400020201

Williams, J.P., Stafford, K.B., Lauer, K.D., Hall, K.M., & Pollini, S. (2009). Embedding reading comprehension training in content-area instruction. *Journal of Educational Psychology, 101*(1), 1–20. doi:10.1037/a0013152

CHAPTER 10

Research on Text Complexity: The Common Core State Standards as Catalyst

James W. Cunningham

Educational policies have a life; a trajectory; a beginning, middle, and end. The Common Core State Standards (CCSS; National Governors Association Center for Best Practices & Council of Chief State School Officers [NGA Center & CCSSO], 2010a) are still in the beginning phase because they are only now being widely implemented. The tests to assess whether students have met the Standards are still being developed.

This chapter addresses what I consider to be the three most significant reading instructional changes called for by the Reading Standards and their associated documents at this crucial point in the life of the CCSS. It also briefly describes the research, especially research on text complexity, which I expect and hope each of the changes will bring about as a catalyst. The chapter also suggests for each change what I believe is a prudent strategy for schools and teachers to pursue in the interim until the needed research is conducted, if it ever is.

Instructional Change 1: More Difficult Texts

The most widely discussed reading instructional change called for by the CCSS is a significant increase in text complexity. If and when the CCSS are fully implemented, the texts students are asked to read across the grades and disciplines will be substantially more difficult. This change is explicitly called for in Appendix A of the CCSS (NGA Center & CCSSO, 2010b), and implicitly in Reading Standard 10 at every grade for both kinds of text, literary and informational. Those who have not read the Standards and only listened to the chatter about them may well have concluded that this is the only major change in reading instruction the CCSS entails.

Quality Reading Instruction in the Age of Common Core Standards, edited by Susan B. Neuman and Linda B. Gambrell. © 2013 by the International Reading Association.

Research Relevant to the Call for More Difficult Texts

The research on text complexity needed to inform evaluation and possible modification of this reading instructional change is research on reader–text match (classically referred to as reading instructional level or zone of proximal development in reading). For a particular reader at a particular time, the text match is the text difficulty that would maximize that student's growth in reading. Studies on this topic attempt to answer the following question: What criteria indicate an optimal reader–text match? The first such criteria were proposed by Betts (1946). He held that a zone of 75–89% reading comprehension and 95–98% oral reading accuracy when reading a text without instruction would indicate a beneficial reader–text match for instructional use. Presumably, for Betts, lower matches in the zone were better than higher ones, as indicated by his identification of "instructional level" with the lowest percentages on the two indicators. More recently, the minimum oral reading accuracy criterion for reader–text match in most classrooms has been reduced to 90% due to the influence of Reading Recovery. So what criteria do existing research support?

Unfortunately, almost all of the studies are dated. Reading Recovery has published few, if any, studies specifically validating their criteria. More regrettably, the studies on reader–text match that have been done are not in agreement. In an excellent and readable review of the research, Johns (2012) concludes that there is no consensus across studies or among researchers as to what specific criteria indicate the best or even an appropriate reader–text match. Perhaps it was this lack of consensus on criteria for reader–text matching that freed the CCSS Committee to increase markedly the standard of difficulty of texts for students across the board.

Hopefully, the CCSS's call for more difficult texts will serve as a catalyst to engender new research on reader–text match. If so, that research must avoid the mistakes of the past that led the set of previous studies to fail to reach or even approach a consensus on criteria. Rather, the field needs creative researchers to "cut the Gordian knot," that is, to address the question from fresher and more productive perspectives.

In the Meantime

In the face of more difficult texts for students to read, two courses of action seem prudent for schools and teachers to take until the needed research on reader–text match is conducted. First, we can carefully monitor our students' engagement and stamina with the texts we ask them to read. Although many and perhaps most of us who have spent extensive time working with struggling readers, their teachers, and their schools are deeply skeptical of the increase in text complexity for grades 1–8, we cannot cite a body of studies to prove we are right and the CCSS Committee was wrong. However, this much surely is not debatable: If students will not read a text or only begin reading it but give up before completing it, they cannot benefit from it. The assumption that the more difficult texts called for by the CCSS will challenge the broad range of students to work harder to read them should receive frequent observation checks in every American classroom.

Second, we should carefully monitor our students' success on the immediate outcome of reading the texts they do read—that is, on the during- or after-reading instructional task. Again, we do not know from research what degree of success on daily reading comprehension or oral reading tasks predicts the best long-term growth in reading ability, but surely something like "C" work is the minimum performance necessary most days for students to consistently improve in reading. Whether regular, short-term success on immediate outcomes will add up to future college and career readiness remains to be seen from future research, but no one ever learned how to be good at anything (especially reading) by doing it poorly every day.

Instructional Change 2: Learning-From-Text Instruction Replaces Comprehension Instruction

Although it has received little scrutiny or discussion, this reading instructional change entailed by the CCSS may be almost as significant as the call for more difficult texts. Traditionally, one important difference between developmental reading instruction and instruction in content area reading has been the former's emphasis on comprehension skills and strategies and the latter's stress on learning from text. In the CCSS, learning from text has become the preferred way of fostering meaningful text reading across the school day.

Indicators of this change are subtle but consistent in the CCSS documents. One of the seven prototypical profiles of students who are meeting the CCSS on their way to college and career readiness is that "they build strong content knowledge" in part by "establish[ing] a base of knowledge across a wide range of subject matter by engaging with works of quality and substance" (NGA Center & CCSSO, 2010a, p. 7), that is, from reading particular texts. None of these seven profiles allude to acquiring or using comprehension skills or strategies. When the K–5 Reading

Standards are introduced, it is the goals of having students build "literary and cultural knowledge" and "a foundation of knowledge" in history/social studies, science, and other disciplines (NGA Center & CCSSO, 2010a, p. 10) that are mentioned. Again, nothing at all is said about learning or applying comprehension skills or strategies. In fact, the Reading Standards themselves generally characterize the results of reading students must manifest and not the means they employ to achieve those results.

That the teaching of comprehension strategies is to be subordinated to the teaching of specific text content in the implementation of the CCSS is made unequivocal in the document by Coleman and Pimentel (2012) for publishers desiring to produce instructional materials consistent with the CCSS:

> Close reading and gathering knowledge from specific texts should be at the heart of classroom activities.... Reading strategies should work in the service of reading comprehension (rather than an end unto themselves) and assist students in building knowledge and insight from specific texts. (p. 9)

Let it be clear the difference this change will make. Tierney and Cunningham (1984) used the distinction between these two kinds of instruction to organize their comprehensive review of research on teaching reading comprehension:

- Learning-from-text instruction—"teacher intervention intended to improve students' ability to understand, recall, or integrate information from a specific text passage or passages." (p. 609)
- Comprehension instruction—"[teacher intervention] whose goal is to improve general and specific reading-comprehension abilities which will transfer to students' reading of passages they later encounter on their own." (p. 609)

Learning-from-text studies assess the impact of instructional interventions on the quantity and quality of learning from the particular texts taught. In contrast, comprehension instructional studies must have one or more "transfer" dependent variables using new texts not taught or read during the interventions.

Procedural Differences Between Learning-From-Text Instruction and Comprehension Instruction

Many studies have been done on each kind of instruction, and many books and articles have been published on teaching comprehension as well as content area reading. Typically, it seems that these distinct kinds of lessons vary along two dimensions. The first is the proportion of time spent on before- or during-reading activities or guidance. Learning-from-text lessons generally spend little time on these phases. This difference seems to occur because any attempt to increase intentional learning by focusing readers' attention before or during reading comes at the expense of incidental learning—a weakness when the text content as a whole is considered important to learn (Tierney & Cunningham, 1984). By contrast, comprehension lessons normally spend considerable time preparing students to read a text in a certain way or provide guidance during reading.

The second dimension along which the two kinds of instruction tend to differ is the thoroughness with which the content of each text is followed up in the after-reading phase of lessons. Learning-from-text lessons are usually more exhaustive. This difference probably occurs because comprehension instructional lessons often choose the aspect(s) of a text that support(s) the application of the particular strategy or strategies being taught and largely ignore other aspects.

Research Relevant to the Call for Replacing Comprehension Instruction With Learning-From-Text Instruction

Interestingly, the CCSS imply that learning-from-text instruction and practice should become modal but still assume it will lead to transfer. One of the "key features" of the Reading Standards is "the growth of comprehension" (NGA Center & CCSSO, 2010a, p. 8). This growth is delineated in some detail:

> Whatever they are reading, students must also show a steadily growing ability to discern more from and make fuller use of text, including making an increasing number of connections among ideas and between texts, considering a wider range of textual evidence, and becoming more sensitive to inconsistencies, ambiguities, and poor reasoning in texts. (NGA Center & CCSSO, 2010a, p. 8)

Obviously, the "steadily growing ability" to comprehend in these ways must result from learning-from-text lessons and independent practice since those are expected to dominate the instructional time once the CCSS are implemented.

There is a considerable body of research on both learning-from-text and reading comprehension instruction. Unfortunately, there are very few studies that employ a learning-from-text intervention but include one or more transfer dependent variables. Consequently, there is very little existing research to support this change brought by implementing the CCSS. Will it work? Certainly, we hope so. However, we need research studies to determine whether transfer is likely, and if so, what is actually transferring.

Research on whether this change is a good idea will attempt to answer two questions: (1) Does close reading, answering questions, discussing, and writing about texts to learn the content of each one thoroughly lead to improved comprehension of transfer texts read independently? and (2) How do effect sizes on transfer texts compare with those in studies of reading comprehension strategy instruction? It will also be important to determine whether this change is equally beneficial or detrimental for all readers or better for some types and levels of readers than others.

The text-complexity research made necessary by this change includes text content analyses so that the potential learning from a text can be quantified. Otherwise, it will be impossible to measure whether lessons and programs to increase learning from text have indeed been successful.

In the Meantime

Implementation of the CCSS is likely to lead us to teach texts more thoroughly and place less emphasis on comprehension skills and strategies. While this change may lead to improved reading comprehension of untaught texts, there is little research to encourage us to expect that outcome. Until such research is done, it seems prudent for us to monitor our students' classroom performance for evidence the change is working for them. In other words, let us observe whether most of our students are improving from a regimen of learning-from-text instruction and practice on similar after-reading discussion and writing tasks over time. If learning-from-text lessons do lead to transfer, student performance on similar instructional tasks should gradually but noticeably improve. Moreover, students' ability and stamina should also increase so that they can handle more challenging and longer texts than they could earlier in the year.

Instructional Change 3: Text-Dependent Questions and Tasks

CCSS's call for close reading, as specified in Reading Anchor Standard 1, has caused much discussion: "Read closely to determine what the text says explicitly and to make logical inferences from it; cite specific textual evidence when writing or speaking to support conclusions drawn from the text" (NGA Center & CCSSO, 2010a, p. 10). However, there has been little acknowledgment that close reading is only one aspect of a broader change throughout the Reading Standards—reliance on text-dependent questions and tasks to focus thinking, discussion, and writing and to evaluate reading. For example, Reading Anchor Standard 2, "Determine central ideas or themes of a text and analyze their development; summarize the key supporting details and ideas" (NGA Center & CCSSO, 2010a, p. 10), also requires methodical scrutiny of a text to analyze the development of a main idea and summarize the details and ideas that support it; likewise for Anchor Standards 3, 4, and beyond. Careful reading of a text and use of textual information in writing and discussion are consistently called for throughout the first nine Reading Standards. In their document outlining criteria for publishers, Coleman and Pimentel (2012) claim, "Eighty to ninety percent of the Reading Standards in each grade require text-dependent analysis" (p. 6).

A Change From What?

This major departure in instructional emphasis stands in striking contrast to two traditions that have shaped reading comprehension instruction and assessment in classrooms for a considerable period of time.

Reader-Response/Response-to-Literature Approaches. The New Criticism that had dominated the teaching of English literature in high school and college for decades was superseded in the late 1960s/early 1970s by reader-response criticism (Makaryk, 1993). By the mid-1980s, this change had trickled down to become an important part of the literature-based reading movement in K–8 that came to dominate American reading instruction from 1987 to 1995 (Cunningham & Creamer, 2003) and continued to influence comprehension teaching in grades 4–8 long after Reading First was implemented. In the quarter century before the CCSS, response-to-literature activities grew to be a common comprehension task for elementary and middle school students to complete after reading. Response-to-literature activities include free-ranging discussions, aesthetic expressions of students' emotional reactions to what they have read (such as drawing or personal writing), and creative productions where characters or settings are fleshed out beyond the specific descriptions given in the text (e.g., building a fort in the classroom after reading James Fenimore Cooper's *The Last of the Mohicans*). For these comprehension instructional tasks, the text frequently serves more as a springboard than a guide for student thinking and work.

Standardized Reading Comprehension Test Questions. Accountability to standardized tests had been a fact of life in schools since the late 1970s but increased in intensity after the 1994 election. This policy transformation brought tremendous pressure on schools and teachers to align their instruction with high-stakes assessments. Consequently, it is informative to examine the ways standardized reading comprehension tests operate to understand how they have refashioned comprehension instruction in many classrooms.

A Classic Study. What are text-dependent questions and tasks? They are questions that cannot be answered correctly (better than chance) and tasks that cannot be successfully performed unless the student has comprehended the text. Tuinman (1973) administered five major standardized reading comprehension tests in two different conditions to 9,451 students in grades 4–6. Half the participants completed the tests as designed; half completed them without access to the passages. The study found that the mean score of the participants in the no-passage condition was significantly higher than chance on all five tests. More tellingly, the participants who did not have any passages averaged 64% as many items correct as those who were given the passages. How could the students who had no passages perform so well relative to those who did have them? That they used a combination of prior knowledge and "test-wiseness" provides the only reasonable explanation.

As dramatically different as they are, response-to-literature activities and traditional standardized comprehension test items share one thing in common: Neither is generally text based. Because of the CCSS Reading Standards' widespread requirement of text-dependent analysis, their implementation can be expected to reduce the incidence in classrooms of both response-to-literature activities and comprehension lessons that promote using prior knowledge and test-taking skills to determine the most probable correct answers on multiple-choice comprehension items.

Research Relevant to the Call for Text-Dependent Questions and Tasks

Like the CCSS's calls for more difficult texts and replacing comprehension instruction with learning from text, the call for text-dependent questions and tasks must be evaluated based on whether the change increases reading achievement on transfer texts in the medium and long term. We also need studies that explore the construct and consequential validity of text-dependent comprehension items. The construct validity studies will be especially important for the text-complexity literature because when it comes to text-dependency of questions and task, it seems that a merger of construct with content validity will be required.

Some of the validity studies will attempt to answer the following research question: How do students' scores on reading comprehension tests with high proportions of text-dependent items compare with their scores on traditional reading comprehension tests? Of course, the results of these studies remain to be seen, but I am tempted to speculate. It seems probable that at least two groups of students will perform differently on more text-dependent comprehension assessments. Those students whose prior knowledge and intelligence are relatively higher than their reading ability will probably score worse. However, those students whose prior knowledge and intelligence are relatively lower than their reading ability will probably score better. If so, and if it is reading comprehension ability proper we want to measure, the text-dependent reading comprehension tests will be more valid and more sensitive to reading instruction.

In the Meantime

Until sufficient research has been conducted on the achievement effects and test validity of predominately text-dependent questions and tasks for comprehension instruction, practice, and assessment, two courses of action seem sensible for schools and classrooms to take.

Practice Formulating Whole-Text and Inferential Text-Dependent Questions. As with having the texts students are asked to read be more difficult and replacing the teaching of comprehension skills and strategies with learning from text, the lack of experience with and research on the use of text-dependent questions in instruction and assessment makes it judicious for us to monitor how our students respond to this change over the course of a school year. Here the biggest challenge may be in assuring ourselves that the questions we ask to guide, follow up, and evaluate reading represent the best that text-dependent questions should be. My fear is that many teachers, perhaps aided by publishers of forthcoming instructional materials and manuals, will overemphasize literal, detail-oriented questions in the name of executing this change. If so, that would be a serious error in judgment because such questions and tasks are inconsistent with the higher order nature of the majority of the CCSS Reading Standards and are unlikely to occur as items on the forthcoming comprehension assessments.

Seek Out Text-Dependent Comprehension Instructional Tasks Like GIST. One of Coleman and Pimentel's (2012) criteria for publishers is "Shorter, challenging texts that elicit close reading and re-reading are provided regularly at each grade" (p. 4). Having shorter texts to use instructionally with students across the grades will make intensive comprehension lesson frameworks such as GIST more practical for classroom use than they have been in the past when reading selections were almost always quite long.

Cunningham (1982) developed the GIST Procedure, an example of a text-dependent reading comprehension task, and conducted an experiment comparing it with a placebo condition. Participants were fourth-graders. GIST was shown to significantly improve students' ability to write succinct and accurate summaries of short texts not used in the treatments. The effect size for this comparison was 0.7, a large effect. Here are the steps in a GIST lesson:

1. Show a group of students the first part of a short text and have them read it to themselves. Hide the text and be their scribe as they orally compose and collectively negotiate a summary in one sentence of X* words. (Show the text portion again if they ask to see it, but always have the students work from memory.)

2. Show the students the first and second parts of the same text and have them read the text so far to themselves. Hide the text and be their scribe as they orally compose and collectively negotiate a new summary in one sentence of X words. (Show this text portion again if they ask to see it, but always have the students work from memory.)

3. Continue as before with the first three parts.

4. Continue as before with the first four parts. (Generally, four parts is the maximum for this lesson. At first, three is enough.)

*X = 10 plus the grade (grades 2–7) (in grades 8–12, X = 18)

When teaching multiple GIST lessons over days or weeks, first fade the number of parts you divide the text into until the group of students can readily compose a one-sentence summary of each entire short text in one step. Then, across multiple lessons, fade from the group task to smaller groups/trios/pairs to an individual task that eventually requires each student to compose a one-sentence summary of each of several short texts in one step. At both the smaller-group and individual stages, have volunteers share a few of their written "gists" aloud and, when there is significant variance, lead a discussion of which ideas seem essential to include and why.

No doubt, there are other text-based comprehension lesson frameworks like GIST that do not merely promote student regurgitation of detailed information. These kinds of lessons should help students gradually acquire the habit and ability to read texts carefully in the higher order way the CCSS Reading Standards require.

Summary

This chapter addresses what I regard as the three most important reading instructional changes called for by the Common Core State Standards and their associated documents. The requirement for students to read more difficult texts across the board is probably the most revolutionary change and is certainly the one I am comfortable with the least. Ideally, it will serve as the impetus for a new generation of better studies on reader–text matching. In the meantime, I encourage schools and teachers to carefully monitor student engagement and short-term success with the new, more challenging texts.

Replacing comprehension instruction with learning-from-text instruction is a less discussed change wrought by the CCSS, but it is one that could have important implications for students' long-term growth in reading ability. It may work, but if it does, research will need to discover *what* is transferring to new and more difficult texts. New and better methods of text-content analysis will be required to measure and elucidate learning from text. In the meantime, educators should be observant of whether improved learning of particular texts is actually teaching their students how to read more difficult and longer untaught texts—that is, whether this reading instructional change is achieving transfer effects.

Increased use of text-dependent questions and tasks is also an underacknowledged change that could transform both reading instruction and assessment. Of the three changes discussed in this chapter, it is the one I believe has the most potential to benefit students. It, too, has implications for research about text complexity beyond the issue of whether it increases reading achievement. For example, what is there that is potentially learnable from a text and how can that best be quantified? In the meantime, I encourage schools and teachers to practice formulating whole-text and inferential text-dependent questions and to seek out text-dependent comprehension instructional tasks like GIST.

No educational policy has ever called for the amount and degree of comprehension instructional changes that the CCSS has mandated. As reading researchers and educators, we have our work cut out for us.

- Use a short text appropriate for your students to read. Break it into three parts and teach a GIST lesson with it. Notice how engaged your students become each time as they attempt to summarize the entire text so far in just one sentence with the maximum number of words or fewer.

- Post a point-of-view chart with characters from a book students have read listed across the top. (For example, from *Charlotte's Web* by E.B. White, the characters would be Wilber, Fern, Arable, Charlotte, and the narrator.) Engage the students in a discussion of each character's "point of view" and fill in the chart as they share their ideas. Make this a text-dependent task by ending the discussion of each character's point of view in this way. Ask the students to search for and read a sentence or two that provides evidence for any idea on the chart for that character. Put the page number after any comment with evidence. Praise students who were able to find appropriate evidence in the text for an idea they or another student had.

DISCUSSION QUESTIONS

1. What is reader–text match, and why is this concept important to consider during the implementation of CCSS's Reading Standards?

2. According to Cunningham, what courses of action are prudent for teachers to take until better research on reader–text match is conducted?

3. For at least the past 30 years, teachers have focused on comprehension instruction in their classrooms. However, the CCSS call for a shift from comprehension instruction to learning-from-text instruction. How do you think this shift will affect classroom teachers and their students?

REFERENCES

Betts, E.A. (1946). *Foundations of reading instruction, with emphasis on differentiated guidance*. New York: American Book Company.

Coleman, D., & Pimentel, S. (2012). *Revised publishers' criteria for the Common Core State Standards in English language arts and literacy, grades 3–12*. Washington, DC: National Governors Association Center for Best Practices & Council of Chief State School Officers. Retrieved from www.core standards.org/assets/Publishers_Criteria_ for_3-12.pdf

Cunningham, J.W. (1982). Generating interactions between schemata and text. In J.A. Niles & L.A Harris (Eds.), *New inquiries in reading research and instruction: Thirty-first yearbook of the National Reading Conference* (pp. 42–47). Rochester, NY: National Reading Conference.

Cunningham, J.W., & Creamer, K.H. (2003). Achieving best practices in literacy instruction. In L.M. Morrow, L.B. Gambrell, & M. Pressley (Eds.), *Best practices in literacy instruction* (2nd ed., pp. 333–346). New York: Guilford.

Johns, J.L. (2012). *Basic reading inventory: Pre-primer through grade twelve and early literacy assessments* (11th ed.). Dubuque, IA: Kendall Hunt.

Makaryk, I.R. (Ed.). (1993). *Encyclopedia of contemporary literary theory: Approaches, scholars, terms.* Toronto, ON: University of Toronto Press.

National Governors Association Center for Best Practices & Council of Chief State School Officers. (2010a). *Common Core State Standards for English language arts and literacy in history/social studies, science, and technical subjects.* Washington, DC: Authors. Retrieved from www.corestandards.org/assets/CCSSI_ELA%20Standards.pdf

National Governors Association Center for Best Practices & Council of Chief State School Officers. (2010b). *Common Core State Standards for English language arts and literacy in history/social studies, science, and technical subjects: Appendix A: Research supporting key elements of the Standards and glossary of key terms.* Washington, DC: Authors. Retrieved from www.corestandards.org/assets/Appendix_A.pdf

Tierney, R.J., & Cunningham, J.W. (1984). Research on teaching reading comprehension. In P.D. Pearson, R. Barr, M.L. Kamil, & P. Mosenthal (Eds.), *Handbook of reading research* (Vol. 1, pp. 609–655). White Plains, NY: Longman.

Tuinman, J.J. (1973). Determining the passage dependency of comprehension questions in 5 major tests. *Reading Research Quarterly, 9*(2), 206–223. doi:10.2307/747135

CHAPTER 11

Core Vocabulary and the Challenge of Complex Text

Elfrieda H. Hiebert

C ollege and Career Readiness Reading Anchor Standard 10—
"Read and comprehend complex literary and informational texts
independently and proficiently"—is the feature that distinguishes
the Common Core State Standards (CCSS; National Governors Association
Center for Best Practices & Council of Chief State School Officers [NGA
Center & CCSSO], 2010, p. 10) from previous standards documents. In
the past, a proficiency such as comparing and contrasting two grade-
level texts might be given as a fifth-grade standard, but what was meant
by "grade-level text" was never defined. Not only do the CCSS include
a Standard devoted specifically to students' ability to read increasingly
more complex text, but explicit guidelines are also given in the form of
quantitative indexes in CCSS Appendix A (NGA Center & CCSSO, 2010b)
and in illustrations of exemplar texts in CCSS Appendix B (NGA Center
& CCSSO, 2010c). An emphasis on increasing capacity with complex text
makes perfect sense, and we can only ask why it has been ignored for the
past several decades.

But the topic *has* been ignored. Consequently, when the CCSS
proposed a three-part system for establishing text complexity, there
were few systems available for evaluating two of the three evaluation
components: qualitative and reader-task dimensions of texts. By contrast,
there is a long history of quantitative systems that typically use some
measure of sentence length and vocabulary difficulty (Klare, 1984). The
CCSS writers drew on a current digital text-difficulty system—the Lexile
Framework—to propose a staircase of text complexity that begins with
grade 2 and extends to college and career readiness (CCR). The staircase
was designed to ensure that students' reading proficiencies increase
across the school years to a level of CCR text by high school graduation.

The CCSS writers based this staircase on the assumption that there
has been a dip in text complexity across all grades over the past 50 years.

Quality Reading Instruction in the Age of Common Core Standards, edited by Susan B. Neuman and
Linda B. Gambrell. © 2013 by the International Reading Association.

Data confirm this assumption in the middle- and high-school grades (Hayes, Wolfer, & Wolfe, 1996; Williamson, 2008) but, as Hiebert and Mesmer (in press) have illustrated, the statement does not apply to texts in the primary grades. Indeed, analyses such as that of Foorman, Francis, Davidson, Harm, and Griffin (2004) have shown that the texts of the primary grades have accelerated in difficulty since *Becoming a Nation of Readers* (Anderson, Hiebert, Scott, & Wilkinson, 1985) called for an end to vocabulary control in reading textbooks.

Many educators question how their students can read even more complex text when a sizable portion of a grade-four cohort already struggles with existing texts that fall below current grade-level expectations (National Center for Education Statistics, 2011). The perspective developed in this chapter is that current performances can partly be explained by the small amounts of reading most American students do in school. Further, when students get "easier" texts, these texts are often simply shorter in length, not substantially different in the load of vocabulary. Finally, when texts are perceived as too difficult, teachers frequently read texts aloud. When this occurs, students have even fewer opportunities to develop independence and proficiency in reading. The task confronting teachers is to support their students in reading more of the texts that are currently available in their classrooms, many of which are sufficiently complex for many students.

The aim of this chapter is to provide teachers with an understanding of why and how movement up the Common Core's staircase of text complexity begins with a focus on the current texts of the elementary school. To accomplish this aim, the chapter addresses three topics: (1) the distribution of vocabulary in texts, (2) students' performances with the core vocabulary, and (3) scaffolds that support students' reading of current texts.

Understanding How Vocabulary Functions in Texts

This section begins with a discussion of the distribution of vocabulary across texts in general and then demonstrates the consistency of the distribution with specific sets of texts.

The Distribution of Vocabulary Within Texts: The 90–10 Phenomenon

Figure 11.1 shows the distribution of words in a sample of K–college schoolbooks (based on the work of Zeno, Ivens, Millard, & Duvvuri, 1995) representing content areas taught in school. Approximately 930 words in

Figure 11.1. Distribution of Words in Written English

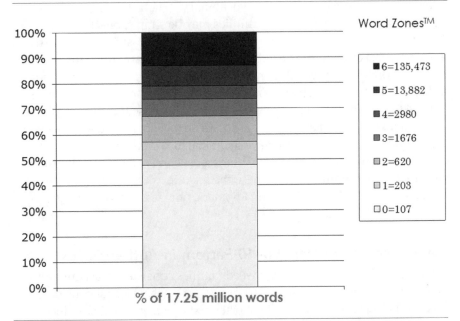

Word Zones™

6=135,473
5=13,882
4=2980
3=1676
2=620
1=203
0=107

% of 17.25 million words

Note. This figure is based on the author's interpretations of the work of Zeno et al. (1995). Copyright TextProject, Inc. (www.textproject.org/), Santa Cruz, CA. Reprinted with permission.

this sample accounted for two thirds of all words in texts. Adding another 4,700 words brings the total to 80% of total words. The remaining words occur much less frequently, with those that occur less than once per million forming the largest group.

I have examined how many words in the most frequent 5,860 words share the same root word (Hiebert, 2012). In my study, word families were defined as the root word and related words with simple derivational endings (e.g., *er, est, ly*), inflected endings, and possessives. Two examples of simple word families are (1) *help, helps, helping, helped,* and *helper* and (2) *locate, locating, located, locates*. This process produced 4,000 word families among the 5,860 words (Hiebert, 2012). The label "simple" is used to distinguish this process from complex word families. For example, the complex word family for *help* would include *helpful* and *helpless*, while the family for *locate* would include *location* and *relocate/relocation*.

The next step was to examine the words in word zones five and six (see Figure 11.1) to identify members of the 4,000 simple word families. Adding rare members to the database brings the percentage of total words accounted for by the simple 4,000 word families to approximately 90% of most texts. Because of its central role in text, this set of 4,000 simple word families can be considered a "core vocabulary" (Hiebert, 2012).

The forms of words in these families may be simple, but the words themselves are not necessarily simple to learn. The most frequent words (e.g., *the, a, of*) often have variant vowel patterns and are quite abstract in meaning. But the core vocabulary includes many words beyond the high-utility words. Words such as *light* and *current* illustrate that many words in the 4,000 simple word families are frequent because they have multiple uses. They take on different parts of speech (e.g., *light* from the sun—noun, a *light* color—adjective). Some have technical meanings (e.g., *current* in electricity) as well as everyday meanings (e.g., *current* fashion). Many are also used in compound words where the meanings are often idiosyncratic (e.g., *light-headed, lightweight*) and idiomatic phrases (e.g., *give the green light, see the light of day*).

Demonstrations of the 90–10 Pattern in Authentic Texts

Verification that the 4,000 simple word families consistently account for the majority of words in texts comes from two analyses. The first considered at least 1,000 words (or all words in shorter texts such as Abraham Lincoln's Gettysburg Address) from all of the text exemplars in Appendix B of the CCSS (NGA Center & CCSSO, 2010c). The information in Table 11.1 shows that, while the percentage of core vocabulary is somewhat lower in high school texts and for informational texts than for elementary and narrative texts, most of the vocabulary of all sets of exemplar texts is accounted for by the core vocabulary.

The second analysis considered the distributions of core vocabulary *across* texts offered for students of different proficiency levels in one grade level of a core reading program (Houghton Mifflin Harcourt, 2008). The StoryTown core reading program, similar to most core reading programs, has an anthology with primary and secondary selections for a week and five guided reading texts designated for readers of different proficiencies (advanced, on-level, below-level, English learner, and intervention). The data in Table 11.2 represent the average percentage for the texts offered for six weeks of instruction.

With one exception, the core vocabulary for texts accounts for 92–94% of all words. The only text that falls outside this range is the text for below-level students. At 89%, much of the vocabulary continues to be from the core, but approximately 11% of the words are rare. Many, although not all, of the rare words in the below-level texts aim to support decoding skills with monosyllabic words (e.g., *plank, daze*) or two-syllable word patterns (e.g., *hinder, indoor*). The percentage of rare words is high, and

Table 11.1. Core Vocabulary Distributions for CCSS Appendix B Text Exemplars

Grade	Narrative	Informational
2–3	.93	.92
4–5	.92	.91
6–8	.93	.87
9–10	.89	.91
11–CCR	.89	.87

Table 11.2. Texts Offered for Different Readers: Six Units/Weeks of Third Grade

	% Core Vocabulary	Word Count
Advanced	93	1010
On level	94	891
Below level	89	541
English learner	94	479
Intervention	93	287
Anthology (primary)	92	1049
Anthology (secondary)	94	153

the rare words are often not repeated, leading to the conclusion that the automaticity of below-level students with the core vocabulary will likely not increase if these texts are their primary learning experience. Texts intended for other levels may support their automaticity to a greater extent.

Students' Performances With the Core Vocabulary

The question of how students are doing with the core vocabulary is a challenging one to answer. Since the late 1980s, when state policies demanded an end to controlled texts, even state assessments stopped using texts controlled for core vocabulary. There is an exception to this pattern—the DIBELS oral reading fluency (ORF) passages. DIBELS developers used the Spache readability formula to establish the difficulty of the ORF passages (Good & Kaminski, 2002). In developing a readability formula, Spache (1953) identified specific sets of high-frequency words for particular grade levels and measured a text's readability against those words. As a result, the core vocabulary accounts for a high percentage of words in exit-level ORF passages: from 97% at the end of grade 2 to 92% at the end of grade 6.

The use of the Spache readability formula in validating ORF passage difficulty means that DIBELS norms can be used to get a sense of how students do with core vocabulary. The following text fits the parameters of the end-of-year DIBELS ORF passage at grade 2:

> Once upon a time a woman was frying some pancakes. As she turned a cake in the pan, she said to her little boy, "If you were a little older, I would send you to the sawmill with some of these cakes for your father's/[10] dinner. But as it is, he must wait till supper for them." "Oh, do let me take them," said the/[20] boy, whose name was Karl. "Do let me go. " And he begged and/[30] begged, till at last his mother selected the brownest/[40] and crispest pancakes. She put them on a/[50] plate with a napkin over them and bade her son take them to the mill. (Lindsay, 1965, p. 207)

The superscript following a slash represents the number of words read by a decile group. Not every student within a decile group would be expected to have read every single word up to that point, but in order to have read 65 words (20th percentile) or 95 words (50th percentile), students needed to read a significant number of words, many of which are in the core vocabulary (Good, Wallin, Simmons, Kame'enui, & Kaminski, 2002). For many students, this reading is often slow, which means that their comprehension is compromised.

In sum, most American students have a fundamental recognition of the core vocabulary by the end of second grade and certainly by the end of third and fourth grades. But as Stanovich (1986) suggested, a lack of automaticity means that students are less likely to read, which decreases reading proficiency even more. To stop this cycle of "the poorer getting poorer" in reading proficiency depends on the use of instructional scaffolds that are carefully and intentionally enacted.

Scaffolds to Support Struggling Readers

The Standards for the grade bands given by the CCSS suggest that there are ways to scaffold students in reading more difficult text, as shown in the following examples:

> Reading Standards for Literature K–5, Grade 4 Students:
> 10. By the end of the year, read and comprehend literature, including stories, dramas, and poetry, in the grades 4–5 text complexity band proficiently, **with scaffolding as needed at the high end of the range.**

Reading Standards for Literature K–5, Grade 5 Students:
10. By the end of the year, read and comprehend literature, including stories, dramas, and poetry, at the high end of the grades 4–5 text complexity band **independently and proficiently.**

(NGA Center & CCSSO, 2010a, p. 12; italics and boldface added)

Scaffold, as commonly defined, refers to a temporary structure that workers use to reach high places as they work on buildings. In a similar vein, the parts of the Standards that have been highlighted suggest that proficient reading can be "scaffolded" in ways that support students' independent reading in subsequent grades.

Before attending to three scaffolds that can support this movement up the staircase of text complexity, the efficacy of one frequently used scaffold in classrooms merits attention: teachers' read-alouds of instructional text. In many classrooms, teacher read-alouds are no longer used only as scaffolds but instead have become permanent parts of the instructional landscape. At the present time, however, there is no evidence showing that teachers' read-alouds of instructional/learning texts lead to increases in students' ability to read more fluently and proficiently in independent contexts. This practice of teacher read-alouds of instructional texts is distinct from teachers' interactional read-alouds of other high-quality texts, which, in contrast, *have* been found to enhance students' vocabulary and comprehension (Greene Brabham & Lynch-Brown, 2002).

Therefore, teacher read-alouds with student read-alongs of short but focused parts of text may be one of the tools in a teacher's toolkit, but it cannot be the primary one. There is research support for three alternate types of scaffolds.

Responsibility

Almost 30 years ago, Pearson and Gallagher (1983) described the critical role of gradual release of responsibility for text guidance from teacher to students. Pearson and Gallagher's cycle can also be applied to tasks with texts. Through intentional instructional steps, a teacher moves students from depending on the teacher for supervision and guidance in a reading task to independent responsibility for the reading task. The goal of reading instruction is to ensure that students read texts independently, not for students to expect their teachers or audio devices to do the reading for them when texts are challenging.

Teachers need to peruse texts to answer the question, Is this a text that this group/class of students should be able to read? If the answer is yes, the teacher should next look at the features that might need an overview prior to students' reading. The prior reading support should not exceed the time spent reading, but an anticipatory set for reading can be created with a few well-chosen comments. Next, the teacher might provide an overview such as the following:

> One of your goals as a third grader is to be able to read texts that have words that you might not know. When you read texts where you learn new words and ideas, you are growing as a reader. This text might look like it is hard, and it may even be on the first read. But I've studied the text, and you know most of the words. We are going to do our word warm-up where we identify new words. I'll also be available to talk with you about words you don't know after you've read the first three pages by yourself. What is important is for you to read to learn the message of the text. After you've read the first three pages by yourself, we'll talk about new words and also about what the text tells you about what school was like in a time long ago.

The DIBELS data suggest that American students, even those in the bottom quartile, can recognize many words. To develop a sense of agency and resilience as readers, students need to take responsibility for appropriate texts. The texts described in Table 11.2 average 7% rare words. Research is unclear as to precise percentages of rare words students can read in scaffolded and unscaffolded settings. However, as the description of the next scaffold—vocabulary—indicates, part of instructional support comes from teachers' review of potentially challenging vocabulary with students.

Vocabulary

There are numerous reasons why vocabulary receives substantial attention in a Common Core classroom. First, while it is not the only dimension that makes texts complex, vocabulary knowledge is closely tied to comprehension (Just & Carpenter, 1987). Unlike syntax, where research has been ambiguous about how it can be strengthened through instruction, there is a rich research base on ways of supporting students' vocabulary growth. There are two levels to this instruction: (1) strengthening vocabulary knowledge overall and (2) addressing the vocabulary of specific texts.

Teaching students about morphological word families is one way to expand students' vocabularies (Carlisle, 2010). Students' vocabularies can also be strengthened by understanding distinctions between unique words (i.e., those not in the 4,000 simple word families) in narrative and informational texts (Hiebert & Cervetti, 2012). The words in narrative texts typically fit into clusters with similar meanings (e.g., *lackadaisical,*

Figure 11.2. Attending to Infrequent Words and Strategies for Addressing These Words

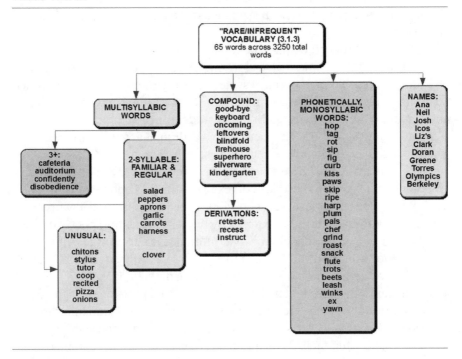

apathetic), while the unique vocabulary in informational texts belong to clusters where words have distinctive but conceptually interrelated meanings (e.g., *acidic, abrasive, alkaline* are all properties of substances).

Students also need to be guided in the specific words that may be unknown in instructional texts. Figure 11.2 is a summary of the infrequent words from a week's worth of guided reading texts (included in the summary in Table 11.2). Very short lessons can be conducted on particular groups of words (e.g., dealing with proper names). Students also need to be aware that the number of new words is finite and that they can figure out almost all but a small percentage of the new words with their already acquired decoding and root word strategies.

Volume

In a study of the amount of time that students spent reading in schools that were part of the No Child Left Behind initiative, Brenner, Hiebert, and Tompkins (2009) found that the amount of time devoted to reading *instruction* doubled in most classrooms, whereas the time spent in reading *practice* increased by only 15%. Much of the increased instructional time was devoted to teachers' talking about reading. True, some of this talk was discussion about what had been read, but students read for less than 20% of the reading period.

The amount that students read in their classrooms needs to be a structural change in American classrooms. Viewed from that perspective, the component is not a temporary structure. However, scaffolds are needed to initiate substantial increases in independent reading time. Increasing the amount of independent reading that students are doing does not happen in one fell swoop. The increase of reading at any point in time needs to occur intentionally and be consistently monitored.

The information in Table 11.2 shows that the distinction between many instructional texts is in the length of texts, not the percentage of core vocabulary. For below-level students, 400 fewer words in a weekly text compared with the length of text read by higher performing peers may not seem great, but over a school year that difference is substantial. Almost 35 years ago, Allington (1977) asked the question, "If they don't read much how they ever gonna get good?" Struggling readers, in particular, need to read substantially more text in school. Because the guided reading texts in a unit typically cluster around a theme, the below-level students can read several texts (e.g., texts geared toward below-level, intervention, and English learner students). By asking below-level students to read three texts rather than one, their opportunities to read over the school year are more than doubled.

Some may argue that repeated reading of single texts will accomplish the same goal. However, in the landmark study of fluency conducted by Kuhn and Schwanenflugel (2008), it was wide reading—which was defined as reading several texts—not simply repeated reading of single texts that proved critical in increasing students' fluency. To ensure that students "get good," students need to read widely and deeply. Wide reading means reading more rather than fewer texts. Deep reading means that students reread portions of these texts for connections and extensions of their knowledge.

Summary

A frequent response of teachers to hearing a call for "complex text" is that this is impossible in their classrooms since their students are far below grade level. The content of this chapter shows that, across all grade levels, the core vocabulary accounts for the majority of the words in texts. By the end of second grade, almost all students can recognize the core vocabulary, but a significant portion of a grade cohort are not very automatic with this vocabulary. Students need to read widely and deeply to become automatic with this vocabulary. When teachers overuse the scaffold of reading texts aloud for students, students' automaticity with the core vocabulary is not aided. Teachers' toolboxes of appropriate scaffolds need to expand to conversations where students take responsibility for the texts themselves, where strategies for unique vocabulary are developed, and where the amount that students read during school time increases substantially. Just as knowledge is the center of the Common Core for students, likewise, teachers' knowledge about how language works can go a long way to providing the foundation for practices that increase students' capacity with complex text.

TRY THIS!

- Before reading a chapter about microorganisms in a life sciences class, have students brainstorm and then use list-group-label to further enhance their knowledge of key ideas. First, identify a key concept that reflects one of the main topics to be studied in the text. Then, have students work in small groups to generate a list of words related to the concept in 60 seconds. List words from each group on the board; then have the class form learning teams to group the words into logical arrangements. Then, have the teams label each arrangement. Finally, ask the students to make predictions about what is to be studied.

- Use a modified cloze passage to reinforce technical vocabulary. Choose a 200- to 500-word text segment that represents one of the most important parts of the reading assignment. Students can supply the missing words either before or after reading the entire assignment. Use discussion to build meaning for key terms and to raise expectations for the entire assignment if students work on the cloze activity before reading. If you assign the cloze passage after reading, the passage will reinforce concepts attained through reading.

DISCUSSION QUESTIONS

1. Vocabulary is a large component of reading comprehension. Given vocabulary's importance within texts, explain vocabulary distribution and the 90–10 phenomenon. Why is this concept vital in students' comprehension of complex texts?

2. Hiebert discusses the reliance on reading aloud instructional texts versus the importance of teachers' read-alouds of high-quality texts. Why should teachers read aloud high-quality texts rather than instructional texts?

3. How do the length of the text selected to read and the time spent reading impact students' success with texts? How can you scaffold your students to spend more time reading in your classroom?

REFERENCES

Allington, R.L. (1977). If they don't read much, how they ever gonna get good? *Journal of Reading, 21*(1), 57–61.

Anderson, R.C., Hiebert, E.H., Scott, J.A., & Wilkinson, I.A.G. (1985). *Becoming a nation of readers: The report of the Commission on Reading.* Washington, DC: The National Institute of Education, U.S. Department of Education.

Brenner, D., Hiebert, E.H., & Tompkins, R. (2009). How much and what are third graders reading? Reading in core programs. In E.H. Hiebert (Ed.), *Reading more, reading better* (pp. 118–140). New York: Guilford.

Carlisle, J.F. (2010). Effects of instruction in morphological awareness on literacy achievement: An integrative review. *Reading Research Quarterly, 45*(4), 464–487. doi:10.1598/RRQ.45.4.5

Foorman, B.R., Francis, D.J., Davidson, K.C., Harm, M.W., & Griffin, J. (2004). Variability in text features in six grade 1 basal reading programs. *Scientific Studies of Reading, 8*(2), 167–197. doi:10.1207/s1532799xssr0802_4

Good, R.H., & Kaminski, R.A. (2002). *DIBELS oral reading fluency passages for first through third grades* (Technical Report No. 10). Eugene, OR: University of Oregon.

Good, R.H., Wallin, J.U., Simmons, D.C., Kame'enui, E.J., & Kaminski, R.A. (2002). *System-wide percentile ranks for DIBELS benchmark assessment* (Technical Report No. 9). Eugene, OR: University of Oregon.

Greene Brabham, E., & Lynch-Brown, C. (2002). Effects of teachers' reading-aloud styles on vocabulary acquisition and comprehension of students in the early elementary grades. *Journal of Educational Psychology, 94*(3), 465–473. doi:10.1037/0022-0663.94.3.465

Hayes, D.P., Wolfer, L.T., & Wolfe, M.F. (1996). Schoolbook simplification and its relation to the decline in SAT-Verbal scores. *American Educational Research Journal, 33*(2), 489–508.

Hiebert, E.H. (2012). *Core vocabulary: The foundation for successful reading of complex text.* Santa Cruz, CA: TextProject. Available at http://textproject.org/assets/text-matters/Text-Matters_Core-Vocabulary.pdf./

Hiebert, E.H., & Cervetti, G.N. (2012). What differences in narrative and informational texts mean for the learning and instruction of vocabulary. In E.J. Kame'enui & J.F. Baumann (Eds.), *Vocabulary instruction: Research to practice* (2nd ed., pp. 322–344). New York: Guilford.

Hiebert, E.H., & Mesmer, H.A. (in press). Upping the ante of text complexity in the Common Core State Standards: Examining its potential impact on young readers. *Educational Researcher.*

Houghton Mifflin Harcourt. (2008). *StoryTown.* Boston: Author.

Just, M.A., & Carpenter, P.A. (1987). *The psychology of reading and language comprehension.* Boston: Allyn & Bacon.

Klare, G.R. (1984). Readability. In P.D. Pearson, R. Barr, M.L. Kamil, & P. Mosenthal (Eds.), *Handbook of reading research* (pp. 681–744). New York: Longman.

Kuhn, M.R., & Schwanenflugel, P.J. (Eds.). (2008). *Fluency in the classroom.* New York: Guilford.

Lindsay, M. (1965). The plate of pancakes. In H.M. Robinson, M. Monroe, A.S. Artley, C.S. Huck, & W.A. Jenkins (Eds.), *More roads to follow* (p. 207). Chicago: Scott, Foresman and Company.

National Center for Education Statistics. (2011). *The Nation's Report Card: Reading 2011* (NCES 2012–457). Washington, DC: Institute of Education Sciences, U.S. Department of Education.

National Governors Association Center for Best Practices & Council of Chief State School Officers. (2010a). *Common Core State Standards for English language arts and literacy in history/social* studies, science, and technical subjects. Washington, DC: Authors. Retrieved from www.corestandards.org/assets/CCSSI_ELA%20Standards.pdf

National Governors Association Center for Best Practices & Council of Chief State School Officers. (2010b). *Common Core State Standards for English language arts and literacy in history/social studies, science, and technical subjects: Appendix A: Research supporting key elements of the Standards and glossary of key terms.* Washington, DC: Authors. Retrieved from www.corestandards.org/assets/Appendix_A.pdf

National Governors Association Center for Best Practices & Council of Chief State School Officers. (2010c). *Common Core State Standards for English language arts and literacy in history/social studies, science, and technical subjects: Appendix B: Text exemplars and sample performance tasks.* Washington, DC: Retrieved from www.corestandards.org/assets/Appendix_B.pdf

Pearson, P.D., & Gallagher, M.C. (1983). The instruction of reading comprehension. *Contemporary Educational Psychology, 8*(3), 317–344. doi:10.1016/0361-476X(83)90019-X

Spache, G. (1953). A new readability formula for primary-grade reading materials. *The Elementary School Journal, 53*(7), 410–413. doi:10.1086/458513

Stanovich, K.E. (1986). Matthew effects in reading: Some consequences of individual differences in the acquisition of literacy. *Reading Research Quarterly, 21*(4), 360–407. doi:10.1598/RRQ.21.4.1

Williamson, G.L. (2008). A text readability continuum for postsecondary readiness. *Journal of Advanced Academics, 19*(4), 602–632.

Zeno, S.M., Ivens, S.H., Millard, R.T., & Duvvuri, R. (1995). *The educator's word frequency guide.* New York: Touchstone Applied Sciences Associates.

CHAPTER 12

Literacy Engagement: The Missing Link

John T. Guthrie & Jennifer McPeake

The basic message of this chapter is that literacy engagement is the missing link for teachers and educators seeking to help students attain the goals outlined in the Common Core State Standards (CCSS; National Governors Association Center for Best Practices & Council of Chief State School Officers [NGA Center & CCSSO], 2010). While many teachers are emphasizing the understanding of complex texts, the use of close-reading activities, and other approaches, we propose that literacy engagement is indispensable to any of these methods. Because complex texts are so challenging, students have to be exceptionally motivated. Therefore, simply giving these advanced materials to students is not enough. Students have to want to unlock the deeper meanings of complex literary informational texts in order to succeed in the CCSS (see College and Career Readiness [CCR] Anchor Standard for Reading 10, NGA Center & CCSSO, 2010, p. 10). Teachers who are moving students forward toward proficiency in the CCSS are providing new motivational supports and new encouragements for extended engagement in reading and writing.

Challenges of Complex Informational Texts

The message that engagement is the key assumes that students' motivation for reading informational text is an issue. In the past four years, we have investigated young adolescents' informational text comprehension and motivation. In interview studies and questionnaires of seventh-grade students, we observed a frequent aversion to reading difficult informational text. Students in our interactions reported that "information texts are boring" more frequently than any other reaction. In a widespread survey of all seventh-grade students in one school district (Guthrie, Wigfield, & Klauda, 2012), 80% named information texts as boring. These texts included science, social studies, math, and other subject matter

Quality Reading Instruction in the Age of Common Core Standards, edited by Susan B. Neuman and Linda B. Gambrell. © 2013 by the International Reading Association.

materials. Beyond a lack of enjoyment in reading informational text, a very high percentage of students actively avoid reading them whenever possible. Our interactions with students showed that 45% converted their negative attitudes to actual avoidant behaviors. These students said they put in minimum effort, attempted not to read, and conspired with their friends to evade reading whenever possible. If students are to reach higher standards, their reading commitments should be increased, and the challenge to teachers is obvious. While interest and commitment are low at present, fostering students' belief in the importance and time for informational text seems imperative for all.

Engagement in reading is driven by the motivations of confidence, interest, and value of reading. Active engagement converts the students' desires and interests into text interactions that create meaningful interpretations. Highly engaged students use what they know while they read to make new meanings, which is fundamental to comprehension. The challenge for teachers is, then, not merely to introduce complex texts with high standards for their students' reasoning about them. Teachers need to give students authentic reasons for digging into the materials. Engagement will not always occur naturally but often depends on teachers' practices.

Designing Classrooms for Engagement

The centerpiece of classroom engagement is a broad plan that can be used in many situations. We present a general lesson plan that follows five essential steps:

1. Select a suitable text.
2. Identify the central concept in the selected text.
3. Provide motivation support.
4. Identify one reading strategy.
5. Give students CCSS-based questions or tasks.

When teachers use each of these five elements, a distinct increase in engagement will appear in the classroom. We recommend that teachers hold this general plan in mind when designing every unit or individual lesson.

This general lesson plan includes two elements that are widespread in classrooms where the CCSS are emphasized. Many teachers are using more complex texts (step 1), and many are orienting to the CCSS (step 5). Distinctive to the general plan are steps 2, 3, and 4, which comprise identifying the concept, providing motivation, and teaching one strategy.

These three steps are the missing links of engagement support. Students are unlikely to reach higher standards without the links that these three ingredients provide. Any lesson and any unit that includes the ingredients of identifying concepts, providing motivation support, and teaching a reading strategy will foster engagement and will yield remarkable dividends in students' informational text comprehension.

Step 1: Select a Suitable Text

The general lesson plan assumes that teachers are working in a curriculum that includes a sequence of conceptual issues or themes in science, social studies, math, or literature. Given the conceptual theme, which has already been created and approved at the district or school level, teachers must first locate texts that are suitable for teaching the broad concept already identified in the curriculum guide. In a unit on the Civil War, examples of text may be the Emancipation Proclamation or a biography of Harriet Tubman. In science, a chapter section on symbiosis, an Internet site on plant–animal relationships, or a diagram that depicts photosynthesis may all be texts that are the target of extended teaching. All of these materials qualify as texts because they represent written language in paper or electronic form that must be understood with knowledge and reasoning skills.

Step 2: Identify the Central Concept in the Selected Text

Examples of the representations of central concepts are symbiosis (science) or slavery (social studies). A concept is not a single person (such as Abraham Lincoln), an individual event (such as the Battle of Antietam), or a specific insect (such as a dragonfly). A concept embraces a range of particular objects or people. For example, slavery is a concept because it encompasses many personal, economic, and political interactions. Reconciliation in literature may refer to connections among people, events, and actions that reflect rejoining what was lost. While the central concept depends upon many facts and connections, it is a major element of knowledge that is imperative for students if they are to progress in understanding future texts that connect to this conceptual subject.

Step 3: Provide Motivation Support

Explicit designs for motivation support may include a range of teacher actions. For young adolescents facing informational text in any subject matter, success with the initial text is a prerequisite to their commitment to learning and reading deeply. Teachers can ensure such success by providing difficulty levels matched to students' competencies, complemented by discussion of crucial literal meanings.

A range of motivation supports may all be beneficial to students, including the teachers' provision of relevance for building students' intrinsic motivation. When students find the text relevant by seeing that it connects to their interests and experiences, they become more intrinsically motivated to read. Affording choices is a key motivator. Teachers can give small but distinct choices throughout a lesson, such as focusing on one diagram, reading for a particular character's perspective, or emphasizing one of several alternative battles in a war. Frequent choices within lessons can motivate students to invest in deeper comprehension.

A widely used motivation support is arranging collaborations, which increases students' social satisfaction in learning. Collaboration fosters students' expression of their ideas and sharing of comprehension or confusion. In either case, students find that they are connected to others, which sustains their effort in making meaning from print. A high priority for teachers should be to emphasize the importance of text in learning as it relates to other forms of information, such as videos, discussion, or social activities. Too often, students do not perceive that texts are useful for them and instead emphasize other sources. While the other sources may be valuable, they cannot convey the explanations and conceptual systems on which subject matter understanding depends. Consequently, students who believe in the importance of the text itself as a contributor to their achievement in a course are likely to grow in achievement. Other motivation supports, such as mastery goals for the classroom, have been shown to be valuable for fostering text interactions, and teachers may find a range of supports for motivation in the classroom through literature reviews and current handbooks published on this topic (Guthrie, Wigfield, & You, 2012.)

Teachers can undertake four simple actions to assure that motivation support is powerful enough to propel learning:

1. *Plan*—Teachers who design motivation support explicitly by assuring success, giving relevance, or affording choices need a plan. Teachers need to know what the choices will be, or what the relevance activity will consist of and how long it will take to complete. Thus, planning explicitly for the design of engagement activities has a big payoff.

2. *Announce the motivation support that may occur for a day or a section of a lesson*—The teacher can announce the support by simply saying, "I am giving you a choice now." He or she would then explain the choice and the students' responsibility. This raises students'

awareness of the value to them and the potential benefit for their reading that choice provides.

3. *Scaffold the motivation support*—Just as teachers adjust lessons to increase students' thinking skills during comprehension instruction, effective teachers adjust motivation support to enable students to successfully experience the motivation activity. For example, if a teacher gives too many choices (say, the choice of six different books for reading about the U.S. Civil War), students may be overwhelmed and unable to select effectively. On the other hand, if teachers give no choice, students will be deprived of input into their learning. Too many or too few choices carry consequences that decrease motivation. The "just right" number of options in a choice situation depends on the students, the nature of the materials, and the teachers' ability to help students make effective choices. Scaffolding choice is as crucial to learning as scaffolding the understanding of literal meanings or drawing appropriate conclusions.

4. *Debrief for one or two minutes at the end of a unit or class period*— Teachers can ask students about which choice they made, which relevance activity they experienced, or which other motivation support occurred and how it impacted their reading activity. Debriefing raises students' awareness and enables them to connect the motivation support to the cognitive effort needed for comprehending complex texts.

Supporting motivation is more fully discussed in a video by the coauthor of this chapter, Jennifer McPeake, in the professional development section of the website www.corilearning.com.

Step 4: Identify One Reading Strategy

On any given day or in any specific unit, teachers should provide instruction in one strategy that will be likely to pay off for this text. Many powerful strategies are available. Examples include previewing the text, drawing inferences between sentences, forming questions during reading, and self-explaining. Strategy instruction has been presented in many teacher education and professional development books that are widely available.

Step 5: Give Students CCSS-Based Questions or Tasks

Referring to one of the Standards or writing a question that reflects the Standard provides closure to the lesson. For example, teachers may ask students to summarize a key text that had been read during the day in ways that include key points and supporting details (see CCR Anchor Standard for Reading 2, NGA Center & CCSSO, 2010, p. 10). A CCSS-based task or question may be presented at the outset of the lesson or may be presented as a culminating activity. Whether it is part of the initial orientation or the closing of the lesson, it should be based on the text that was selected, using the central concept of the text. Motivated students who use the strategy should be more likely to be successful in the CCSS task than other students.

Interdisciplinary Units

Although the general lesson plan is valuable, a broader design for literacy engagement is to build interdisciplinary units. This unit described in the following sections illustrates how the motivation principles can be used in classrooms. We believe teachers can most effectively increase literacy engagement through these units. Thus, we next describe several features of units that enable teachers to boost engagement in ways that will increase performance of the CCSS. Following these unit features, we provide an example of one interdisciplinary unit for seventh-grade students.

The main aim of interdisciplinary units is to foster a high volume of deep reading. The units are designed to be interesting and relevant forms of reading complex text. However, it is not the interest itself that increases informational text comprehension but rather the extended reading activity that involves reasoning and thinking that moves students forward into higher proficiencies.

Interdisciplinary units are organized around a compelling theme. The theme may be approximately four to six weeks in length for upper elementary and middle school students and may encompass the big ideas in an existing curriculum. For example, in science, themes of biodiversity or adaptation may be used. In social studies, colonial life or the U.S. Civil War may be themes that offer opportunities for multiple types of reading activities.

Text Selection

Texts in a theme should include a wide range of print and digital materials. These may be pulled from a variety of genres, including original writings, textbooks, reports, diaries, charts and tables, and academically specific forms of reading. For example, reading in science may include identifying means and reviewing diagrams and flowcharts, whereas reading in history may require students to examine a letter from one of the U.S. founding fathers in its historical context.

Texts should be differentiated for students at the diverse levels that may be found from grades 3 to 12 because a major barrier to reading informational text for young adolescents is that they see it as too difficult. When students perceive texts as impossible to understand, their avoidance may be immediate. They may pay little attention, invest minimum effort, and neglect reading. Providing student–text matches that are appropriate at the outset of learning reduces this avoidance. Challenge can be accelerated after students' initial proficiency with text is established.

Motivation Support

This section describes the main types of motivation support for an interdisciplinary unit. Relevance of the text will determine how fully students pursue deep text meanings. If students can relate personally to the content, connect information to their background knowledge, and bring meanings to new materials through inferencing, they find them relevant. This relevance boosts their efforts to go beyond memorizing and to connect the text to what they already know. Relevance can be increased especially through hands-on activities, but also through videos and multimedia events. (A video describing how to bring relevance into teaching is provided on the website www.corilearning.com.)

Providing choice as a form of motivation support (as discussed earlier in this chapter) is well known to educators, and interdisciplinary units are ideal contexts in which to provide options for students that will enable them to select texts, identify tasks of reading that will be valuable or interesting to them, and specialize in subcontents of a domain. Through these selections, students increase their interest and thus their commitment to comprehending informational texts. For example, teachers may enable students to choose between specializing in two key battles of the U.S. Civil War. While students may read about both battles, they may specialize in one of them, learning more deeply about the leadership, economics, and politics of that battle, which gives them an expertise that is gratifying.

When students believe reading is important, they invest effort in understanding. Conversely, when students believe that reading is not useful, their effort wanes and their commitments are hard to restore. Although discussion, supplementary videos, and writing activities may enhance understanding, teachers can point to the text as their single most powerful ally in gaining content knowledge.

Collaboration among students energizes the classroom. Collaborations can empower students to comprehend more deeply and enjoy the process of unlocking complex texts. Many forms of student groupings allow for collaboration, including partnerships, small-team projects, larger debates within the classroom, or enactments of historical periods in a whole-class activity. As with other motivation supports, a collaborative activity does not directly benefit comprehension, but it is useful when it generates high amounts of extended, engaged reading. Activities should be organized to assure that students must read extensively to explain to their team or their partner the meanings of one or several texts. The social expectation to make sense of multiple texts gives students a reason to pursue their reading at a new level of intensity.

Scaffolding Motivation

Scaffolding is essential to effective motivation support. For instance, a teacher may scaffold choice by giving high support initially. With a class unfamiliar with making choices during learning, teachers may begin with one minor choice of selecting one of two key reading examples, or a teacher may give a choice in literature of which character to focus on in a story. While they read about both characters, students may specialize in one of them and be prepared to explain that character's qualities to the team or the class. When a teacher begins with a small choice, the scope of students' choices can be expanded during the course of a 4- to 6-week unit. Students who are familiar with making and being responsible for choices may be given a increasingly wide range of texts, tasks to perform, student groups in which to participate, and even choices of how to display their learning through writing and illustrating.

A culminating product should be the aim of an interdisciplinary unit. Each aspect of the unit should point toward a project or activity that enables students to integrate their reading, writing, knowledge, and multimedia resources. The product could be a PowerPoint slide deck, an essay, or an artistic effect that is aimed at an authentic audience. The audience may be within class or within school, or may also reach out to the local community. The product that integrates multiple forms of literacy, while also enabling students' artistic effects to display their expertise in the subject matter domain and their comprehension of a diversity of complex texts, will be a memorable outcome of the unit.

Grading

Grading during an interdisciplinary unit may seem daunting to teachers. However, it is relatively easy to identify several student projects that may be graded, including writings, summaries, maps, debates, or read-alouds. If students are drawing concept maps or building timelines of text, these may be graded for thoroughness, accuracy, and clarity. The culminating product may be graded using a rubric that teachers design and may include characteristics suggested by students. In this way, grading is capturing a variety of key elements in an interdisciplinary unit, embracing the content, reading skills, and motivational aspects of engagement, including interest and commitment to thorough work.

At least four to eight CCSS that are related to a particular interdisciplinary unit should be identified and stated. These Standards may be represented as goals and objectives for subsections of the unit. Each literacy activity of the week may contain a CCSS goal that accompanies other goals of content learning and reading development. At the conclusion of the interdisciplinary unit, when culminating projects are presented by students or reviewed by teachers, the extent that students participated in activities pertinent to the CCSS can be recognized.

Example of an Interdisciplinary Unit

This example was taken from a seventh-grade interdisciplinary unit in social studies (Guthrie, McRae, & Klauda, 2007) based on Concept-Oriented Reading Instruction (CORI; see www.corilearning.com for more information on this instructional method). It covers the curriculum goal of teaching about the U.S. Civil War. As shown in Figure 12.1, this unit and corresponding activities spanned four weeks in the spring of the seventh-grade year. In the "content" row, the first two weeks were devoted to causes of the Civil War while the last two weeks referred to outcomes of the Civil War for both the North and the South. Key concepts are shown in the next row of the unit framework. These central ideas included economics, culture, slavery, politics, leadership beliefs, and military actions; all of these concepts were integrated. In the integration, students used all of the concepts first to describe the causes of the Civil War and second to characterize the outcomes of the Civil War. As the next row in the unit framework depicts, comprehension instruction was provided across the four weeks including inferencing, summarizing, concept mapping, and the use of multiple strategies, in that order.

Motivation was supported throughout the unit, but individual motivation encouragements were emphasized each week. At the outset of the unit, teachers focused on the relevance of the texts for students, which consisted of discussing Civil War locations within 50 miles of the classroom. In one case, a barn used in the Underground Railroad was

Figure 12.1. Sample Interdisciplinary Unit in Social Studies

	Week 1	Week 2	Week 3	Week 4
Content	Causes of the Civil War: A Nation Divided	Causes of the Civil War: Unity vs. States' Rights	Military Conduct and Events of War	Impact of War
Concepts	Economics, Culture, Slavery, Politics	Leadership, Beliefs	Military	(All)
Comprehension Instruction	Inferencing	Summarizing	Concept Mapping	Multiple Strategies
Motivation	Relevance	Choice	Reading Importance	Collaboration
Whole-Class Text	*The Causes of the Civil War*	*The Causes of the Civil War*	*Key Battles of the Civil War*	*The Aftermath of the Civil War*
Guided Reading: On-Grade Learners	*A Nation Divided* *The Causes of the Civil War*	*The Home Front in the North* *The Home Front in the South*	*The Civil War in the East* *Key Battles of the Civil War*	*The Aftermath of the Civil War*
Guided Reading: Struggling Readers	*Secession*	*Key People of the Civil War*	*Battles of the Civil War*	*Reconstruction* *The Carpetbaggers*
Guided Reading: Advanced Readers	*CORI Information Text Enrichment*	*CORI Information Text Enrichment*	*CORI Information Text Enrichment*	*CORI Information Text Enrichment*
Writing	Inferences: Integrating Knowledge and Ideas	Summaries, Persuasive Essay	Concept Mapping: Key Ideas and Concepts	Culminating Project: Inferences, Summary, Concept Map

found in the school district. Knowing about this building made reading about the Underground Railroad and Harriet Tubman's biography meaningful. In addition, students viewed brief video clips of the enactments of Civil War events, such as speeches and debates.

Choices were the centerpiece of motivation for week 2. Teachers provided choices of which Civil War battle in which to specialize, which biography of a Civil War leader to read for an independent reading activity, which partners to work with, and whether to display knowledge through summaries or graphic illustrations of Civil War events.

In week 3, students' values for texts were emphasized. Teachers pointed to the usefulness of texts for developing explanations of why the North won a given battle and why the South won a different battle. Although students viewed videos and discussed texts, teachers reminded them about the centrality of text in forming their knowledge, as well as the benefits of peer interactions and writing to enhance that knowledge.

Collaborative activity was featured in the culminating project. In this unit, students made large posters of an aspect of the Civil War, explaining why the North or South had dominated a particular battle or a piece of Civil War–related legislation. Thus, the motivation supports shifted across the unit, although they were all present throughout.

The texts to be used are listed in the unit framework. The whole-class text was the same for weeks 1 and 2, and a different text was used in weeks 3 and 4. These were trade books with informative illustrations. Generally, teachers utilized the whole-class text for modeling and establishing the key concepts. Three additional texts were provided in classrooms for guided reading, including texts for on-grade learners, struggling readers, and advanced readers. In each week, focused writing activities were presented in the unit framework and evolved from text-specific to complex essays.

Research Base Supporting Engagement as a Missing Link

The research base abundantly supports our suggestion that engagement in reading is a missing link for teachers who are aiming to improve students' performance of the CCSS. Students with sustained motivation and engagement increase in reading achievement more rapidly than students with lower engagement (Guthrie, Wigfield, & You, 2012). Beyond this link, interdisciplinary units have been shown not only to foster engagement and motivation, but also to increase achievement directly (Guthrie, Klauda, & Ho, 2013). Abundant evidence undergirds the position that interdisciplinary units are the strongest framework for building long-term engagement that accelerates reading achievement.

The contribution of engagement to achievement seems obvious. Students who read longer and more deeply with more determination will achieve higher than their peers. But this may often be lost in the scramble to teach individual skills. Too often, students gain a reading competency but lack the opportunity to put the new skill into practice over an extended time so that it becomes part of their reading repertoire. Time, effort, and persistence in reading are essential to fusing skills into a student's daily reading. Evidence points not only to the positive value of dedication but also to the barriers that avoidance presents for students. Avoidance of reading is the biggest obstacle to achievement. If students decide not to read and to minimize effort, their opportunities to gain skill and knowledge from reading and language arts activities decrease into nonexistence.

Because many studies of engagement and achievement are correlational, it is possible that engagement may not causally increase achievement. However, many experiments have been done. When students are enabled to increase their engagement through excellent instruction, they outperform other students who did not receive this instruction. For example, if teachers provide choices during learning, students' engagement is increased and comprehension of the text in an instructional unit is increased compared with students in control groups. This was documented in a research literature of K–2 students sponsored by the Institute of Education Sciences (Shanahan et al., 2010).

If engagement is a link to achievement in reading complex texts, how can we increase engagement consistently? A broad array of research shows that interdisciplinary units are powerful tools for teachers. At the elementary school level in grades 3 to 5, interdisciplinary units in CORI have been shown to increase engagement, illustrated by large amounts of reading; motivation in the forms of interest, self-efficacy, and social motivation; and motivation and achievement in comprehension. This evidence is derived from 11 studies over 10 years (Guthrie et al., 2007) in which one group of students was provided with interdisciplinary units in CORI while other students were not provided this instruction but attended traditional reading and language arts classes in school. The students receiving CORI scored higher in tested reading achievement than those receiving traditional instruction, and they also outperformed control students in intrinsic motivation for reading. The units were provided over six weeks of teaching toward science goals approved by the school district using trade books, textbooks, and Internet materials for all students including advanced, on-grade-level, and struggling readers.

More broadly, a review of literature sponsored by the Institute of Education Sciences identified five components of effective comprehension instruction for K–2 students (Shanahan et al., 2010). One of these elements was motivation and engagement in reading. The review identified a range of studies supporting the value of teachers encouraging self-efficacy, fostering relevance for interest in reading, and building social motivations through collaborative activities. (This review and a video explaining these principles are available as links on www.corilearning.com.)

At the middle school level, interdisciplinary units and connections of reading and language arts to the content areas of history and science have also been found to increase engagement. A review of research sponsored by the Institute of Education Sciences on adolescent reading comprehension (Kamil et al., 2008) underscored motivation and engagement as critical ingredients in effective reading programs. Their review showed that the principles of interdisciplinary units—including relevance, choice, collaboration, and thematic teaching—are likely to have a strong positive effect in the classroom. For seventh-grade students who received CORI as an interdisciplinary unit in science during reading/ language arts, the instructed group increased in achievement directly and also increased in engagement and motivation, which likewise boosted achievement (Guthrie et al., 2013). Interdisciplinary units are fascinating investigations of intriguing topics, which motivate students to want to read widely and deeply.

TRY THIS!

- Choice—Give students a choice every day for a week in each reading lesson:

    Day 1: Allow students to choose which book to read for a 20-minute independent reading activity.

    Day 2: Give students a choice of which character or concept to become an expert on.

    Day 3: Let students choose which partner to work with for a 15-minute read-and-summarize activity.

    Day 4: Give students a choice of questions to answer about reading after you put one teacher question and three student questions on the board or overhead.

    Day 5: Give students a choice about how to show understanding of a text, either by drawing, summarizing, or mapping.

• Relevance—Have students write three to five sentences on how a text they are reading for class connects to their experience. Is a character very similar or very different from someone they are familiar with? Is a place discussed in a social studies lesson similar or different from a place they have visited? Do they agree with the attitudes or beliefs of a person they read about in a novel or social studies unit?

DISCUSSION QUESTIONS

1. In their opening paragraph, Guthrie and McPeake emphasize the importance of literacy engagement. Define literacy engagement and its significant relationship to CCSS.

2. Using the five ingredients in the centerpiece of classroom engagement as described by Guthrie and McPeake, sketch a general lesson plan.

3. What is CORI, and what is its role in literacy engagement?

REFERENCES

Guthrie, J.T., Klauda, S.L., & Ho, A.N. (2013). Modeling the relationships among reading instruction, motivation, engagement, and achievement for adolescents. *Reading Research Quarterly, 48*(1), 6–29. doi:10.1002/rrq.035

Guthrie, J.T., McRae, A.C., & Klauda, S.L. (2007). Contributions of Concept-Oriented Reading Instruction to knowledge about interventions for motivations in reading. *Educational Psychologist, 42*(4), 237–250.

Guthrie, J.T., Wigfield, A., & Klauda, S.L. (2012). *Adolescents' engagement in academic literacy* (Rep. No. 7). College Park: University of Maryland. Retrieved from www.corilearning.com/research-publications/2012_adolescents_engagement_ebook.pdf

Guthrie, J.T., Wigfield, A., & You, W. (2012). Instructional contexts for engagement and achievement in reading. In S.L. Christensen, A.L. Reschly, & C. Wylie (Eds.), *Handbook of research on student engagement* (pp. 601–634). New York: Springer Science. doi:10.1007/978-1-4614-2018-7_29

Kamil, M.L., Borman, G.D., Dole, J., Kral, C.C., Salinger, T., & Torgeson, J. (2008). *Improving adolescent literacy: Effective classroom and intervention practices* (NCEE 2008-4027). Washington, DC: National Center for Education Evaluation and Regional Assistance, Institute of Education Sciences, U.S. Department of Education. Retrieved from ies.ed.gov/ncee/wwc/pdf/practice_guides/adlit_pg_082608.pdf

National Governors Association Center for Best Practices & Council of Chief State School Officers. (2010). *Common Core State Standards for English language arts and literacy in history/social studies, science, and technical subjects*. Washington, DC: Authors. Retrieved from www.core standards.org/assets/CCSSI_ELA%20 Standards.pdf

Shanahan, T., Callison, K., Carriere, C., Duke, N.K., Pearson, P.D., Schatschneider, C., et al. (2010). *Improving reading comprehension in kindergarten through 3rd grade: A practice guide* (NCEE 2010-4038). Washington, DC: National Center for Education Evaluation and Regional Assistance, Institute of Education Sciences, U.S. Department of Education. Retrieved from ies.ed.gov/ncee/wwc/PracticeGuide .aspx?sid=14

CHAPTER 13

Picture Storybooks Go Digital: Pros and Cons

Daisy Smeets & Adriana Bus

An increasing number of picture storybooks for young children have become available electronically, and there has been an explosion in children's storybook apps, especially since tablet computers such as iPads have become popular. Today's e-books have evolved significantly from platforms that once only displayed simple digitized versions of print books to tools that can now support highly interactive, multimedia experiences. At a minimum, multimedia additions to electronic picture storybooks include at least an oral reading of the story text. In addition, they may involve symbolic elements typically not used with print books: live-action video, digital graphics, animations, music, sound effects, and interactivity of text (e.g., highlighting of text while it is narrated). Some educators are of the opinion that the multimedia additions are unnecessary and may even work counterproductively. Interaction with adults is still considered to be the optimal way to familiarize children with stories and the varied and rich vocabulary in picture storybooks. On the other hand, additional features may provide new opportunities for text comprehension.

In the age of Common Core State Standards (National Governors Association Center for Best Practices & Council of Chief State School Officers, 2010), teachers may wonder whether e-books are appropriate tools for familiarizing 4- to 6-year-olds with children's literature and contributing to a positive relationship with reading that lasts a lifetime: When young children have learned to enjoy books, they will continue to read, whereby technical reading and oral language skills keep improving, resulting in sustained motivation to read (Mol & Bus, 2011). The gold standard of book reading to 4- to 6-year-olds is interactive reading that combines an oral rendition of text with clarification about the story text through the actions of pointing at pictures and highlighting details mentioned in the text (Whitehurst & Lonigan, 2001). In addition to building comprehension skills, shared book reading may also promote print knowledge, especially when parents actively focus children's

Quality Reading Instruction in the Age of Common Core Standards, edited by Susan B. Neuman and Linda B. Gambrell. © 2013 by the International Reading Association.

attention on print features (e.g., Justice & Ezell, 2000). Therefore, teachers of preschoolers and kindergarten children may want to explore whether additional multimedia features can bolster similar or additional beneficial effects of e-book reading. As the number of living storybooks available on the Internet and through apps and other digital media increases, it becomes more and more imperative to examine effects of electronic books that allow young children to hear a story and explore a range of activities while the tale moves along.

Shared Book Reading

One of the first studies of the Leiden group appeared to give interactive, multimedia books on the computer the green light (de Jong & Bus, 2004). The study compared the gold standard of *shared* print book reading with *independent* reading of interactive books on the computer. In the shared reading condition, the adult stimulated children to make inferences (e.g., "Do you see why the bride cannot sit on the luggage carrier?") or to make a connection between the text and picture (e.g., paraphrasing the text the experimenter pointed to the picture, saying, "See, Little Tiger is carried first by Little Bear, and then by the strong wolf and the strong goat"). In the independent e-book condition, children "read" a story from the same book series on their own. The digitized Janosch books (1998a, 1998b) included, apart from an oral rendition of the tale, click-accessible hotspots that revealed a sound or animation, mostly inconsistent with the story text (e.g., a tea towel turns into a dove). With simple filmic means, the illustrations in the book were animated to dramatize events highlighted in the story text (e.g., the doctor bends toward the X-ray saying: "Ah, a faulty stripe."). Other depictions in the illustration that were not highlighted in the text were not animated.

Children's retellings of the story text were of the same quality whether children shared the book with an adult who actively involved the children by asking questions (the gold standard of reading) or "read" the animated, interactive computer version on their own. There was no evidence that the added eye and ear candy (the hotspots revealing effects that were surprising but mostly not helpful for understanding the story text) distracted children to the detriment of story comprehension. Apparently, for parents or teachers looking for viable options for children to listen to stories, e-books can meet the need without placing a heavy burden on the adult. Researchers from the Joan Ganz Cooney Center (Chiong, Ree, Takeuchi, & Erickson, 2012) even conclude that attempts by adults to share interactive e-books with their child may distort the e-book reading experience. Interactive e-books are mostly designed in a way that does not allow adults to access and control settings to customize a shared reading.

The researchers asked 32 pairs of parents and their 3- to 6-year-old children to share both a print book and an e-book. Half of the pairs read a *basic* e-book (where pictures appear on the computer but no multimedia features are included), and the other half read an *enhanced* e-book (which included highly interactive, multimedia experiences). The results buttressed the argument that it is preferable to choose print or basic e-books when you read to children and want to prioritize literacy-building experiences over ones intended "just for fun." The enhanced e-book was much less effective than a print and basic e-book in supporting the benefits of shared reading, probably because the e-book enhancements in the target book were not designed in a way that allows parents to customize interactive experiences. Apps included fun animations that may easily provoke *non-content related actions* (e.g., behavior- or device-focused talk, pushing hands away). In sum, the extra features of enhanced e-books appeared to distract adults and children alike from the story, negatively affecting the nature of conversation and the amount of detail children recall.

Bells and Whistles in Enhanced E-Books

Unlike traditional printed picture storybooks, electronic storybooks show less homogeneity in design features due to a variety of bells and whistles (de Jong & Bus, 2003; Korat & Shamir, 2004; Roskos, Brueck, & Widman, 2009). In some books, pictures are similar to those in the printed version of the book, but other books may include animated (details of) pictures. Apart from an oral rendition of text, electronic picture storybooks may include sound effects and background music. Furthermore, some electronic stories include games or other interactive features such as hotspots, often revealing some kind of audio or visual effect when clicked on. How do these e-book features affect children's language and literacy development?

Animated Illustrations

The Leiden group found beneficial effects of e-books that presented animated illustrations instead of static ones in addition to an oral rendition of text (e.g., Smeets & Bus, 2012b; Verhallen & Bus, 2010; Verhallen, Bus, & de Jong, 2006). In these studies, first- and second-language learners repeatedly heard either a storybook with animated illustrations that dramatize the story, as in the Janosch series (e.g., 1998a, 1998b), or an electronic version of a similar story with merely static pictures. Text comprehension—especially vocabulary—improved when children "read" the animated e-book. We assume that the animated parts of pictures make it easier for children to match relevant details in illustrations with oral text, thus facilitating word and text comprehension. Animated details attract more visual attention than other parts, which may promote contiguity between oral text and illustration; that is, corresponding text is pronounced simultaneously with animated details in the illustration. For example, the text "Winnie is furious" in the story *Winnie the Witch* (Thomas & Gorky, 1996) is accompanied by an illustration showing an angry-looking witch making wild movements, which may help to coordinate the text with Winnie's behavior. Likewise, camera effects, such as zoom, may help to match relevant details in illustrations with oral text, thereby supporting children's text comprehension.

Normally, children fixate more than 90% of their time on the illustrations in picture storybooks while they listen to an oral reading of text (e.g., Evans & Saint-Aubin, 2005) and, what probably is most important, they fixate more often and longer on details in illustrations that are highlighted in the story text than on elements that are not (Verhallen & Bus, 2011). That is, while looking at illustrations in books, children search for elements that are highlighted in the story text. For example, while listening to a story about a mouse who wants to pick strawberries and therefore brought his wheelbarrow with him, we see their eyes successively fixate on the mouse, the strawberries, and the wheelbarrow. Lavishly illustrated storybooks for young children may complicate children's finding their way through the illustration and may instead coordinate *what* children look at in illustrations with the oral text. Take, for instance, the storybook *Rokko the Crocodile* (de Wijs, 2001). One of the illustrations shows Rokko and his parents watching a dozen crocodile eggs, waiting for Rokko's siblings to appear. The illustration shows, in addition to intact eggs, some eggs that are broken. Sometimes a baby crocodile's snout is visible, which demonstrates how young crocodiles appear from an egg. However, other broken eggs show a tail, which could also mean that a crocodile is crawling inside the egg. By and large, there is much room for errors in interpreting the story language (e.g., what is meant by *siblings* and what does *appearing* mean?).

Simultaneous processing of story text and illustrations, as is facilitated by animated e-books (Schnotz & Rasch, 2005), may explain why animated versions of picture storybooks were preferable to versions with only static pictures. Holding verbal and visual information in working memory at the same time may help children build stronger connections between visual and verbal information. When a word is processed through both the verbal and visual channels, this stimulates dual coding of information (Paivio, 1986), which facilitates storing and retaining word meanings. It seems evident that the quality of animations is vital. Film-like presentations of stories may not have the same effects when they include "wild" animations that do not match the story text. The "crowdedness" of animated presentations, requiring children to process simultaneously through multiple modalities that do not match, may even cause overload of the brain, which may reduce learning about the story language. We expect, therefore, negative results for cartoon-like e-books that include numerous animations that do not match the story language.

Sound Effects and Music

Likewise, additional audio features in electronic books are perceptually salient and thus likely to elicit and sustain children's attention (e.g., Barr, Zack, Garcia, & Muentener, 2008). Moreover, background music may lend support to story comprehension, for instance by stressing the characters' moods (e.g., sadness or happiness). Adding the sound of *knocking* on a door, birds *whistling*, or a motor *humming* may help clarify these words' meanings. When sounds are coded simultaneously with the oral text, dual coding may facilitate storage and retrieval of unknown words (Paivio, 1986).

A recent study (Smeets, van Dijken, & Bus, 2012) shows that background music and sounds are not beneficial for all children, however. When children are diagnosed with severe language impairments (SLI), aural multimedia additions distort the beneficial effects of video stories. Instead of supporting text comprehension by emphasizing suspense, stressing moods (such as happiness or sadness), and clarifying the meanings of words, the addition of music and sounds seems to complicate the perception of speech by these children. Differential effects of video and music as this study revealed for SLI children have not been examined in normal populations, but it may be worth the effort to find out which elements of video storybooks make these e-books more or less effective in other groups (for instance in easily distractible groups).

The finding that music and sounds were detrimental for word learning in children with SLI has far-reaching implications for e-book development. In many storybook apps, the volume of the soundtrack is loud and not adjustable, which may be a problem for children with language delays in particular. In Disney's *Cars 2*, the narration can barely be heard with the exciting background music and sound effects of race cars driving by. The storybook app *Magic Gold Fish* by Yasmin Studios includes hotspots with sound effects (e.g., a fish splashing in the water) that are very loud in comparison with the narration. Interestingly, the app *Pansjo Tummy* developed by ThenQ includes an option to turn off background music and narration separately; such a feature makes an e-book more adaptive to support learning in different target groups.

Interactivity in Enhanced E-Books

Games—Too Many Choices?

Largely due to the increased popularity of touch screen devices, a considerable quantity of e-books includes interactive features such as puzzles, coloring, or memory games, but there is concern for the educational quality of these stories (e.g., de Jong & Bus, 2003; Korat & Shamir, 2004; Roskos et al., 2009; Zucker, Moody, & McKenna, 2009). These activities might be entertaining and increase children's motivation (e.g., Ricci & Beal, 2002), but they may also promote a "game-playing mode" rather than stimulate children to focus on the story (de Jong & Bus, 2002; Labbo & Kuhn, 2000).

A study targeting one of the first digitized picture storybooks that appeared on the Dutch market, *P.B. Bear's Birthday Party* (Davis, 1996), showed that too many choices of interactive options is risky given that most young children bring a game-playing mentality to the computer (personal communication with Linda Labbo, April 19, 2004). Each screen of *P.B. Bear's Birthday Party* offered a choice of hotspots to click on resulting in one or more of the following:

- Speech feedback for the complete text on the screen or speech feedback for single-text phrases or individual words
- A film-like presentation of the events (e.g., P.B. Bear starts unwrapping the package as described by the text)
- Animations (clicking on rebus-like icons that replace the nouns in the printed text, the written word appears simultaneously with short, 4.5-second animations and their pronunciation)

As none of the actions happened automatically, the program opened up the possibility to revert to game playing without paying attention to the story text. The result, as concluded by de Jong and Bus (2002), was that the iconic modes of this book (e.g., animated illustrations, animations, games) attracted the 4- and 5-year-old participants' attention at the expense of listening to the oral story text. After six 15-minute sessions, only a minority of the children in this study had listened to the entire story text more than once, even though they had sufficient opportunity to read the story six times. Actually, children explored *P.B. Bear's Birthday Party* in bits and pieces, activating animations, accessing text fragments, and ignoring connected text. As a result, the children in the experimental condition did not know the story content better than those in a control condition, who played some other computer game and did not hear the story about P.B. Bear. A game-playing disposition may dominate with such books unless teachers carefully establish what students are expected to do with their time with e-books.

Hotspots

In general it is assumed that interactivity is especially effective due to children's active involvement in extracting meanings (Sénéchal, 1997; Sénéchal et al., 1995). Television shows for young children that promote active involvement have been demonstrated to support learning more than programs without this feature (e.g., Crawley, Anderson, Wilder, Williams, & Santomero, 1999). Nickelodeon's Dora the Explorer and Blue's Clues e-books include, therefore, a "tutor" who makes eye contact with children, asks them questions, pauses for the child to respond, and reacts to the child's answer. Likewise, the first generation of enhanced e-books included hotspots that elaborated on story events or on words in the text. For instance, the story *'I'll Make You Well Again,' Said the Bear* (Janosch, 1998b) contained a scene where Tiger is given an injection prior to an operation. A click on the needle triggers a visualization of how the fluid spreads out in the body. Exploring more recent e-books, we came across many more examples of hotspots that support comprehension of text and story events. In the Dr. Seuss series developed by Oceanhouse Media and Dr. Seuss Enterprises (e.g., *A Cat in the Hat*), objects are defined when clicked on, similar to how parents or teachers may explain the meanings of difficult words (e.g., Biemiller & Boote, 2006; Dickinson & Smith, 1994; Elley, 1989).

Korat and colleagues have reported that e-books with a built-in option to receive word definitions on demand promote word learning (e.g., Shamir & Korat, 2009) in both typically developing children (Shamir, Korat, & Shlafer, 2011) and children at risk for language delays (Shamir et al., 2011). The studies reveal significant pre- to posttest gains in word learning but do not offer concrete evidence for the effects of interactive word-meaning explanations beyond exposure to text alone. Therefore, in a recent study (Smeets & Bus, 2012a), we tested the effectiveness of hotspots that trigger a definition of a difficult word when clicked in comparison with a read-only control condition. For instance, in *Bear Is in Love With Butterfly* (van Haeringen, 2004), a definition of the word *shy* was audio recorded and linked to a hotspot in the illustration. When the mouse touches Bear's red head, a green circle appears around Bear's head, which means that the child has found a hotspot. After clicking on the hotspot, the voiceover explains Bear's mindset: "Bear is shy, his cheeks have turned red."

These hotspots enhanced growth in vocabulary beyond encounters with words in text (e.g., Biemiller & Boote, 2006; Blewitt et al., 2009). Hotspots were especially beneficial when words were somewhat familiar and children succeeded at the pretest to select a picture that reflects the target word. That is, when words were receptively familiar prior to the intervention, hotspots improved expressive word knowledge (i.e., saying the word and using it in a sentence). We did not find evidence for (expressive) word learning when the words were completely unknown at pretest.

Questions

Children are more actively involved when they are prompted to answer questions. Segers and Verhoeven (2002; 2003), for instance, let children work independently with e-books that included vocabulary games. Children could be asked to place a cup of coffee on the kitchen table, to answer a question (such as, Can a carrot be bought in a bakery?), or to point out or color a certain object in the illustration.

Multiple-choice questions were presented in the e-books focused on in our study (Smeets & Bus, 2012a). For instance, when Bear in the story *Bear Is in Love With Butterfly* (van Haeringen, 2004) is fanning the fire, the story is interrupted for a question by the computer assistant: "Bear is fanning the fire. In which picture can you see that?" To answer the question, children can click on one of three pictures that appear on screen (the correct image among two distracters). The assistant gives feedback regarding the correctness of the response and provides clues in the cases of incorrect responses. We compared a questioning approach with hotspots that provide definitions after clicking on the hotspot. Our findings provide evidence for the assumption that effects are superior for multiple-choice questions that encourage children to make—rather than take—meaning (Moreno & Valdez, 2005). Even when words were completely unfamiliar prior to listening to the story, questions promoted growth in word knowledge.

Highlighting Print

Many enhanced e-books are furnished with tools of digital guidance that may focus children's attention on print. When printed text is available, it might change while it is read by either turning blue (e.g., *P.B. Bear's Birthday Party* [Davis, 1996]), highlighting, increasing in size, or underlining. In some multimedia e-books, the iconic modes of words are visible in combination with the written word. In *P.B. Bear's Birthday Party*, for instance, a small-sized picture replaces the printed form of objects (e.g., bed, orange juice, and marmalade). The printed word appears after a click on the small-sized picture, simultaneously with a short animation and pronunciation of the word. Most animations represent the meaning of the noun. For example, the drum starts to move and sounds like a drum. From an experiment with *P.B. Bear's Birthday Party,* it appeared that this multimedia feature may stimulate interaction with text, resulting in internalization of orthographic features of words (de Jong & Bus, 2002).

A feature that is present in many e-books is a "karaoke-bar" that emphasizes words in synchrony with the reader's voice. For instance, in Disney's storybook apps *Cars 2* and *Pooh's Birthday Surprise*, words are highlighted when they are read aloud. In an eye-tracking study, de Jong and Bus (2012) have demonstrated that highlighted text attracts children's visual attention tremendously and more so when children are more advanced in print knowledge. More importantly, such features have been demonstrated to improve print knowledge such as word recognition (de Jong & Bus, 2012; Korat, 2010) and letter-reading skills (Gong & Levy, 2009).

Besides a reading of the whole text, stories often include options to hear individual words read aloud, either entirely or in segments, which is designed to increase children's awareness of the relation between letters and sounds. For instance, touching words in a storybook app activates a read-aloud of that particular word. For beginning or struggling readers, whole-word reading software can lead to significant gains in written-word recognition, written-word naming, and phonological awareness (e.g., de Jong & Bus, 2002) and can even be equally effective as one-to-one tutoring with an adult in terms of phonological attainment. Especially considering that the most frequent cause of reading difficulties is weaknesses in phonological decoding skills, text-to-speech options can be valuable additions in the earliest years of reading education.

From Research to Practice

A nonstarter of a story cannot wow as an app, no matter how fabulous its bells and whistles are (Smith, 2011). However, the firm belief that children benefit most from sharing traditional print books with an adult has yet to be proved, as there is growing evidence to suggest that some of the promising features of optimally designed e-books may even outperform traditional shared print book reading.

So far, the search for interactive, multimedia features to enrich "good" storybooks has revealed the following:

- Animated pictures that include motion and zoomshots provide more clues from which children can extract meanings of difficult words than static pictures, especially when animations highlight elements from the oral text and nonverbal elements are coordinated with verbal elements in text.

- Effects of visual and audio features in enhanced e-books are not yet unraveled, with the exception of SLI children, in which the music and sounds (though not the animated pictures) may interfere with learning.

- Choices between iconic features and text reading have the disadvantage that children mostly prefer the animations and iconic elements at the expense of listening to the book's story text.

- Interactive features like hotspots and questions targeting complex words in the story text support growth in vocabulary more than listening to text alone.

- When children have become active participants in the interaction with the e-reader device by answering multiple-choice questions, interactivity is particularly beneficial (word learning improved by almost 20%).

While 4- and 5-year-old children might dislike print book reading sessions when they are frequently interrupted for questions, questions within interactive e-books may increase children's motivation (Kamil, Intrator, & Kim, 2000). Parents might not know which words to comment on or which events to discuss. E-books, on the other hand, are often designed in collaboration with educators, which results in age-appropriate and more challenging interactions.

However, without a model of book reading routines built up by prior encounters with books read to children by adults, interaction with electronic books might not be possible. In the early stages of book reading, children enjoy interaction with adults more than the book; they need adults to narrow the gap between their everyday world and the world of the book, and caregivers typically read the pictorial content of an illustrated story and its accompanying text more idiosyncratically to younger or less experienced children than to older or more experienced ones (Bus & de Jong, 2006). Also because it is fun and supportive of the emotional bonding with the child, it is important that parents and preschool teachers continue reading to younger age groups.

In sum, this chapter has described that e-books can provide benefits over printed books. However, a lot depends on the quality of e-books, as cutting-edge research in this area has revealed. It is parents' and teachers' responsibility to guide children in their activities with e-books and on the Internet, because children's own choices might not be the ones that should be preferred in a learning context. Young children show an almost universal preference for the exciting commercial programs that fail necessary qualities (Bus & Neuman, 2009).

Many teachers are not that comfortable with technology and fail the expectation and disposition that they can use technology for their own purposes. In the Netherlands, teachers rarely incorporate computer stories into their curriculum or encourage targeted viewing of television stories as an at-home activity. They qualify e-books rather as edutainment than serious learning materials. However, our findings concerning the effects of electronic stories on emergent literacy skills suggest that alternative ways of encountering stories may be a profitable addition to adult-led book reading at home and in kindergarten classrooms. Electronic stories are useful in allowing children to engage in independent reading before they are capable of reading conventional printed texts on their own.

TRY THIS!

- Illustrations in picture storybooks are works of art that must be interpreted (Schickedanz & Collins, 2012). Think of ways in which technology may help with this.

- Try out an interactive e-book for yourself. Experiment with the interactive features and think about how these features affect your reading of the text. (For a demo of interactive videobooks with questions posed by a built-in tutor, you can visit the bereslim website at web.bereslim.nl/bereslim/bereslimme-boeken/demo-bereslimme-boeken.html.)

DISCUSSION QUESTIONS

1. After reading this chapter, are you convinced that in the age of the CCSS, electronic storybooks can contribute to a positive experience with literacy development that lasts a lifetime?

2. The authors note that e-books are designed for children to "read" independently and that e-books' designs do not match the experiences of shared adult–child reading. Discuss the role of parents and teachers in young children's e-book reading activities.

REFERENCES

Barr, R., Zack, E., Garcia, A., & Muentener, P. (2008). Infants' attention and responsiveness to television increases with prior exposure and parental interaction. *Infancy, 13*(1), 30–56. doi:10.1080/15250000701779378

Biemiller, A., & Boote, C. (2006). An effective method for building meaning vocabulary in primary grades. *Journal of Educational Psychology, 98*(1), 44–62. doi:10.1037/0022-0663.98.1.44

Blewitt, P., Rump, K.M., Shealy, S.E., & Cook, S.A. (2009). Shared book reading: When and how questions affect young children's word learning. *Journal of Educational Psychology, 101*(2), 294–304. doi:10.1037/a0013844

Bus, A.G., & de Jong, M.T. (2006). Book sharing: A developmentally appropriate way to foster pre-academic growth. In S. Rosenkoetter & J. Knapp-Philo (Eds.), *Learning to read the world: Language and literacy in the first three years* (pp. 123–144). Washington, DC: ZERO TO THREE.

Bus, A.G., & Neuman, S.B. (2009). Afterword. In A.G. Bus & S.B. Neuman (Eds.), *Multimedia and literacy development: Improving achievement for young learners* (pp. 273–278). New York: Routledge.

Chiong, C., Ree, J., Takeuchi, L., & Erickson, I. (2012). *Print books vs. e-books: Comparing parent-child co-reading on print, basic and enhanced e-book platforms.* New York: The Joan Ganz Cooney Center at Sesame Workshop.

Crawley, A.M., Anderson, D.R., Wilder, A., Williams, M., & Santomero, A. (1999). Effects of repeated exposures to a single episode of the television program Blue's Clues on the viewing behaviors and comprehension of preschool children. *Journal of Educational Psychology, 91*(4), 630–637. doi:10.1037/0022-0663.91.4.630

de Jong, M.T., & Bus, A.G. (2002). Quality of book-reading matters for emergent readers: An experiment with the same book in a regular or electronic format. *Journal of Educational Psychology, 94*(1), 145–155. doi:10.1037/0022-0663.94.1.145

de Jong, M.T., & Bus, A.G. (2003). How well suited are electronic books to supporting literacy? *Journal of Early Childhood Literacy, 3*(2), 147–164. doi:10.1177/14687984030032002

de Jong, M.T., & Bus, A.G. (2004). The efficacy of electronic books in fostering kindergarten children's emergent story understanding. *Reading Research Quarterly, 39*(4), 378–393. doi: 10.1598/RRQ.39.4.2

de Jong, M.T., & Bus, A.G. (2012). *AVI gaat digitaal: oefenboekjes voor beginnende lezers op tablet* [Practice material for beginning readers on tablet]. Leiden, Netherlands: Leiden University/ Association of Reading.

Dickinson, D.K., & Smith, M.W. (1994). Long-term effects of preschool teachers' book readings on low-income children's vocabulary and story comprehension. *Reading Research Quarterly, 29*(2), 104–122. doi:10.2307/747807

Elley, W.B. (1989). Vocabulary acquisition from listening to stories. *Reading Research Quarterly, 24*(2), 174–186. doi:10.2307/747863

Evans, M.A., & Saint-Aubin, J. (2005). What children are looking at during shared storybook reading: Evidence from eye movement monitoring. *Psychological Science, 16*(11), 913–920. doi:10.1111/j.1467-9280.2005.01636.x

Gong, Z., & Levy, B.A. (2009). Four year old children's acquisition of print knowledge during electronic storybook reading. *Reading and Writing, 22*(8), 889–905. doi:10.1007/s11145-008-9130-1

Justice, L.M., & Ezell, H.K. (2000). Enhancing children's print and word awareness through home-based parent intervention. *American Journal of Speech-Language Pathology, 9*(3), 257–269.

Kamil, M.L., Intrator, S.M., & Kim, H.S. (2000). The effects of other technologies on literacy and literacy learning. In M.L. Kamil, P.B. Mosenthal, P.D. Pearson, & R. Barr (Eds.), *Handbook of reading research* (Vol. 3, pp. 771–778). Mahwah, NJ: Erlbaum.

Korat, O. (2010). Reading electronic books as a support for vocabulary, story comprehension and word reading in kindergarten and first grade. *Computers & Education, 55*(1), 24–31. doi:10.1016/j.compedu.2009.11.014

Korat, O., & Shamir, A. (2004). Do Hebrew electronic books differ from Dutch electronic books? A replication of a Dutch content analysis. *Journal of Computer Assisted Learning, 20*(4), 257–268. doi:10.1111/j.1365-2729.2004.00078.x

Labbo, L.D., & Kuhn, M.R. (2000). Weaving chains of affect and cognition: A young child's understanding of CD-ROM talking books. *Journal of Literacy Research, 32*(2), 187–210. doi:10.1080/10862960009548073

Mol, S.E., & Bus, A.G. (2011). To read or not to read: A meta-analysis of print exposure from infancy to early adulthood. *Psychological Bulletin, 137*(2), 267–296. doi:10.1037/a0021890

Moreno, R., & Valdez, A. (2005). Cognitive load and learning effects of having students organize pictures and words in multimedia environments: The role of student interactivity and feedback. *Educational Technology Research & Development, 53*(3), 35–45. doi:10.1007/BF02504796

National Governors Association Center for Best Practices & Council of Chief State School Officers. (2010). *Common Core State Standards for English language arts and literacy in history/social studies, science, and technical subjects.* Washington, DC: Authors. Available at www.corestandards.org/assets/CCSSI_ELA%20Standards.pdf

Paivio, A. (1986). *Mental representations: A dual coding approach.* New York: Oxford University Press.

Ricci, C.M., & Beal, C.R. (2002). The effect of interactive media on children's story memory. *Journal of Educational Psychology, 94*(1), 138–144. doi:10.1037/0022-0663.94.1.138

Roskos, K., Brueck, J., & Widman, S. (2009). Investigating analytic tools for e-book design in early literacy learning. *Journal of Interactive Online Learning, 8*(3), 218–240.

Schickedanz, J.A., & Collins, M.F. (2012). For young children, pictures in storybooks are rarely worth a thousand words. *The Reading Teacher, 65*(8), 539–549. doi:10.1002/TRTR.01080

Schnotz, W., & Rasch, T. (2005). Enabling, facilitating, and inhibiting effects of animations in multimedia learning: Why reduction of cognitive load can have negative results on learning. *Educational Technology Research and Development, 53*(3), 47–58. doi:10.1007/BF02504797

Segers, E., & Verhoeven, L. (2002). Multimedia support of early literacy learning. *Computers & Education, 39*(3), 207–221. doi:10.1016/S0360-1315(02)00034-9

Segers, E., & Verhoeven, L. (2003). Effects of vocabulary training by computer in kindergarten. *Journal of Computer Assisted Learning, 19*(4), 557–566. doi:10.1046/j.0266-4909.2003.00058.x

Sénéchal, M. (1997). The differential effect of storybook reading on preschoolers'acquisition of expressive and receptive vocabulary. *Journal of Child Language, 24*(1), 123–138. doi:10.1017/S0305000996003005

Sénéchal, M., Thomas, E., & Monker, J.A. (1995). Individual differences in 4-year-old children's acquisition of vocabulary during storybook reading. *Journal of Educational Psychology, 87*(2), 218–229. doi:10.1037/0022-0663.87.2.218

Shamir, A., & Korat, O. (2009). The educational electronic book as a tool for supporting children's emergent literacy. In A. Bus & S.B. Neuman (Eds.), *Multimedia and literacy development: Improving achievement for young learners* (pp. 168–181). New York: Routledge.

Shamir, A., Korat, O., & Shlafer, I. (2011). The effect of activity with e-book on vocabulary and story comprehension: A comparison between kindergarteners at risk of learning disabilities and typically developing kindergarteners. *European Journal of Special Needs Education, 26*(3), 311–322. doi:10.1080/08856257.2011.593824

Smeets, D.J.H., & Bus, A.G. (2012a). Interactive electronic storybooks for kindergartners to promote vocabulary growth. *Journal of Experimental Child Psychology, 112*(1), 36–55. doi:10.1016/j.jecp.2011.12.003

Smeets, D.J.H., & Bus, A.G. (2012b). *The interactive video book as a word learning device for kindergartners.* Under review.

Smeets, D.J.H., van Dijken, M.J., & Bus, A.G. (2012). Using electronic storybooks to support word learning in children with severe language impairments. *Journal of Learning Disabilities, 00*(0), 000–000. doi:10.1177/0022219412467069

Smith, V. (2011, December 18). What makes a great app? Kirkus Reviews Children's (blog). Retrieved December 3, 2012, from www.kirkusreviews.com/blog/childrens/what-makes-great-app/

Verhallen, M.J.A.J., & Bus, A.G. (2010). Low-income immigrant pupils learning vocabulary through digital picture storybooks. *Journal of Educational Psychology, 102*(1), 54–61. doi:10.1037/a0017133

Verhallen, M.J.A.J., & Bus, A.G. (2011). Young second language learners' visual attention to illustrations in storybooks. *Journal of Early Childhood Literacy, 11*(4), 480–500. doi:10.1177/1468798411416785

Verhallen, M.J.A.J., Bus, A.G., & de Jong, M.T. (2006). The promise of multimedia stories for kindergarten children at risk. *Journal of Educational Psychology, 98*(2), 410–419. doi:10.1037/0022-0663.98.2.410

Whitehurst, G.J., & Lonigan, C.J. (2001). Emergent literacy: Development from prereaders to readers. In S.B. Neuman & D.K. Dickinson (Eds.), *Handbook of early literacy research* (Vol. 1, pp. 11–29). New York: Guilford.

Zucker, T.A., Moody, A.K., & McKenna, M.C. (2009). The effects of electronic books on pre-kindergarten-to-grade-5 students' literacy and language outcomes: A research synthesis. *Journal of Educational Computing Research, 40*(1), 47–87. doi:10.2190/EC.40.1.c

LITERATURE AND MULTIMEDIA CITED

Davis, L. (1996). *P.B. is jarig* [P.B. Bear's birthday party] [CD-ROM]. Nieuwegein, Netherlands: Bombilla/VNU Interactive Media.

de Wijs, I. (2001). *Rokko krokodil* [Rokko the crocodile]. Rotterdam, Netherlands: Ziederis.

Janosch. (1998a). *Groot feest voor Tijger* [Big party for Tiger] [CD-ROM]. Baarn, Netherlands: Het Spectrum Electronic Publishing.

Janosch. (1998b). *'Ik maak je weer beter,' zei Beer* ['I'll make you well again,' said the Bear] [CD-ROM]. Baarn, Netherlands: Het Spectrum Electronic Publishing.

Thomas, V., & Gorky, P. (1996). *Heksenspul met Hennie de Heks en de Kat Helmer* [Winnie the Witch] [CD-ROM]. Nieuwegein, Netherlands: Bombilla.

van Haeringen, A. (2004). *Beer is op Vlinder* [Bear is in love with butterfly]. Amsterdam: Leopold.

CHAPTER 14

The E-Book Goes to School: Shared Book Reading 3.0

Kathleen Roskos

There's no doubt about it—e-books are rapidly spreading into the early childhood classroom, inviting young children to interact with books in ways they have not done before. E-book sales have dramatically increased within the last few years, cornering about 18% of the children's book market (Peckham, 2012). Intent on winning over a new generation of readers, Barnes & Noble recently launched a digital collection of more than 12,000 books (Association of American Publishers, 2010). Not to be left behind, most commercial reading programs now include e-books for reading development and instruction (e.g., the Storia app produced by Scholastic Books [store.scholastic.com]). Needless to say, e-books are novel and fresh, offering different ways of touching (swipe, tap, drag, drop), listening (music, narrator voices), looking (animated illustrations and words, videos) and reading texts (up, down, all around). Presently awed by their wizardry (some are very cool apps), we nonetheless know relatively little about e-books as tools for learning to read and for reading in a Common Core State Standards (CCSS) context.

This chapter takes a closer look at the pedagogic future of e-books intended for our young readers. Implicit in the discussion is the emerging role of the e-book as a curricular resource that supports the implementation of the CCSS for English Language Arts in the early grades (National Governors Association Center for Best Practices & Council of Chief State School Officers [NGA Center & CCSSO], 2010). In order to achieve these rigorous Standards for beginning reading, teachers need to be equipped to promote and support foundational reading skills (letter knowledge, sounds, and word reading) *and* build meaning-based skills (comprehension, conceptual knowledge, and vocabulary) in varied genres. They need 21st-century tools that invigorate instruction and strengthen its intensity on a daily basis so that children can truly achieve these Standards. They need resources that not only upgrade the

Quality Reading Instruction in the Age of Common Core Standards, edited by Susan B. Neuman and Linda B. Gambrell. © 2013 by the International Reading Association.

text complexity of learning materials and align with standards, but also that motivate children to read a lot in an online world. The e-book is a newcomer in the panoply of reading instructional materials, but a dazzling one that shows promise for helping teachers implement the CCSS. The chapter explores the design quality of e-books as children's *first* readers, describes the potential of good e-books for learning to read and reading in prekindergarten through grade 2 classrooms, and presents an e-book routine (Shared Book Reading 3.0) that guides the use of e-books in early childhood reading instruction.

E-Book Quality

At the outset of any discussion of e-books, it is important to understand that an e-book is both an object (an electronic mechanism) and a text source (a book). The electronics interface with the text, meaning there are points of interaction between the "e" (electronics) and the content (book). This interface profoundly influences the reader–text relationship, because the "e" (the electronic part) is impressive. Narration, music, animation, color, hyperlinks, and motion are powerful attractors that can capture and influence viewer/reader attention.

Types of E-Books

The "e" capacity of e-books is fundamental to their quality and the basis of categorizing different e-book types. The simplest type of e-book is in a portable document format (PDF) that, in short, "travels well" across a range of electronic devices (Kindle, NOOK, iPhone, iPod, iPad, and desktop computers). It has the basics: start/stop buttons and front/back arrows for pagination. It may include bookmarking and annotating features plus an audio function. This type of e-book looks, feels, and acts a lot like the traditional print book, and in some cases consists of pages directly scanned from a printed book. There are large numbers available for downloading from sites such as the New York Public Library website or through public online libraries (e.g., via OverDrive, a public e-book vendor).

Rapidly increasing in availability at school, a garden-variety type of e-book includes more advanced features, such as music, animation, print highlights, hotspots (hyperlinks that leave the page), and embedded games; it may contain word decoding and word-search assistance. Tumblebooks (www.tumble-books.com) is a representative example of this e-book type, following a standard format yet offering more hands-on interactivity than a PDF or a print book (unless that book has textured illustrations, audio or music components, or pop-up features).

The most complex type of e-book (to date) is the interactive e-book or animated story. It presents a film-like version of content (sometimes even in 3-D) and allows a full range of multisensory interactions with the illustrations and text—visual, auditory, haptic (touch), and kinesthetic (bodily movement). Take, for example, the e-book titled *The Going to Bed Book* (Boynton, 2011). This bedtime story is modeled on a board book, and in addition to calming narration and soothing music effects, the app accommodates lots of exploration by small, chubby fingers: page turning, tapping (to poke bath bubbles), swiping (to get pajamas from a drawer), sounds (running water for the bath), and even "steam" (to trace with your finger). Interactive e-books include sophisticated and creative multimodal interfaces, such as toolbars, virtual assistants, reading-level adjusters, embedded video, and activities (e.g., coloring an illustration, doing an experiment, listening to a song). The "e" in this e-book type is highly engaging and provides a glimpse into the future of children's publishing as children's books transition from print to digital (McLeod, 2011).

Qualities of Design

What are the qualities of a good, workable, instructive, enjoyable e-book for young children? A good book is a good book, and quality criteria for traditional and print-based children's literature certainly apply to e-books as couriers of stories and information; therefore, criteria include age-appropriateness; cultural sensitivity; satisfying plots; content/concept accuracy; and rich expressions of human values, traits, and struggles (Norton & Norton, 2010). Of course, they should also offer children increasingly complex, genre-varied texts to challenge and stretch their reading abilities at school. In this respect, e-books—like print books—are held to Anchor Standard for Reading 10 of the CCSS, which describes the importance of range, quality, and complexity of student reading materials (NGA Center & CCSSO, 2010, p. 10). Increasingly, vendors, publishers, and library services provide information on the reading levels of digital content. Tumblebooks, for example, is in the process of assigning a Lexile level on all e-books in its library.

Yet e-books are different from print books because their electronics operate interactively on a *screen page*. This is to say, the "e" carries some of the reading load—and thus has the power to help or hinder the reader's comprehension. Although standards of performance for e-books have not been established by the book industry, there are a few basic principles of effective design (Gonzalez, 2010; Krozser, 2010):

- Multimedia—The multimedia characteristic of digital books should enhance the reading experience. Audio, video, and image assets should be well integrated with the content and support the construction of meaning. Visuals should incorporate quality images that inform the message.

- Interactivity—The digital medium should be fully used to allow readers choice and participation; it should support the flow of text from one screen page to the next. It should allow for augmentations that reach beyond the immediate display of the screen page.

- Usability—The digital book should be easy to navigate and use; it should employ conventions appropriate to books (e.g., a cover page) yet include adaptations best suited to the electronic environment in terms of physical interaction (e.g., touching, orienting to print, scrolling, locating, adjusting).

Guided by these principles, Buckleitner (2011) developed the Children's E-book Evaluation Instrument and used it to review 125 children's e-book releases between April and December 2010. (Reviews are available on the Children's Technology Review website at childrenstech.com; subscription required.) The instrument consists of five general criteria that rate items on a 4-point scale to generate quantitative ratings for children's interactive media. The *ease of use* criteria, for example, include items related to children's sense of control (e.g., *page turn icons are easy to spot*). Criteria related to *educational value* describe the outcomes of the experience (e.g., *games and animations support the story*). An *entertainment category* rates the "fun" in the experience (e.g., *hotspots provide surprises*). Finally, a *features* category considers the e-book design (e.g., *fonts are easy to read*). Ratings indicate the overall *value* of the e-book on a scale of 1 (low) to 10 (high).

Increasingly, publications and journals associated with the book industry also include reviews (but not critiques) of e-book apps for children. *Kirkus Reviews,* for example, provides a list of the Best Book Apps for toddlers to teens (www.kirkusreviews.com/lists/). According to Vicki Smith (2011), children's and teen editor at *Kirkus*, a "great" e-book app (a) first succeeds as a book on its own terms, (b) uses "bells and whistles" that enhance the story, (c) provides interactions that make sense and are developmentally appropriate, (d) maximizes the media to surprise and delight the reader, and (e) uses the "e" format effectively to retain the "bookness" of the reading experience. *Wild About Books* by Judy Sierra for preschoolers through second graders and *Van Gogh and the Sunflowers* by Laurence Anholt for primary graders are notable examples.

Some early literacy researchers, however, remain generally unimpressed (if not deeply concerned) with the design quality of many e-books for young children, citing that there is too much of everything—animations, sounds, text features, and activities; frequent and annoying mismatches between print and illustrations; distractions that pull readers away from the story; and poor aesthetics (Adriana Bus, personal communication, August 7, 2012; de Jong & Bus, 2003; Roskos, Brueck, & Widman, 2009). Teachers need to be wary of e-book apps that try to do too much because the time spent may not cultivate the close reading that the CCSS and other standards require nor develop essential skills for integrating text content with pictures and words.

E-Book Potential for Learning to Read

Can e-books of reasonably good quality help children learn to read? This is a critical question as e-books proliferate in children's early literacy experiences. To build the literary, expository, and foundational reading skills described in the CCSS, young children need book experiences that will help them to read words with sufficient accuracy and speed to comprehend texts well by the end of third grade. Equally important, children need to *want* to read! E-books, as a curricular resource, should support, if not advance, these expectations. Therefore, is there evidence of their effects?

Research on the role of e-books in young children's literacy development and skills is in its infancy, and much of it is lab-based research, not applied research. Lab-based studies, however, show some promising results, but not without some cautions. In a series of experiments using specially designed e-books and story-like games, Bus and colleagues found that children at risk for literacy delays benefit from the enriched reading environment that e-books provide, showing gains in phonological awareness, phoneme awareness, and vocabulary (Kegel & Bus, 2012; Kegel, van der Kooy-Hofland, & Bus, 2009; Smeets & Bus, 2012; van der Kooy-Hofland, Kegel, & Bus, 2011). The highlighting of print and the temporal contiguity of audio (narration, music) with visual information (illustrations) draw children's visual attention to pictures and print in ways that concretize the text, making it more real for them and more memorable (Verhallen & Bus, 2011, 2012).

There are subtle individual behavioral variations, however, that influence the potential learning quality of children's e-book interactions.

Children with poor regulation skills, for example, do not benefit from the interactions as much as their peers, more often resorting to random clicking in stories and games (Kegel et al., 2009). At the same time, children with neurobiological issues (e.g., mild perinatal adversities), who are especially susceptible to environmental factors, gained ground in the enriched e-book environment (Kegel, Bus, & van IJzendoorn, 2011). In short, the e-book environment differentially impacts its users, which has major implications for its electronic design. Some children may need more pedagogic supports than others to keep their attention focused on the instructional content, and some may benefit from more multimedia than others to stimulate and enrich their experience. The work of Korat and Shamir (2004; Shamir & Korat, 2009) corroborates many of these findings. Focused on the dictionary hotspot as a resource for developing children's phonological awareness and vocabulary, they observed its benefits for at-risk young readers, especially in the presence of adult mediation.

In the applied research arena, several promising studies have been conducted recently. For example, Chiong, Ree, Takeuchi, and Erickson (2012) compared parent–child partners (in which children were 3 to 6 years old) coreading across three book formats: print books, basic e-books (e-book on a tablet with minimal interactive features), and enhanced e-books (e-book on a tablet with many interactive features). In general, the results suggest that the print books and the basic e-book were more advantageous for literacy-building coreading, whereas the enhanced e-book was more advantageous for engaging children and prompting physical interaction. Comparing shared book reading with print books versus e-books in preschool classrooms, Moody, Justice, and Cabell (2010) observed that with adult-led e-book reading, children demonstrated more persistence, an indicator of engagement; however, there were more talk initiations in the adult-led traditional shared book reading. In short, these studies suggest that the complexity and reading manner may matter in e-book shared reading to promote early literacy.

Examining e-book implementation in Early Reading First Head Start classrooms, our own series of field studies yielded several helpful classroom-based observations (Roskos, Burstein, You, Brueck & O'Brien, 2011). One of these is the urgent need for validated evaluation tools that help parents and teachers choose quality e-books for sharing with young children as discussed previously (Roskos & Brueck, 2011; Roskos, Brueck, & Widman, 2009). Research-based rating tools can support a rigorous review process that not only informs consumers but also builds a corpus of quality e-book literature for children.

Another important, albeit often overlooked, observation is the need to design rich physical environments that support young children's interactions with e-books. Relatively little is known about the impact of e-book devices—such as touch screen computers, interactive whiteboards, and mobile devices—on the arrangement and allocation of classroom space. The architectural goal is to weave e-book browsing and reading into already well-designed physical learning spaces of the classroom, and not to isolate this way of reading from traditional book-reading areas, such as the book corner or library center (Lackney, 2007). When educators begin to blend physical, digital, learner, and play spaces together, the overlap opens up new arenas for innovation, referred to as "edges" or "peripheral areas with high growth potential" (Hagel, Brown, & Davidson, 2009). Our research suggests several criteria for creating appealing spaces for e-book browsing and reading, including the following:

- Clearly defined space in the book or library area
- Signage related to e-book titles, usage, and storage
- Inviting café-like surroundings for sharing e-books with friends or enjoying them in private
- Good acoustics to hear stories
- Access to headphones, adequate Wi-Fi, and power outlets for devices and recharging stations

Inviting e-book nooks and niches, we have observed, are popular places that children flock to at center time and enjoy, supporting their literacy motivations and interests (Burstein & Roskos, 2011).

We also examined the impact of different instructional formats (e.g., shared book, book browsing) and device type (e.g., touch screens, mobiles) on children's engagement with e-books. Results show that the type of device used for e-reading has an impact on several key multisensory behaviors that contribute to children's engagement with e-books. In general, mobiles appear to afford more looking and touching but less moving and gesturing than the touch screen, which we might expect given that e-book reading at the touch screen is often adult led (Roskos, Burstein, & You, 2012). Given the increasing role of haptic perception (e.g., touch) in digital reading, access to mobile devices may favor behaviors that nurture literacy motivation and participation, especially for less attentive children, and support ongoing engagement with e-books for all children—an observation also noted in the Chiong et al. (2012) research.

Finally, we gathered descriptive information on the use of e-books in the shared book reading routine at preschool. Observations focused on teachers' implementation of shared book reading with small groups of children at a tabletop touch screen device with an emphasis on learning target words, followed by independent reading of the e-book app on a mobile device. Results suggested a relatively easy transition from print book to e-book shared reading that supported children's word learning (Roskos & Burstein, 2012). Teachers readily applied the familiar before-during-after framework of the shared book routine and employed evidence-based instructional techniques (e.g., making predictions). Applying the known to the new during the e-reading however, was often used to a fault in that the teachers did not capitalize on the robust text features of e-books very well to enlarge, enrich, or expand the literacy experience. Print highlights, for example, were not pointed out; dictionary hotspots were only cursorily explored; powerful media links between picture and print were overlooked; and the "hand over" of touching, tapping, swiping, and other interactive activities to children was limited (perhaps due to issues of control). Further research is definitely needed in order to define, describe, and examine transitioning instructional techniques to the media-rich e-book environment, and to generate new ones that maximize its potential.

On the whole, this small but growing body of lab-based and field research suggests that the signature characteristics of e-books—visuals, sound effects, narration, animation, print highlights/features, music effects, embedded tutors/activities—do not appear to interfere with the emerging literacy skills of most children, and in fact may be promoting essential skill development for some children, especially those who benefit from enriched reading environments. However, we need to know much more about how the new, alluring text features of e-books become well aligned, well timed, well placed, and aesthetically well constructed to produce substantive, intelligent, and instructive e-texts for children.

Shared Book Reading 3.0

At school, e-books must be more than "edutainment"; they must serve an authentic instructional purpose in the literacy program and substantively contribute to the achievement of the CCSS College and Career Readiness Anchor Standards in Reading (NGA Center & CCSSO, 2010, p. 10). For this to happen, they must become an integral part of shared book reading—the sine qua non of early literacy instruction. Founded on the commonplace bedtime story routine, Don Holdaway (1979) articulated a preschool story learning cycle where newly read storybooks became old favorites after repeated readings, and in the process, primed children for literacy through modeling, participating, attempting, and playing out reading-like behaviors. This cycle served as the original version of the shared book routine at school (pointer and all).

By the late 1990s, the shared book routine had been fully incorporated into early and beginning literacy instruction, organized around a "Read To, Read With, You Try" approach with Big Books and replicated with little books. This more expanded (and considerably more detailed) version of the shared book experience offered a primary means of instructing young children in early literacy skills. Today the shared book experience is extensive and elaborate, lasting up to five days where children are introduced to a book (e.g., title, author, illustrator), read and reread the book with teacher support to develop word-level and comprehension skills, and read the book on their own while completing extension activities (e.g., innovating on the text). The routine is widely used in early childhood classrooms and supported as a best practice in early literacy instruction.

The question is, however, does a shared book routine work when there is no tangible book? How does it work when the book is narrated and presented on a computer screen that can be large (like a smartboard), small (like an iPod), or somewhere in between (like a touch screen or an iPad)? How does it work when the reader can leave the screen page and view or do something else?

Presently there are no definitive answers to these questions. There are, however, descriptive observations and teacher accounts that shed light on shared book reading with e-books–or what we might term Shared Book Reading 3.0—in this day and age (Buckleitner, 2011; Roskos & Burstein, 2012; Zucker, Moody, & McKenna, 2009). Figure 14.1 summarizes what we are learning from this research, offering guidance on shared e-book reading for early childhood educators.

We can observe several familiar shared book reading elements in this model—the presence of the before-during-after framework, for example, and the introduction to the title, author, and illustrator on the initial screen page. Evidence-based instructional techniques are preserved, such as making predictions, asking/answering questions, learning new words, linking to prior experience, and discussing print and picture. There are also some notable augmentations that are important in a digital reading environment.

Consider first the gray-highlighted items in Figure 14.1 for the before-reading phase. Previewing an e-book, for example, may take more time, as teachers will need to evaluate its quality both as a piece of literature and also as an electronic book. The teacher will need to pay particular attention to the scaffolds provided for learning to read (e.g., decoding helpers),

Figure 14.1. Shared Book Reading 3.0

Phase	Considerations	Guidance
Before	• Ease of use • Multimedia features • Interactivity • Listen/view mode • Read/view mode • Interactive whiteboard • Touch screen • iPad	• Preview e-book for quality. • Explore text features and digital assets (several times). • Select pause points for instructional episodes. • Select the auto or manual mode for initial reading. • Use the interactive whiteboard for whole-group shared book reading. • Use a touch screen (mounted or tabletop) or iPad for small-group shared book reading.
	• Title • Author/illustrator • Predictions	• Use traditional shared reading procedures.
During	• Listen/view or read/view the entire e-book together. • Demonstrate and explore the text features. • Provide word-level as well as text-level instruction. • Invite children to participate in control of the e-book.	**Day 1:** Pause and discuss the content at strategic points. Explore word meanings and print/picture highlights. **Day 2:** Show and explain the text features; teach skills. **Days 3–5:** • Ask children to page-turn (click arrow). • Ask children to tap specific text features. • Ask children to tell about text pushes (beyond the screen page) and pulls (on the screen page). • Ask children to respond to the pedagogic agent or tutor (if present).
After	• Ask/answer questions to check for listening and reading comprehension. • Revisit some text features for instructional purposes. • Show favorite part(s). • Connect to prior experiences at school and home. • Prepare for independent book browsing/reading with mobiles (e.g., NOOKs, Kindles, iPads, iPods).	**Day 1:** Reinforce story theme or informational content. **Day 2:** • Walk through text structure. • Use some text features to teach literacy concepts and skills. • Connect to prior experience. **Day 3:** • Focus on specific text features to teach specific skills. • Demonstrate e-book or an old favorite on mobile devices. • Invite children to browse/read stories on a mobile with a friend or alone.

(continued)

Figure 14.1. Shared Book Reading 3.0 (*continued*)

Phase	Considerations	Guidance
You Try	• Provide comfortable space in the classroom library or book corner. • Encourage children to browse, listen, and read. • Remind them to handle devices with care. • Hold children accountable for their independent e-book reading.	• Locate mobile devices and headphones in the classroom book area. • Post simple directions for usage. • Use signage to feature e-book titles. • Provide children with ways to share their favorites (e.g., posters and rating charts).

ensuring that common e-book design mistakes are avoided (such as confusing taps, swipes, and page turns or lack of easy access to the menu and controls). The teacher will also need to make instructional decisions about what mode to use (listen or read) and on what device to maximize children's participation at the outset and throughout the experience.

There are also new considerations in the during-reading phase, especially around demonstrating text features and explaining how they are linked to the content of the book or text. Inviting and monitoring children's active participation with text features, however, may introduce new management challenges. For instance, young children's taps, swipes, pushes, pulls, and tilts can be quite vigorous (and rough), and they can influence their effort to be in control. Having to wait in the face of so many opportunities may also prove overwhelming for some children, and they can get upset when the teacher chooses to move on.

After-reading time requires the added step of modeling the proper use of devices for independent book browsing and reading, and helping children to engage in responsible e-book reading on their own or with a friend. Just as Big Books are often placed in the classroom's library corner for children to read and enjoy on their own (including a pointer), new e-book selections and old favorites should be highlighted and available on a range of devices that children have learned to use with care for their own reading pleasure.

E-Books Into the Future

Over time, each emerging and new technology and curricular literacy resource generates a pedagogy, or set of practices, that attempts to maximize its instructional use with learners. The medieval-age hornbook called for instructional techniques and strategies that emphasized pronouncing letters and sounds correctly and articulately. Teaching, therefore, focused on recitation. The basal reader system led to a host of oral- and silent-reading teaching techniques collapsed into the directed reading lesson, which consisted of multiple steps (and hefty workbooks for practice). The Big Book introduced the idea of collaborative or shared reading, neatly summed in the Read To, Read With, You Try procedure. It also emphasized after-reading activities as innovative extensions (not workbooks) and connecting texts and reading experiences to one another as well as to children's lives. Today we face a new challenge: to use e-books effectively with print books to reach higher levels of literacy than ever before.

TRY THIS!

- Using Figure 14.1, choose an informational e-book and develop a lesson for your students. Remember to include all four phases: before, during, after, and you try.

- Locate 10 e-books and download them to an e-reader device. Now, use your lesson plan from the first "Try This!" activity and develop a template that can be used with most e-books. Then, apply this template to your 10 e-books. Now, you have more practice with e-books and a template as well as 10 lessons that you can use with your students when they want to read an e-book.

DISCUSSION QUESTIONS

1. According to Roskos, how are e-books reflected within the CCSS?

2. Roskos asserts that little research has been done to explore the relationship between e-books and physical spaces within classrooms that foster students' reading engagement. Why is the relationship an important one?

3. Roskos discusses familiar elements in the before-during-after reading model that also apply to e-books. List these elements and discuss the similarities and differences between e-books and traditional print books.

REFERENCES

Association of American Publishers. (2010). *Bookstats publishing formats highlights.* New York: Author. Retrieved from publishers. org/bookstats/formats

Buckleitner, W. (2011). The children's e-book revisited. *Children's Technology Review, 19*(1), 6–11. Retrieved from www .childrenssoftware.com/pdf/g1.pdf

Burstein, K., & Roskos, K. (2011, April). *Design considerations for an effective e-book physical environment.* Paper presented at the Annual Meeting of the American Educational Research Association, New Orleans, LA.

Chiong, C., Ree, J., Takeuchi, L., & Erickson, I. (2012). *Print books vs. e-books: Comparing parent-child co-reading on print, basic and enhanced e-book platforms.* New York: The Joan Ganz Cooney Center at Sesame Workshop.

de Jong, M.T., & Bus, A.G. (2003). How well suited are electronic books to supporting literacy? *Journal of Early Childhood Literacy, 3*(2), 147–164. doi:10.1177/14687984030032002

Gonzalez, G.L. (2010, January 14). "E" is for experiment (not e-books). *Publishing Perspectives.* Retrieved December 3, 2012, from publishingperspectives. com/2010/01/"e"-is-for-experiment-not-e-Books

Hagel, J., Brown, J.S., & Davidson, L. (2009, February 6). How to bring the core to the edge. *HBR Blog Network* (blog). Retrieved December 3, 2012, from blogs.hbr.org/ bigshift/2009/02/how-to-bring-the-edge-to-the-c.html

Holdaway, D. (1979). *The foundations of literacy.* Portsmouth, NH: Heinemann.

Kegel, C.A.T., & Bus, A.G. (2012). Online tutoring as a pivotal quality of web-based early literacy programs. *Journal of Educational Psychology, 104*(1), 182–192. doi:10.1037/a0025849

Kegel, C.A.T., Bus, A.G., & van IJzendoorn, M.H. (2011). Differential susceptibility in early literacy instruction through computer games: The role of the dopamine D4 receptor gene (DRD4). *Mind, Brain, and Education, 5*(2), 71–78. doi:10.1111/j.1751-228X.2011.01112.x

Kegel, C.A.T., van der Kooy-Hofland, V., & Bus, A.G. (2009). Improving early phoneme skills with a computer program: Differential effects of regulatory skills. *Learning and Individual Differences, 19*(4), 549–554. doi:10.1016/j.lindif.2009.07.002

Korat, O., & Shamir, A. (2004). Do Hebrew electronic books differ from Dutch electronic books? A replication of a Dutch content analysis. *Journal of Computer Assisted Learning, 20*(4), 257–268. doi:10.1111/j.1365-2729.2004.00078.x

Krozser, K. (2010, January 25). Before e-book experimentation, how about a little back to basics? *Publishing Perspectives.* Retrieved December 3, 2012, from publishingperspectives.com/2010/01/ before-e-book-experimentation-how-about-a-little-back-to-basics

Lackney, J.A. (2007). 33 educational design principles for schools and community learning centers. *School Design Studio* (blog). Retrieved December 3, 2012, from schoolstudio.typepad.com/school_design_ studio/33-educational-design-pri.html

McLeod, S. (2011, May 2). The future of print: 21 interesting e-books for kids. *Big Think.* Retrieved December 3, 2012, from bigthink.com/ideas/the-future-of-print-21-interesting-e-books-for-kids

Moody, A.K., Justice, L.M., & Cabell, S.Q. (2010). Electronic versus traditional storybooks: Relative influence on preschool children's engagement and communication. *Journal of Early Childhood Literacy, 10*(3), 294–313. doi:10.1177/1468798410372162

National Governors Association Center for Best Practices & Council of Chief State School Officers. (2010). *Common Core State Standards for English language arts and literacy in history/social studies, science, and technical subjects.* Washington, DC: Authors. Retrieved from www.core standards.org/assets/CCSSI_ELA%20 Standards.pdf

Norton, D.E., & Norton, S. (2010). *Through the eyes of a child: An introduction to children's literature* (8th ed.). Upper Saddle River, NJ: Prentice Hall.

Peckham, M. (2012, April 5). Report: E-reading soars, shift from print to e-books continues. *PC World.* Retrieved December 3, 2012, from www.pcworld.com/article/ 253277/report_ereading_soars_shift_ from_print_to_e-books_continues.html

Roskos, K., & Brueck. J. (2011, April). *Developing an e-book quality rating tool.* Paper presented at the annual meeting of the American Educational Research Association, New Orleans, LA.

Roskos, K., Brueck, J., & Widman, S. (2009). Investigating analytic tools for e-book design in early literacy learning. *Journal of Interactive Online Learning, 8*(3), 218–240.

Roskos, K., & Burstein, K. (2012). Descriptive observations of e-book shared reading at preschool. *Journal of Literacy and Technology, 13*(3), 27–57.

Roskos, K., Burstein, K., & You, B.-K. (2012). A typology for observing children's engagement with ebooks at preschool. *Journal of Interactive Online Learning, 11*(2), 47–66.

Roskos, K., Burstein, K., You, B.-K., Brueck, J., & O'Brien, C. (2011). A formative study of an e-book instructional model in early literacy. *Creative Education, 2*(1), 10–17.

Shamir, A., & Korat, O. (2009). The educational electronic book as a tool for supporting children's emergent literacy. In A. Bus & S.B. Neuman (Eds.), *Multimedia and literacy development* (pp. 168–181). New York: Routledge.

Smeets, D.J.H., & Bus, A.G. (2012). Interactive electronic storybooks for kindergarteners to promote vocabulary growth. *Journal of Experimental Child Psychology, 112*(1), 36–55. doi:10.1016/j.jecp.2011.12.003

Smith, V. (2011, December 18). What makes a great app? Kirkus Reviews Children's (blog). Retrieved December 3, 2012, from www.kirkusreviews.com/blog/childrens/what-makes-great-app

van der Kooy-Hofland, V., Kegel, C.A.T., & Bus, A.G. (2011). Evidence-based computer interventions targeting phonological awareness to prevent reading problems in at-risk young students. In S.B. Neuman & D.K. Dickinson (Eds.), *Handbook of early literacy research* (Vol. 3, pp. 214–227). New York: Guilford.

Verhallen, M.J.A.J., & Bus, A.G. (2011). Young second language learners' visual attention to illustrations in storybooks. *Journal of Early Childhood Literacy, 11*(4), 480–500. doi:10.1177/1468798411416785

Verhallen, M.J.A.J., & Bus, A.G. (2012, July). *Beneficial effects of illustrations in picture storybooks for storing and retaining story text.* Paper presented at the annual meeting of the Society for the Scientific Studies of Reading, Montreal, ON, Canada.

Zucker, T.A., Moody, A.K., & McKenna, M.C. (2009). The effects of electronic books on pre-kindergarten-to-grade-5 students' literacy and language outcomes: A research synthesis. *Journal of Educational Computing Research, 40*(1), 47–87. doi:10.2190/EC.40.1.c

LITERATURE AND MULTIMEDIA CITED

Boynton, S. (2011). *The going to bed book* (Boynton Moo Media series). Vancouver, BC, Canada: Loud Crow Interactive.

CHAPTER 15

Common Core State Standards: Productivity Is Key

Marilyn Jager Adams

A major trigger for the development of the Common Core State Standards (CCSS; National Governors Association Center for Best Practices & Council of Chief State School Officers [NGA Center & CCSSO], 2010) was the static and stubbornly lackluster educational performance of young adults in the United States. Yet, if educational productivity in the United States is, in fact, stable and unchanging, one might well ask, Where's the crisis? What's the urgency? Why change?

Part of the problem is that educational growth is tightly linked with economic growth, like chicken and egg. Over the first two thirds of the 20th century, educational attainment in the United States increased by a whopping 6.7 years and, in parallel, the country's economic productivity increased by 2.5% per year. By contrast, increases in educational attainment within the United States began to slow in the 1970s, such that high school and college completion rates have barely changed since. Alongside, the fraction of U.S. productivity growth attributable to education fell by a third between 1980 and 2000 and, absent some dramatic change, is estimated to fall by half again in the next two decades (Goldin & Katz, 2008).

But the problem is worse than that, for economic growth is increasingly a function of international competitiveness. In most European countries, high school enrollment was less than 40% in the 1950s. Today, by contrast, educational attainment of young adults in most European and several Asian countries equals or exceeds that of young adults in the United States (Provasnik, Gonzales, & Miller, 2009). Until recently, public high schools were rare in less developed countries. Today, by contrast, they are growing rapidly in quantity and quality (Goldin & Katz, 2008).

Given the surge in educational growth in the rest of the world, the slowing of educational growth within the United States amounts to an ever-steeper relative decline. Bear in mind, too, that the population of the

---

Quality Reading Instruction in the Age of Common Core Standards, edited by Susan B. Neuman and Linda B. Gambrell. © 2013 by the International Reading Association.

United States is less than 5% of the world and shrinking. The United States will never again compete solely by having more people who are educated. Its economic future depends on having enough people who are *better* educated.

But the problem is still worse than that, for competitiveness ultimately depends on productivity. Productivity means getting more done in less time and possibly with a lower cost, and, these days, productivity is about technology. The capacity to store information electronically has added enormously to the efficiency of many tasks by reducing the human labor required for their execution as much as possible. Thus, as technology grows in distribution and sophistication, and as it is increasingly adapted for and adopted by different sectors of the economy, it is increasingly reshaping the labor market.

Back in the 1970s, just as educational attainment was beginning to plateau in the United States, growth in the technology sector was beginning to take off. Just as the flow of new college graduates was abating, the demand for them was accelerating. By the mid-1990s, there arose an acute demand, a "wage premium," for people with the knowledge and skills required to develop and deploy the new technological capabilities. Alongside, the number (though not the pay) of jobs requiring minimal education increased, too. However, the number of in-between jobs began to fall and has continued to fall (Autor, Katz, & Krueger, 2008; Autor, Levy, & Murnane, 2003). Mid-wage occupations constituted 60% of job losses during the 2008 recession but only 22% of recovery growth in the years since (National Employment Law Project, 2012).

Over the last decade or so, the U.S. middle class has been economically bruised in many ways that seem incomprehensible. However, one factor that must be considered very seriously is that the kinds of occupations on which the middle class was anchored are vanishing. We must educate our children for the opportunities of the future.

Reforming Literacy Education

Among students taking the ACT college-entrance test, roughly half are shown to read too poorly to succeed without remediation in first-year courses offered by two- or four-year colleges or by technical and trade schools. Toward understanding why, ACT (2006) conducted an analysis of the students' response profiles. Most of the factors examined—including literal versus inferential comprehension, and such textual elements as identifying main ideas, supporting details, and types of relationships (sequential, comparative, or cause and effect)—were found not to be causal factors. However, there was an exception. The analysis showed that all but the very strongest readers—the top 1%—demonstrated great difficulty in comprehending more complex texts. For the 51% whose scores fell below the college and career readiness cutoff, performance on more complex texts was at chance, no better than random guessing.

Given its original charge of increasing the college and career readiness of students, the emphasis within the CCSS on complex text follows directly. All high school students are to be engaged in ample close reading of texts that are rich in information, argument, and literate language (for example, see NGA Center & CCSSO, 2010, p. 8, and College and Career Readiness Anchor Standard for Reading 10 on p. 10). The problem with this plan, of course, is that its success depends unforgivingly on ensuring students can rise to the challenge. It depends, in other words, on significantly increasing the literacy levels with which students enter high school.

With that in mind, the Standards, originally set forth for high school only, were extended downward, first to the intermediate grades, and then to the primary grades. The goal was to create a single, developmentally coherent, and well-integrated suite of standards extending from kindergarten through grade 12, designed with the objective that *if* students met the expectations of each grade, they would be ready for the challenges of the next. A problem with this plan is that its success depends critically on the "if," and here we encounter another impasse.

The K–5 Standards for English Language Arts presented by the CCSS were by and large gathered from existing state standards. As such, they are by and large very similar to existing state standards. Yet the fourth-grade reading assessment from the National Assessment of Educational Progress (NAEP) shows that 60% of students are reading below grade level upon exiting the primary grades and, worse, that half of those children are barely able to read at all (National Center for Education Statistics, 2009).

The argument made here is that even if the CCSS were perfect, and even if every early childhood teacher in the United States were perfectly prepared and pursued the Standards with unflagging energy and discipline, the learning prescribed by the K–5 Standards would still remain out of reach of the majority of students. More specifically, the argument is that the Standards' requirements exceed the maximum productivity of the conventional classroom. To monitor and respond to the individual educational needs of every one of the children in a classroom requires far more time, labor, and resources than one teacher can offer.

If it is possible to significantly increase the number of children who meet or exceed the requirements only by significantly increasing the productivity of the classroom, then how might we do that? The answer is technology. In education, as in any other sector, productivity is about technology. If the United States needs its schools to educate students for the new technologies—and it urgently does—then it must provide its schools with the technologies necessary for doing so.

Help Needed: Examples

In this section, I turn the attention to four core literacy challenges:

1. Understanding complex informational texts
2. Developing reading fluency
3. Conquering phonics
4. Enjoying preschool read-alouds

Discussion is centered on how appropriate technology could multiply the efficiency and effectiveness of each.

Understanding Complex Informational Texts

Learning—whether it is about a pattern, a spelling, a concept, an event, a theory, an attribution, or the information in a text—consists in creating or modifying associations among its familiar parts. Not even the simplest passage can be understood without some basic familiarity with its conceptual building blocks. Moreover, the richer a student's knowledge of the words and concepts in a text, the richer the understanding gained through reading it (Dochy, Segers, & Buehl, 1999; Shapiro, 2004). To be sure, students' comprehension and learning is also influenced by their reading skills (such as decoding and fluency). But even the advantage of strong reading skills turns out to be greatest for students with strong domain knowledge (O'Reilly & McNamara, 2007).

Conversely, research shows that how much one knows about academic topics depends strongly on how much one has read about them (Cunningham & Stanovich, 1991; Stanovich, 1993). Our students, collectively, do not know enough. The NAEP shows that 71%, 76%, 78%, and 87% of high school students are currently below grade level in math, civics, science, and U.S. history, respectively (National Center for Education Statistics, 2010, 2011a, 2011b, 2011c). Similarly, as measured through the Programme for International Student Assessment, the ability of U.S. high school students to read and understand scientific material falls within the bottom third as compared with other Organisation for Economic Co-operation and Development (OECD) countries (Provasnik et al., 2009). As Hirsch (2006) has argued, the reading deficit is integrally tied to a knowledge deficit.

The CCSS's recommendation for greater emphasis on informational texts is thus well motivated. Our students need to read more informational texts so that they will learn more information, and they need to learn more information so that they can more productively read to be informed. As students' knowledge about each topic grows through reading, they will become better able to read, understand, think, and learn still more about it on their own for the rest of their lives. Better still, reading deeply about any given topic is shown to significantly advance one's ability to grasp the language, logic, and modes of thought that arise within many other topics to the extent that they are conceptually related topics (see Adams, 2010). As examples, learning about Mars makes it easier to learn about the rest of the solar system; learning about invasive plants may ground an understanding of certain diseases; and learning about the Federalist and Anti-Federalist quarrels in the signing of the U.S. Constitution makes it easier to understand contemporary issues of states' rights and individual liberties.

In short, reading more results in learning more, and knowing more results in reading better. However, the converse holds equally: Students who have read little will know little, and students who know little will comprehend little when they read.

When the students don't know enough about a topic to manage the text at hand, what do we do? The time-honored solution is to give them an easier text. In itself, however, offering easier texts can only make the root problem worse, for it denies students the very language, information, and modes of thought that they need most to move up and on. Alas, the linguistic complexity of textbooks for students in grades 8 through 12 has fallen to the level of the fifth-grade textbooks of 50 years ago (Hayes, Wolfer, & Wolfe, 1996).

To be sure, simpler texts are useful and appropriate for purposes of introducing a topic. The problem is that, even for any such introduction to be useful or memorable, the mind needs more information. But, aha! Therein lies the solution to the dilemma: The key to accelerating students' growth with informational texts lies in choosing a topic and then organizing the reading regimen such that each text bootstraps the language and knowledge that will be needed for the next. Let the students begin with a short, easy overview of the topic, and then choose each successive text such that it expands on the information so far established. As the students learn the core vocabulary, basic concepts, and overarching schemata of the domain, they will become ready to explore its subtopics. Gradually and seamlessly, they will find themselves ready for texts of increasingly greater depth and complexity. Their reading proficiency and confidence will grow as their knowledge grows.

A problem with this plan, of course, is that it depends on the availability of appropriate sets of topical texts. True, texts for such sets surely exist on the Web. But asking teachers to put the sets together themselves is unfair and unwise. For one thing, finding good materials on the Web even for just *one* such set of readings is a hugely time-intensive undertaking, and teachers already have a full-time job. For another, *most* teachers need such materials and many more besides. Asking each individual teacher to construct such materials—in effect to arduously reduplicate, for better or for worse, the efforts of thousands of others—is unconscionably inefficient and uneconomical. Creating each unit for grades K–12, will depend on the judicious selection not just of topics but also equally of the reading materials comprising each unit. From the billions of pages of print that are available, finding those that capture a supportive array of information and complexity and that are suitably well written and informative is a task that should involve teams of scholars, educators, and librarians and will require much time and effort and the best minds and sensibilities available.

Developing Reading Fluency

In moving through challenging texts, teacher-moderated discussion is indispensable toward helping children gain command of the information and argument offered and giving them the opportunity to reflect, enjoy, and wonder about what they have learned. Even so, the amount of text that can be covered during such sessions is limited. To become readers, students must read far more, and they must read closely and thoughtfully.

The NAEP special study on fluency (Daane, Campbell, Grigg, Goodman, & Oranje, 2005) shows that only 10% of fourth-graders were able to read "with phrasing that was consistent with the author's syntax and with some degree of expressiveness," (p. v) and *only* this group obtained reading comprehension scores that were at or above grade level (a "proficient" scoring on the NAEP). At the other end of the distribution, 40% of fourth graders were unable to read with minimal fluency; the comprehension scores of these children fell below NAEP's "basic" cutoff, indicating an inability to understand or learn from grade-level texts (Daane et al., 2005).

Just as there are two levels of fluency, there are two layers of learning that enable fluency. The first layer consists of gaining word-recognition automaticity, and the second involves gaining the linguistic and background knowledge needed to interpret the words both separately and in their ensemble.

To most, it is obvious that learning to recognize printed words involves skills and practice that are specific to the written domain. Yet research shows this to be equally true of the vocabulary, syntax, background knowledge, and modes of thought that characterize texts. Moreover, because the knowledge and skills required for reading and understanding text are specific to text, their acquisition comes about only through experience in reading and understanding text.

The prescription, then, is to require children to read more text and, in order to promote new learning, to centrally include text that is challenging. The problem is that a text read without fluency can barely be understood, and what has not been understood cannot be learned. It follows that unless and until children can read and understand texts on their own, they need support and instruction to help them through it.

Indeed, research shows that the single best practice for developing reading fluency is guided oral reading—the practice of engaging students in reading aloud, one-on-one to a helpful listener (National Institute of Child Health and Human Development, 2000). But again, no matter how they try, classroom teachers cannot give each of their 20 or so students the individual, guided oral reading support on which learning to read depends.

As I have argued elsewhere (Adams, 2011a, 2011b), the United States needs to get serious about developing speech recognition–based reading software for its schools. This is not a "pie-in-the-sky" proposal. Today, people around the world speaking in dozens of languages depend on automatic speech recognition for telephone call routing and directory assistance. It is widely used for dictation and information capture in the defense, health care, and legal sectors. It is used for captioning live television so we can watch our favorite games in noisy sports bars, and it is used by unnamed agencies for transcribing suspicious communications. It is employed by people as they talk to their computers, mobile devices, and cell phones while browsing the Web, managing their bookmarks, or in reverse, asking their cell phones to transcribe their voicemail and send written copy to their e-mail. They also use it to talk to their televisions, their music players, their cars, and their navigation systems. And, of course, speech recognition is very hot in the gaming industry.

In other words, automatic speech recognition is a technology that is mature and even commonplace in industry after industry with the salient exception of where it is needed most: in education. Whatever the economic or social value of the applications mentioned previously, most pale in comparison to the potential of speech recognition as it could and should be used to help people learn to read and read to learn.

Given "ears," the computer can listen to students as they read, offering help or prompting further thought at just the right moments while making records of their progress and difficulties in the background. Such technology, in other words, could cost effectively provide the individualized, one-on-one, interactive support and guidance on which becoming a reader so integrally depends.

Conquering Phonics

Nearly all delayed readers in the middle and upper grades have failed to develop adequate reading fluency. Of those, research indicates that roughly half are still struggling with word-recognition skills (Brasseur-Hock, Hock, Kieffer, Biancarosa, & Deshler, 2011; Hock et al., 2009; Leach, Scarborough, & Rescorla, 2003). Unless and until students are quickly and accurately able to recognize most of the individual words of a text, both fluency and productive comprehension of more complex materials remain out of reach.

With this in mind, the Reading First program gave absolute priority to supporting children's alphabet skills in the primary grades. In response, the reading scores of primary-grade students did indeed rise. But not enough. Why not?

One reason is that the spelling–sound correspondences of English are extraordinarily complicated. As documented in a recent study of 14 different countries (Seymour, Aro, & Erskine, 2003), most European children are able to accurately read nearly any one- or two-syllable word in their speaking vocabulary by the end of first grade. By contrast, the performance of the (well-heeled, above-average) English-speaking children in the study was but 34%. The researchers concluded that it would not be until third grade that the decoding facility of the English-speaking children would reach the level of first graders in countries with less complicated spelling systems.

Second, the complexity of English spelling–sound rules is such that it must be taught and learned in layers. To make sense, each element and each layer must be assimilated in proper, functional relation to others, and even then the system is rife with exceptions and inconsistencies that must be learned as instances or categories in themselves.

Third, in striving to impart each element, layer, and relationship to every one of the children in their classrooms, teachers must continually repeat, recast, contrast, and then probe each aspect of each lesson, and therein lies another major problem with phonics instruction. Done conscientiously, this effort absorbs an enormous amount of classroom time—and, even still, some children will not keep up.

In short, phonics instruction—decoding, spelling, and word recognition—is an ideal candidate for individual adaptive, computer-based instruction. With response time and accuracy as metrics, software could be designed such that every learning opportunity is equally an assessment point. No child would miss out on critical information for the reason of inattention or misunderstanding, nor would any child need to sit idly waiting for others to catch up. Providing instruction, extensions, and practice in deference to each student's continually monitored needs, good software should significantly increase the efficacy of phonics instruction. This is critically important because every child must conquer phonics in order to be able to learn to read and write. Avoiding unnecessary repetition and practice, such software should also be significantly more efficient, reducing the time required by each individual and the class as a whole to progress. This, too, is critically important, for it would free up time so direly needed for lending proper support to other core dimensions of language and literacy development.

Enjoying Preschool Read-Alouds

Research shows that having a rich experience of read-alouds at home is one of the greatest assets that students entering kindergarten and first grade can bring to the classroom for learning to read. Reading books regularly with young children is shown to increase their print knowledge, vocabulary, book language, and interest in learning to read (for reviews, see Bus, van IJzendoorn, & Pellegrini, 1995; Scarborough & Dobrich, 1994; Sénéchal & LeFevre, 2002). In the classic study of "dialogic" reading, for example, Whitehurst et al. (1988) found that teaching parents to ask their 3-year-olds open-ended questions during storybook reading resulted, over a period of just one month, in more than half a year's growth more than reading as usual.

Based on such findings, reading aloud to preschoolers became a priority recommendation within the Early Reading First program for preschool centers. How well do read-alouds work in preschool settings? Even under formal study conditions with a careful training of teachers and monitored implementation, published research shows that the impact of read-alouds within preschool centers is far smaller than in-home studies (e.g., Whitehurst et al., 1994). Perhaps related to this, read-alouds are not a favored activity in many centers, frequently neglected by teachers even when they are being evaluated for compliance (Dickinson & Sprague, 2002; Lonigan & Whitehurst, 1998).

And no wonder. Have you ever watched a read-aloud session in a preschool? Typically, having gathered the children around her, the teacher reads a page and then pans the book to subsets of two or three children, in turn, asking questions to engage them more closely (e.g., "Do you see the mouse? Where's the mouse? Yes, there's a frog, but we're looking for the mouse. Do you see the mouse? She did? Well, let's talk about that later. Joshua, hands in lap, please....") To be sure, the teacher is busy for the duration. But the individual children are not. Teachers openly voice concern that management of these sessions is difficult. Worse, reading even one book takes a lot of time, and often the story's flow and language are effectively lost.

Preschool classrooms need large projection screens at least as much as do office conference rooms. With a projection screen, the pictures and print would be big enough for all of the children to see at once, allowing for attentive, whole-book reading, as well as rich, whole-group discussion and exploration of the story and of the print.

In complement to adequate visual display facilities, preschools need good acoustical support. Such technology should include multiple electronic speakers and should be configured to accept input from wireless microphones and from other audio sources such as computers, both separately and in tandem.

Research shows that young children are especially poor at discerning speech with a background of even moderate noise (American Speech-Language-Hearing Association, 2005; Crandell & Smaldino, 2004; Nelson, Soli, & Seltz, 2003). Importantly, it is not that adults can hear better. Rather, adults are better able to compensate for what they can't hear by using their knowledge about the speaker's topic and their familiarity with the syntax, the vocabulary, and the phonology of the language (Stelmachowicz et al., 2000). For children, by contrast, a major purpose of such sessions—and, indeed, of nearly every classroom lesson—is to offer them an opportunity to *learn* about new topics and language. Consistently, poor acoustics are even more disruptive for children who are learning English as a second language in school (Crandell & Smaldino, 1996; Nelson, Kohnert, Sabur, & Shaw, 2005).

Technology for Our Classrooms

High-quality audio-amplification technology should be required in every classroom. It should be obvious that audibility is of paramount importance to students. It is also vital for teachers. Problems due to vocal fatigue and abuse are a near-universal occupational hazard in the teaching profession, accounting for 10% of sick days (Voice Academy, 2010).

Similarly, every classroom should be equipped with large-screen projection systems or, better yet, interactive projection systems. Many important lessons are just too hard to describe, discuss, or explore without visual support. At least as important, people are neurologically wired to attend to what they look at (Henderson & Ferriera, 2004; Kristjansson, 2011).

Not all primary-grade teachers embraced the Reading First challenge equally. Nevertheless, the Reading First program collectively represents the most aggressive, disciplined, multipronged effort to teach all children the alphabetic basics that has ever been and, very likely, ever again will be undertaken in this country. And still, too many children fared poorly. The hope driving the Reading First effort was that a strong foundation of phonics would enable students to independently acquire new words encountered in print, such that its impact would snowball, compounding itself and growing with each successive year in school. But that did not happen either. Even where the growth of less advantaged students was strongly accelerated over the primary grades, growth in later grades was not, and the biggest weakness among these children was poor reading fluency (Adams, 2008). Without phonics and fluency, reading is exhausting and unproductive. And again, both phonics and fluency depend integrally on individual support that is beyond the capacity of the conventional classroom. In no other challenge is the potential productivity of technology more urgent.

Finally, there is the issue of content and connectivity. Beyond the informational text sets discussed in the previous section, there are many educational resources that could and should be available for teachers, students, parents, and the public, as appropriate, on the Web. Many are there already, but they are just too hard to find, and unacceptable materials abound. The United States should commit itself to a serious and ongoing national effort to create, maintain, and update not just a website, but a top-level domain that is full of websites and that is entirely devoted to education, from preschool through high school. Doing so will require expertise and effort—which is to say, it will require funding. In terms of lost productivity, however, the real cost of the current situation is unsupportable. Equally, the potential advantages of such a system as it evolves are of insuperable importance to the country.

- Log in to Project Gutenberg (www.promo.net/pg) and download one of their free e-books as an addition to an existing text set. Select one that you feel will especially contribute to students building their knowledge about the core vocabulary, basic concepts, and overarching schemata of the unit.

- Supplement information presented in a read-aloud with a clip carefully chosen from YouTube or another website. The clip can extend key concepts and build students' schemas. For example, after hearing a read-aloud about elephants, students might view a clip about elephants.

DISCUSSION QUESTIONS

1. Adams identifies four core literacy challenges: (1) understanding complex informational texts, (2) developing reading fluency, (3) conquering phonics, and (4) enjoying preschool read-alouds. For Adams, the key to integrating these challenges with the CCSS lies in proper utilization of technology to increase efficiency within classrooms. Discuss each of the four literacy challenges and the solutions posited by Adams.

2. Adams, as well as many authors in other chapters of this book, mentions that those who read become better readers, while those who do not read ultimately will not become better readers. How is this effect related with the CCSS? That is, if the CCSS suggest that teachers increase the complexity of texts, what should teachers do when students are ill-fitted to take on texts with additional complexity?

3. What specific technology equipment that every classroom needs does Adams discuss? Why is this technology important in the era of CCSS?

REFERENCES

ACT. (2006). *Reading between the lines: What the ACT reveals about college readiness in reading.* Iowa City, IA: Author.

Adams, M.J. (2008). The limits of the self-teaching hypothesis. In S.B. Neuman (Ed.), *Educating the other America: Top experts tackle poverty, literacy, and achievement in our schools* (pp. 277–300). Baltimore: Paul H. Brookes.

Adams, M.J. (2010). Advancing our students' language and literacy: The challenge of complex texts. *American Educator, 34*(4), 3–11.

Adams, M.J. (2011a, November 29). Bringing speech recognition to reading instruction. *Education Week, 31*(13). Retrieved December 7, 2012, from www.edweek.org/ew/articles/2011/11/29/13adams.h31.html

Adams, M.J. (2011b, September 21). *Technology for developing children's language and literacy: Bringing speech recognition to the classroom.* New York: Joan Ganz Cooney Center at Sesame Workshop. Retrieved December 7, 2012, from joanganzcooneycenter.org/Reports-30.html

American Speech-Language-Hearing Association. (2005). *Acoustics in educational settings: Technical report.* Washington, DC: Author. Retrieved December 7, 2012, from www.asha.org/policy/TR2005-00042.htm. doi:10.1044/policy.TR2005-00042

Autor, D.H., Katz, L.F., & Krueger, A.B. (1998). Computing inequality: Have computers changed the labor market? *The Quarterly Journal of Economics, 113*(4), 1169–1213. doi:10.1162/003355398555874

Autor, D.H., Levy, F., & Murnane, R.J. (2003). The skill content of recent technological change: An empirical exploration. *The Quarterly Journal of Economics, 118*(4), 1279–1333. doi:10.1162/003355303322552801

Brasseur-Hock, I.F., Hock, M.F., Kieffer, M.J., Biancarosa, G., & Deshler, D.D. (2011). Adolescent struggling readers in urban schools: Results of a latent class analysis. *Learning and Individual Differences, 21*(4), 438–452. doi:10.1016/j.lindif.2011.01.008

Bus, A.G., van IJzendoorn, M.H., & Pellegrini, A.D. (1995). Joint book reading makes success in learning to read: A meta-analysis on intergenerational transmission of literacy. *Review of Educational Research, 65*(1), 1–21.

Crandell, C.C., & Smaldino, J.J. (1996). Speech perception in noise by children for whom English is a second language. *American Journal of Audiology, 5*(1), 47–51.

Crandell, C.C., & Smaldino, J.J. (2004). Classroom acoustics. In R.J. Roeser & M.P. Downs (Eds.), *Auditory disorders in school children: The law, identification, and remediation* (pp. 269–283). New York: Thieme.

Cunningham, A.E., & Stanovich, K.E. (1991). Tracking the unique effects of print exposure in children: Associations with vocabulary, general knowledge, and spelling. *Journal of Educational Psychology, 83*(2), 264–274. doi:10.1037/0022-0663.83.2.264

Daane, M.C., Campbell, J.R., Grigg, W.S., Goodman, M.J., & Oranje, A. (2005). *Fourth-grade students reading aloud: NAEP 2002 special study of oral reading (NCES 2006–469).* Washington, DC: Institute of Education Sciences, National Center for Education Statistics, U.S. Department of Education.

Dickinson, D.K., & Sprague, K.E. (2002). The nature and impact of early childhood care environments on the language and early literacy development of children from low-income families. In S.B. Neuman & D.K. Dickinson (Eds.), *Handbook of early literacy research* (Vol. 1, pp. 263–280). New York: Guilford.

Dochy, F., Segers, M., & Buehl, M.M. (1999). The relation between assessment practices and outcomes of studies: The case of research on prior knowledge. *Review of Educational Research, 69*(2), 145–186. doi:10.3102/00346543069002145

Goldin, C.D., & Katz, L.F. (2008). *The race between education and technology.* Cambridge, MA: Harvard University Press.

Hayes, D.P., Wolfer, L.T., & Wolfe, M.F. (1996). Schoolbook simplification and its relation to the decline in SAT-Verbal scores. *American Educational Research Journal, 33*(2), 489–508. doi:10.3102/00028312033002489

Henderson, J.M., & Ferriera, F. (Eds.). (2004). *The interface of language, vision, and action: Eye movements and the visual world.* New York: Taylor & Francis.

Hirsch, E.D., Jr. (2006). *The knowledge deficit: Closing the shocking education gap for American children.* New York: Houghton Mifflin.

Hock, M.F., Brasseur, I.F., Deshler, D.D., Catts, H.W., Marquis, J.G., Mark, C.A., et al. (2009). What is the reading component skill profile of adolescent struggling readers in urban schools? *Learning Disability Quarterly, 32*(1), 21–38.

Kristjánsson, A. (2011). The intriguing relationship between visual attention and saccadic eye movements. In S.P. Liversedge, I.D. Gilchrist, & S. Everling (Eds.), *The Oxford handbook of eye movements* (pp. 455–470). New York: Oxford University Press.

Leach, J.M., Scarborough, H.S., & Rescorla, L. (2003). Late-emerging reading disabilities. *Journal of Educational Psychology, 95*(2), 211–224. doi:10.1037/0022-0663.95.2.211

Lonigan, C.J., & Whitehurst, G.J. (1998). Relative efficacy of parent and teacher involvement in a shared-reading intervention for preschool children from low-income backgrounds. *Early Childhood Research Quarterly, 13*(2), 263–290. doi:10.1016/S0885-2006(99)80038-6

National Center for Education Statistics. (2009). *The nation's report card: Reading 2009: National Assessment of Educational Progress at grades 4 and 8* (NCES 2010–458). Washington, DC: Institute of Education Sciences, U.S. Department of Education. Retrieved December 7, 2012, from nces.ed.gov/nationsreportcard/reading

National Center for Education Statistics. (2010). *The nation's report card: Grade 12 reading and mathematics 2009 national and pilot state results* (NCES 2011–455). Washington, DC: Institute of Education Sciences, U.S. Department of Education. Retrieved December 7, 2012, from nces.ed.gov/nationsreportcard/pdf/main2009/2011455.pdf

National Center for Education Statistics. (2011a). *The nation's report card: Civics 2010: National Assessment of Educational Progress at grades 4 and 8* (NCES 2011–466). Washington, DC: Institute of Education Sciences, U.S. Department of Education. Retrieved December 7, 2012, from nces.ed.gov/nationsreportcard/pdf/main2010/2011466.pdf

National Center for Education Statistics. (2011b). *The nation's report card: Science 2009: National Assessment of Educational Progress at grades 4 and 8* (NCES 2011–451). Washington, DC: Institute of Education Sciences, U.S. Department of Education. Retrieved December 7, 2012, from nces.ed.gov/nationsreportcard/pdf/main2009/2011451.pdf

National Center for Education Statistics. (2011c). *The nation's report card: U.S. history 2010: National Assessment of Educational Progress at grades 4 and 8* (NCES 2011–468). Washington, DC: Institute of Education Sciences, U.S. Department of Education. Retrieved December 7, 2012, from nces.ed.gov/nationsreportcard/pdf/main2010/2011468.pdf

National Employment Law Project. (2012). *Report: The low-wage recovery and growth inequality.* New York: Author.

National Governors Association Center for Best Practices & Council of Chief State School Officers. (2010). *Common Core State Standards for English language arts and literacy in history/social studies, science, and technical subjects.* Washington, DC: Authors. Retrieved from www.corestandards.org/assets/CCSSI_ELA%20Standards.pdf

National Institute of Child Health and Human Development. (2000). *Report of the National Reading Panel. Teaching children to read: An evidence-based assessment of the scientific research literature on reading and its implications for reading instruction: Reports of the subgroups* (NIH Publication No. 00–4754). Washington, DC: U.S. Government Printing Office.

Nelson, P., Kohnert, K., Sabur, S., & Shaw, D. (2005). Classroom noise and children learning through a second language: Double jeopardy? *Language, Speech, and Hearing Services in Schools, 36,* 219–229. doi:10.1044/0161-1461(2005/022)

Nelson, P.B., Soli, S.D., & Seltz, A. (2003). *Classroom acoustics II: Acoustical barriers to learning.* Melville, NY: Acoustical Society of America.

O'Reilly, T., & McNamara, D.S. (2007). The impact of science knowledge, reading skill, and reading strategy knowledge on more traditional "high-stakes" measures of high school students' science achievement. *American Educational Research Journal, 44*(1), 161–196. doi:10.3102/0002831206298171

Provasnik, S., Gonzales, P., & Miller, D. (2009). *U.S. performance across international assessments of student achievement: Special supplement to the condition of education 2009 (NCES 2009–083).* Washington, DC: National Center for Education Statistics, Institute of Education Sciences, U.S. Department of Education.

Scarborough, H.S., & Dobrich, W. (1994). On the efficacy of reading to preschoolers. *Developmental Review, 14*(3), 245–302. doi:10.1006/drev.1994.1010

Sénéchal, M., & LeFevre, J. (2002). Parental involvement in the development of children's reading skill: A five-year longitudinal study. *Child Development, 73*(2), 445–460. doi:10.1111/1467-8624.00417

Seymour, P.H.K., Aro, M., & Erskine, J.M. (2003). Foundation literacy acquisition in European orthographies. *The British Journal of Psychology, 94*(2), 143–174. doi:10.1348/000712603321661859

Shapiro, A.M. (2004). How including prior knowledge as a subject variable may change outcomes of learning research. *American Educational Research Journal, 41*(1), 159–189. doi:10.3102/00028312041001159

Stanovich, K.E. (1993). Does reading make you smarter? Literacy and the development of verbal intelligence. In H.W. Reese (Ed.), *Advances in child development and behavior* (Vol. 24, pp. 133–180). San Diego, CA: Academic Press. doi:10.1016/S0065-2407(08)60302-X

Stelmachowicz, P.G., Hoover, B.M., Lewis, D.E., Kortekaas, R., & Pittman, A.L. (2000). The relation between stimulus context, speech audibility, and perception for normal-hearing and hearing-impaired children. *Journal of Speech, Language, and Hearing Research, 43*(4), 902–914.

Voice Academy, University of Iowa. (2010). *More FAQ's about amplification systems.* Retrieved December 7, 2012, from www.uiowa.edu/~shcvoice/media-faq.html

Whitehurst, G.J., Arnold, D.S., Epstein, J.N., Angell, A.L., Smith, M., & Fischel, J.E. (1994). A picture book reading intervention in day care and home for children from low-income families. *Developmental Psychology, 30*(5), 679–689. doi:10.1037/0012-1649.30.5.679

Whitehurst, G.J., Falco, F.L., Lonigan, C.J., Fischel, J.E., DeBaryshe, B.D., Valdez-Menchaca, M.C., et al. (1988). Accelerating language development through picture book reading. *Developmental Psychology, 24*(4), 552–559. doi:10.1037/0012-1649.24.4.552

The New Literacies of Online Research and Comprehension: Assessing and Preparing Students for the 21st Century With Common Core State Standards

Donald J. Leu, Elena Forzani, Cheryl Burlingame, Jonna M. Kulikowich, Nell Sedransk, Julie Coiro, & Clint Kennedy

As literacy educators, we live in new times with new literacies. The Internet, a central aspect of literacy and life, continually generates new technologies for information and communication, repeatedly requiring new literacies (Baker, 2010; Lankshear & Knobel, 2006). Being literate today does not necessarily ensure that one will be fully literate tomorrow since new technologies will always appear, regularly requiring additional new literacies. Thus, when we speak of new literacies in an online age, we mean that literacy is not just *new* today; it becomes *new* every day of our lives. How we adapt to new literacies in these new times will define us as literacy educators. Most importantly, how we adapt in the classroom will define our students' futures.

During this period of change, nations around the world have begun to develop specific educational plans, often with a special focus on literacy. Arguably, the most visible have been the Australian Curriculum (Australian Curriculum, Assessment and Reporting Authority, 2012) and the Common Core State Standards (CCSS) Initiative in the United States (National Governors Association Center for Best Practices & Council of Chief State School Officers [NGA Center & CCSSO], 2010). Initiatives like these seek to provide nations with systems of developmental standards to inform instruction. In the United States, the CCSS replace the "big five" of reading (phonemic awareness, phonics, fluency, vocabulary, and comprehension) with a richer, more complex English language arts framework. Two elements of the CCSS in particular are likely to impact classroom literacy instruction in profound ways:

1. An emphasis on higher level thinking during reading and writing instruction
2. A focus on acquiring skills in the new, digital literacies of online research and comprehension

This chapter explores both of these areas, recognizing that the digital literacies of online research and comprehension require, perhaps, even larger amounts and more complex types of higher level thinking than offline reading and writing. First, the chapter explains why the Common Core Standards have appeared and why the digital literacies of online research and comprehension as well as higher level thinking are emphasized. It also shares innovative assessments that evaluate students' abilities to conduct research online and write a short report. Finally, it explores how we might think about evaluating students' abilities with online research and comprehension in ways to inform instruction.

Why Have the CCSS Appeared Now?

Why is it at *this* time that the CCSS have appeared? Why do they include higher level thinking skills and new digital literacies that are important for online research and comprehension? One answer to both of these questions is a simple one—the literacy demands in the workplace have changed because the organization of workplace settings has changed (Kirsch, Braun, Yamamoto, & Sum, 2007; Reich, 1992; Rouet, 2006). Traditionally, industrial-age organizations were organized in a vertical, top-down fashion, where most decisions were made at the highest levels and then communicated to lower levels, limiting innovative or creative contributions throughout the chain of command. However, this approach wasted large amounts of intellectual capital within an organization, limited innovation, and, as a result, failed to maximize either creativity or productivity. Because employees at lower levels of the organization tended to simply follow directions, they were not required to possess or use higher level thinking skills or digital literacies.

Today, global economic competition requires that organizations abandon these traditional command-and-control structures and instead harness all of their intellectual capital, unleash innovation and creativity, and generate greater productivity. Otherwise, in a highly competitive global economy, they are literally out of business.

Organizations in post-industrial economies (Reich, 1992) achieve greater productivity and become more competitive by reorganizing themselves horizontally and organizing much of their work within collaborative teams. In addition to their regular duties, each team is charged with identifying and solving important problems that lead to better ways of producing goods or providing services within their team. High-performance workplaces take advantage of the literacy and problem-solving skills of every employee to increase creativity, innovation, and productivity (Smith et al., 2000). This economic change has important consequences for education.

Schools now need to prepare students with a wider range of higher level thinking and digital literacy skills important to the new workplace settings that have emerged. Skills such as the following become important for schools to consider:

- Identifying important problems
- Locating useful information related to the problems that are identified
- Critically evaluating information that is found, often online
- Synthesizing multiple sources of online information and evaluating arguments to determine a solution
- Communicating effectively to others with digital technologies
- Monitoring and evaluating the results of decisions, modifying these as needed

The transition from an industrial to a post-industrial society has happened rapidly in the United States. Within a single year, for example, Internet use in U.S. workplaces increased by nearly 60% among all employed adults 25 years of age and older (U.S. Department of Commerce, 2002). Companies have had to rapidly restructure into more flattened decision-making organizations in order to survive. Given the changing nature of the workplace, it is not surprising that the CCSS have emerged today and include an emphasis on both higher level thinking and the digital literacies of online research and comprehension.

It is important to recognize that these changes for school are not confined to a goal of simply creating more productive workers and workplaces. Even more importantly, the Internet provides individuals with opportunities to make their personal lives richer and more fulfilling. This happens while advocating for social justice, refinancing a home, selecting a university to attend, managing a medical crisis, purchasing books, or any one of hundreds of other tasks important to daily life. The CCSS have emerged as the nation has recognized the changing nature of work and life, and the need for schools to prepare students in new ways.

Higher Level Thinking Skills

The changing nature of work and life make it essential now to prepare students to transcend a simple, factual level of understanding and actually use information in creative and innovative ways to develop new ideas and solve complex problems. This requires higher level thinking skills. What are these? Many (Anderson & Krathwohl, 2001; Geertsen, 2003; Hopson, Simms, & Knezek, 2001) consider higher level thinking skills to include evaluation, synthesis, analysis, interpretation, and application. Viewing reading and writing from this perspective suggests it is important to teach students how to use information to create new knowledge and to communicate new ideas far beyond the simple, literal understanding of a passage. This is why the CCSS now include Anchor Standards (AS) for Reading (R) and Writing (W) that include elements of higher level thinking (see Table 16.1, specifically AS-R 6 and 8 and AS-W 7 and 9).

The New Literacies of Online Research and Comprehension

The CCSS also include digital literacies. How does the nature of reading and writing change on the Internet? What, if any, new literacies do we require? We are just discovering the answers to these questions (Afflerbach & Cho, 2010). Online reading comprehension, it appears, typically takes place within a research and problem-solving task (Coiro & Castek, 2011). Rather than simply reading for a general purpose, online reading comprehension is specifically focused to solve a particular problem or answer a particular question. In short, online reading comprehension is online research. Of course, you may also do this offline, but it is almost always done online.

Online reading also differs from traditional reading because it becomes tightly integrated with writing as we communicate with others to learn more about the questions we explore and as we communicate our own interpretations. E-mail, text messages, blogs, wikis, and many other new tools become important elements of online research and comprehension. Again, you may also do this offline, but it is almost always done online.

Table 16.1. Common Core Anchor Standards (AS) in Reading (R) and Writing (W) That Reflect Higher Level Thinking and the Digital Literacies of Online Research and Comprehension

Reading

AS-R 1. Read closely to determine what the text says explicitly and to make logical inferences from it; cite specific textual evidence when writing or speaking to support conclusions drawn from the text.

AS-R 2. Determine central ideas or themes of a text and analyze their development; summarize the key supporting details and ideas.

AS-R 4. Interpret words and phrases as they are used in a text, including determining technical, connotative, and figurative meanings, and analyze how specific word choices shape meaning or tone.

AS-R 5. Analyze the structure of texts, including how specific sentences, paragraphs, and larger portions of the text (e.g., a section, chapter, scene, or stanza) relate to each other and the whole.

AS-R 6. Assess how point of view or purpose shapes the content and style of a text.

AS-R 7. Integrate and evaluate content presented in diverse media and formats, including visually and quantitatively, as well as in words.

AS-R 8. Delineate and evaluate the argument and specific claims in a text, including the validity of the reasoning as well as the relevance and sufficiency of the evidence.

AS-R 9. Analyze how two or more texts address similar themes or topics in order to build knowledge or to compare the approaches the authors take.

AS-R 10. Read and comprehend complex literary and informational texts independently and proficiently.

(NGA Center & CCSSO, 2010, p. 10)

Writing

AS-W 1. Write arguments to support claims in an analysis of substantive topics or texts, using valid reasoning and relevant and sufficient evidence.

AS-W 2. Write informative/explanatory texts to examine and convey complex ideas and information clearly and accurately through the effective selection, organization, and analysis of content.

AS-W 6. Use technology, including the Internet, to produce and publish writing and to interact and collaborate with others.

AS-W 7. Conduct short as well as more sustained research projects based on focused questions, demonstrating understanding of the subject under investigation.

AS-W 8. Gather relevant information from multiple print and digital sources, assess the credibility and accuracy of each source, and integrate the information while avoiding plagiarism.

AS-W 9. Draw evidence from literary or informational texts to support analysis, reflection, and research.

AS-W 10. Write routinely over extended time frames (time for research, reflection, and revision) and shorter time frames (a single sitting or a day or two) for a range of tasks, purposes, and audiences.

(NGA Center & CCSSO, 2010, p. 18).

Furthermore, additional skills are required to effectively use new technologies such as browsers, search engines, wikis, blogs, and many others that are used online. Keyword entry in a search engine, for example, becomes an important new literacy skill because search engines are an important new technology for locating information. Other online technologies require additional new strategies during online reading.

Finally, and perhaps most importantly, online reading may require even greater amounts of higher level thinking than offline reading. In a context in which anyone may publish anything, higher level thinking skills—such as critical evaluation of source material and understanding an author's point of view—become especially important online. Moreover, rapid access to many different sources increases the importance of being able to logically integrate multiple source materials. One can quickly see that online reading may require even more higher level thinking than offline reading.

Therefore, a view of online reading comprehension is emerging as one that requires additional new skills, strategies, dispositions, and social practices as we increasingly rely on the Internet to conduct research, solve problems, and answer questions (Leu, Kinzer, Coiro, Castek, & Henry, 2013). In this chapter, we shall refer to this as online research and comprehension. At least five processing practices occur during online research and comprehension: (1) reading to identify important questions, (2) reading to locate information, (3) reading to evaluate information critically, (4) reading to synthesize information, and (5) reading and writing to communicate information (Leu, Kinzer, Coiro, & Cammack, 2004). Within these five areas reside the skills, strategies, and dispositions that are distinctive to online research and reading comprehension as well as others commonly found during offline reading in a complex blending that has yet to be fully understood.

Emerging research in the new literacies of online research and comprehension has provided us with a number of preliminary insights:

- Online research and comprehension are not isomorphic with offline reading comprehension; additional reading comprehension skills appear to be required (Afflerbach & Cho, 2010; Coiro, 2011).

- Some challenged offline readers who possess online research and reading comprehension skills may read online better than other students who lack online reading skills (Castek et al., 2011).

- Prior knowledge may contribute less to online research and reading comprehension than offline reading comprehension because readers may gather required prior knowledge online as a part of the reading paths they follow (Coiro, 2011).

- While adolescent "digital natives" may be skilled with social networking, texting, video downloads, MP3 downloads, and smashups, they are not generally skilled with online information use, including locating and critically evaluating information (Bennett, Maton, & Kervin, 2008).
- Students often learn many online research and comprehension skills from other students within the context of challenging activities designed by the teacher (Kiili, Laurinen, Marttunen, & Leu, 2012; Zawilinski, 2012).

How Are We Doing?

How have we been doing with incorporating these digital and informational literacy skills into our curriculum? As of now, we are not doing very well. While the United States awaits full implementation of the CCSS, state reading standards and state reading assessments have yet to include any online research and comprehension skills. This is surprising, given the fact that several international assessments have already begun to include these skills, such as PISA (Organisation for Economic Co-operation and Development, 2011) and the Programme for the International Assessment of Adult Competencies (PIAAC Expert Group on Problem Solving in Technology-Rich Environments, 2009).

Moreover, the following observations have not substantially changed since they were first observed a decade ago (Leu, Ataya, & Coiro, 2002):

1. Not a single state in the United States measures students' abilities to read search engine results during state reading assessments.
2. Not a single state in the United States measures students' abilities to critically evaluate information that is found online to determine its reliability.
3. In the United States, no state writing assessment measures students' abilities to compose effective e-mail messages.
4. Few, if any, states in the United States permit all students to use a word processor on their state writing assessments.

The New Literacies of Online Research and Comprehension Are Now Blended Into the CCSS

Perhaps the failure of states to include any digital literacies in their standards is one of many reasons that the CCSS have emerged. We see a conscious awareness of the need to include online research and comprehension skills and higher level thinking in one of the Common Core's "key design considerations," which is "research and media skills blended into the Standards as a whole" (NGA Center & CCSSO, 2010, p. 4). It states,

> To be ready for college, workforce training, and life in a technological society, students need the ability to gather, comprehend, evaluate, synthesize, and report on information and ideas, to conduct original research in order to answer questions or solve problems, and to analyze and create a high volume and extensive range of print and nonprint texts in media forms old and new. The need to conduct research and to produce and consume media is embedded into every aspect of today's curriculum. (NGA Center & CCSSO, 2010, p. 4)

In addition, the Common Core's "portrait of students" who are "college and career ready" also describes the need to include online research and comprehension skills. A key element of this description of students who are college and career ready is as follows:

> They use technology and digital media strategically and capably. Students employ technology thoughtfully to enhance their reading, writing, speaking, listening, and language use. They tailor their searches online to acquire useful information efficiently, and they integrate what they learn using technology with what they learn offline. (NGA Center & CCSSO, 2010, p. 7)

At least half of the Common Core Anchor Standards contain items, in both reading and writing, that reflect the shift to higher level thinking and online research and comprehension (see Table 16.1).

How Should We Assess Online Research and Comprehension That Requires Higher Level Thinking?

At the time of writing this chapter, assessments for the CCSS had not yet been presented. Therefore, we share here an initial model for assessing higher level thinking and online research and comprehension. The assessments are being developed by the Online Research and Comprehension Assessment (ORCA) Project (Leu, Kulikowich, Sedransk, & Coiro, 2009). This project is developing valid, reliable, and practical performance-based assessments of students' ability to conduct Internet research in science and write a short report of their results. A series of assessments in two different formats (Closed Internet and Scenario-Based,

Multiple Choice) have been developed, tested in cognitive labs, and pilot-tested among 1,200 students. They are now undergoing a final validation trial among representative state samples of 1,600 seventh-grade students in two states (Leu et al., 2012). These assessments are consistent with Common Core's Anchor Standards for Reading and Writing that focus on higher level thinking and the use of digital literacies for online research (see Table 16.1).

The Closed Internet Format (ORCA-Closed) asks students to conduct research and write a short report within a closed online environment, a simulation of the Internet, including a social network with chat capabilities, a search engine, e-mail, blogs, wikis, and over 400 websites. The Scenario-Based, Multiple Choice format (ORCA-Multiple Choice) provides students with the same set of research problems to solve within scenarios where decisions are evaluated from multiple-choice responses. The research problems in both formats come from science and focus on human body systems, a common curricular area for the seventh grade in every state.

During their research, students are evaluated in four areas of the online research and comprehension process: locating information, evaluating information, synthesizing information, and communicating information. You may view a video of one student taking the ORCA-Closed assessment, "Are Energy Drinks Heart Healthy?" by visiting this URL: neag.uconn.edu/orca-video-ira. The beginning sequence of this research activity is illustrated in Figure 16.1.

Locating Information

Figure 16.1 shows the opening sequence of chat messages from Brianna, a system-generated avatar, within a social network. Brianna presents a problem and the research question, directing each student to an e-mail where additional information about the research project may be found. When the student follows Brianna's directions and clicks on the text "Click here," an e-mail inbox appears with several possible messages from which to select. Here we assess the student's ability to evaluate the inbox message list and locate the correct e-mail message to open on the first click. Each student's actions are captured on a "back end" data capture system and scored.

Figure 16.1 also shows the window that appears, containing the e-mail message from the principal that defines the problem and research project. The principal asks the student to conduct research online on the question, "How do energy drinks affect heart health?" and then send a short report to the School Board President, Mrs. Kira Marin, via e-mail.

Figure 16.1. The Beginning Screen Sequences in the Assessment,
"Are Energy Drinks Heart Healthy?"

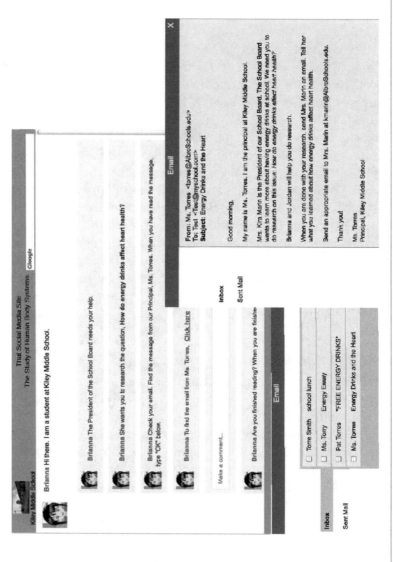

Note. To view a video of this assessment, please visit neag.uconn.edu/orca-video-ira.

Next, Brianna takes each student through several search tasks to locate relevant information for the research project. In each, students are asked to use keywords and a search engine to locate websites. During this portion of the research project, we capture and score students' abilities to define appropriate keywords for different types of search tasks. We also evaluate their ability to read search engine results by capturing and scoring their "first click" choice from the list of search results. Finally, students are evaluated on their ability to locate the URLs of two different sites and send these URLs to Brianna, via chat, when she requests them. "Locate" tasks require higher level thinking skills of evaluation and analysis. The following is a list of the four Locate skills that we evaluate, each related to Common Core AS-R and AS-W (see Table 16.1). We also identify the primary AS-R and AS-W that each skill most closely represents in **boldface,** with related Anchor skills in *italics*:

1. Given a problem in science and a specific social context, can the student locate the correct e-mail message in an inbox on the first click? (**AS-R 1;** *AS-R 7;* **AS-W 6**)

2. Given a problem in science and a specified informational context, can the student use appropriate keywords in a search engine? (*AS-R 1;* **AS-R 4;** *AS-W 6; AS-W 7;* **AS-W 8;** *AS-W 9*)

3. Given a problem in science and a specified informational context, can the student locate the best site for a task from a set of search engine results on the first click? (*AS-R 1;* **AS-R 7;** *AS-W 6; AS-W 7;* **AS-W 8;** *AS-W 9*)

4. Given a problem in science and a specified informational context, can the student locate and communicate the correct website addresses from two different search tasks? (AS-R 1; **AS-R 4;** AS-R 10; AS-W 6; **AS-W 7;** AS-W 8)

Evaluating Information

In the course of the research project, another avatar appears, and the student is asked to evaluate the source and reliability of one of the websites they located. "Evaluate" tasks require the higher level thinking skills of analysis and evaluation. The following is a list of the four Evaluate skills that we evaluate, each related to Common Core AS-R and AS-W (see Table 16.1). We also identify the primary Anchor skills for reading and writing that each most closely represents in **boldface,** with related Anchor skills in *italics*:

1. Can the student identify the author of the website? (**AS-R 1;** *AS-W 6;* **AS-W 9**)

2. Can the student evaluate the author's level of expertise? (**AS-R 1;** *AS-R 4; AS-R 8; AS-W 6; AS-W 7; AS-W 8;* **AS-W 9**)

3. Can the student identify the author's point of view? (*AS-R 5;* **AS-R 6;** *AS-W 1; AS-W 6; AS-W 8;* **AS-W 9**)

4. Can the student evaluate the reliability of a website? (*AS-R 4; AS-R 5; AS-R 6;* **AS-R 8;** *AS-R 10; AS-W 1; AS-W 2; AS-W 6; AS-W 7;* **AS-W 8;** *AS-W 9*)

Synthesizing Information

For each of the sites that students locate, Brianna asks students to summarize (synthesize) the most important information related to the research question in a notepad that appears. Students are also asked to synthesize information that they recorded in their notepads across two websites and finally provide a final summary, or synthesis, of what they read, across all four sites. In each of these tasks, the information they record in their notepad is captured and scored. "Synthesis" tasks require the higher level thinking skills of analysis and synthesis. The following is a list of the four Synthesis skills that we evaluate, each related to Common Core AS-R and AS-W (see Table 16.1). Primary Anchor skills for reading and writing that each task most closely represents appear in **boldface,** with related Anchor skills in *italics*:

1. Can students provide a summary of one important element from the first website using their own words that is relevant to the topic or that supports the given claim? (**AS-R 2;** *AS-R 7; AS-W 2; AS-W 6;* **AS-W 9;** *AS-W 10*)

2. Using notes from the notepad or information from the sites themselves, can students use their own words to integrate one detail from each of the first two websites relevant to the topic or that supports the given claim? (**AS-R 7;** *AS-W 2; AS-W 6;* **AS-W 9;** *AS-W 10*)

3. Using notes from the notepad or information from the sites themselves, can students use their own words to integrate one detail from each of the second two websites that is relevant to the topic or supports the given claim? (**AS-R 7;** *AS-W 2; AS-W 6;* **AS-W 9;** *AS-W 10*)

4. Using notes from the notepad or information from the sites themselves, can students use their own words to develop an argument after reading all four websites? (**AS-R 7;** *AS-W 1; AS-W 2; AS-W 6; AS-W 7;* **AS-W 8;** *AS-W 9; AS-W 10*)

Communicating Information

At the conclusion of their online research project, students are asked to write a short report, presenting their results to the President of the School Board, Mrs. Marin. During the e-mail task, four "Communicate" skills are assessed and are listed in the section that follows. Each is related to Common Core AS-R and AS-W (see Table 16.1). We also identify the primary Anchor skill for writing that each most closely represents in **boldface,** with related Anchor skills in *italics*:

1. Knowing the social content and the audience, does the student include the correct e-mail address in an e-mail message? (**AS-W 6**)

2. Knowing the social content and the audience, does the student include an appropriate subject line in an e-mail message? (**AS-W 6**)

3. Knowing the social content and the audience, does the student include an appropriate greeting in an e-mail message to an important, unfamiliar person? (**AS-W 6**)

4. Does the student compose and send a well-structured, short report of their research in an e-mail with sources and appropriate argument structure, containing at least one relevant claim and at least two pieces of evidence? (**AS-W 7;** *AS-W 8; AS-W 9; AS-W 10*)

Assessments of Online Research and Comprehension: A Double-Edged Sword

Effective instruction cannot take place without effective assessment to inform that instruction, but this can only happen when assessment is used appropriately. Used inappropriately, assessment can corrupt instruction and distort learning toward the mastery of specific, ungeneralizable knowledge. Thus, any literacy assessment is a double-edged sword; its utility is defined by how it is used.

Currently, we have few assessments of online research and comprehension. Without knowing how students perform in these important areas, teachers have little data with which to plan instruction. While assessment is not the only component of effective instruction, it is certainly one important element. Valid and reliable assessments of online research and comprehension that are also practical for teachers to use are essential if we are to effectively prepare students for the new opportunities that define work and life in this century.

The initial assessments developed in the ORCA Project have demonstrated good estimates of reliability and validity (Leu et al., 2012).

We also believe them to be innovative, taking a performance-based approach. Assessments developed in the ORCA Project measure actual online research and comprehension performance within the context of a complete research project, including keyword and search engine use as well as e-mail and wiki communication.

Nevertheless, ORCA Project assessments are not without their limitations. Most prominent, perhaps, is the need to score many of the constructed response items in the ORCA-Closed by hand. We have worked to streamline this task, but many items still require scorers trained to an adequate level of reliability, and each assessment takes about 10 minutes to score. To this end, we have developed similar scenario-based ORCA-Multiple Choice assessments that are quickly auto-scored by our system. We are evaluating this format in relation to the constructed responses of the ORCA-Closed assessments.

It is also important to recognize that any assessment of online research and comprehension will always have a more limited "shelf-life" compared with assessments of offline reading because ever-evolving new literacies are involved. The assessments we have developed will become dated over time. Additional technologies and new literacy practices will appear and become essential to the workplace and to daily life, prompting the need for revising the assessments on a regular basis and also, it should be noted, for revising the Common Core Standards regularly.

As the ORCA Project continues and as we learn more about the assessment of online research and comprehension, we are likely to discover additional limitations that are equally important. Nevertheless, the current assessments provide a useful starting point to understanding the assessment of online research and comprehension within authentic, performance-based tasks.

If used appropriately, assessments of online research and comprehension may lead to more effective instruction in at least two important ways. First, they may be especially useful in helping teachers and parents see and understand the types of higher level thinking and the types of literacy practices that are important to online research and comprehension. It is hard to teach something that is unfamiliar. Perhaps seeing activities such as those involved in the ORCA Project will yield greater understanding by teachers and parents about the types of skills, strategies, and literacy practices that are required during online research and comprehension.

Second, good instruction depends on knowing what students can do and what they have difficulty doing. Assessments of online research and comprehension that are connected to the CCSS provide teachers with a better understanding of their students' abilities in important new areas for literacy development. They will provide starting points for instruction in classrooms and can support the development of additional skills, strategies, and practices in classroom lessons and activities. Used inappropriately, however, they will only serve to limit our students' abilities, not expand them. This would happen, for example, if the topics in these assessments were the only online research topics assigned during the year or if the assessment's target websites were the only ones used to teach the critical evaluation of source information.

In the very best of worlds, assessments of online research and comprehension will serve to support teachers, parents, and students, showing them what is possible far beyond the specifics of any particular assessment. Good assessments of online research and comprehension demonstrate how skilled online readers may use their online research ability to develop a rich and sophisticated understanding of any area of knowledge that interests them and follow any dreams that they have for their future. It is essential that we quickly develop these to help both teachers and students make these dreams a reality.

TRY THIS!

- Teach the evaluation of search engine results by playing "One Click." Identify a current topic that you are studying in class, such as Japan. Use a search engine to conduct a search using this topic as a keyword. Print out enough hard copies of the search results to provide each student or student pair with a copy. Begin asking questions that require students to make inferences from the search results page to select the one site that meets the criteria you provide (e.g., "Which site would you pick if you wanted to find information that came from the Japanese government about Japanese history?"). Continue asking similar questions, and each time a student answers, ask the student, "How did you figure that out?" This will help identify valuable strategies that students can use during the evaluation of search engine results. After one or two sessions, ask students or teams of students to come up with the "One Click" questions to ask.

- Help students become better searchers by directing them to the resources at Google: Search Education at www.google.com/insidesearch/searcheducation. This site contains lesson plans, live training sessions, and a Google a Day Challenge.

DISCUSSION QUESTIONS

1. We live in a world filled with continually emerging new technologies, each requiring additional new literacies (e.g., Google Docs, Skype, Contribute, Basecamp, Dropbox, Facebook, Foursquare, Chrome, or any one of thousands of mobile apps). Identify the latest new online technology that you have encountered. Which new literacies and strategies does it require? Describe how you are acquiring them. What does this suggest for classroom learning?

2. Visit neag.uconn.edu/orca-video-ira and view the seventh-grade student completing the assessment of online research and comprehension, "Are Energy Drinks Heart Healthy?" What online research and comprehension skills do you see in this video? How is each important for online readers? Do your students have these skills? What might you do to support their development in your classroom?

3. You want to help your students develop communication skills with e-mail, blogs, and wikis, but all are blocked by your school district's filter. You have conducted online research and discovered two child-safe products that you like: ePals and Gaggle. You have set up a meeting with your principal to request that your district conduct a "pilot" of these tools in your classroom. What information will you provide your principal with when you make your request and how would you set up and evaluate the pilot use of these tools in your classroom?

NOTE

Portions of this material are based upon work supported by the U.S. Department of Education under Award No. R305G050154 and No. R305A090608. Opinions expressed herein are solely those of the authors and do not necessarily represent the position of the U.S. Department of Education.

REFERENCES

Afflerbach, P.A., & Cho, B.-Y. (2010). Determining and describing reading strategies: Internet and traditional forms of reading. In H.S. Waters & W. Schneider (Eds.), *Metacognition, strategy use, and instruction* (pp. 201–225). New York: Guilford.

Anderson, L.W., & Krathwohl, D.R. (Eds.). (2001). *A taxonomy for learning, teaching and assessing: A revision of Bloom's Taxonomy of educational objectives: Complete edition*. New York: Longman.

Australian Curriculum, Assessment and Reporting Authority. (2012). *The Australian Curriculum, version 3.0*. Retrieved December 9, 2012, from www.australiancurriculum.edu.au/Home

Baker, E.A. (2010). *The new literacies: Multiple perspectives on research and practice*. New York: Guilford.

Bennett, S., Maton, K., & Kervin, L. (2008). The 'digital natives' debate: A critical review of the evidence. *British Journal of*

Educational Technology, 39(5), 775–786. doi:10.1111/j.1467-8535.2007.00793.x

Castek, J., Zawilinski, L., McVerry, J.G., O'Byrne, W.I., & Leu, D.J. (2011). The new literacies of online reading comprehension: New opportunities and challenges for students with learning difficulties. In C. Wyatt-Smith, J. Elkins, & S. Gunn (Eds.), Multiple perspectives on difficulties in learning literacy and numeracy (pp. 91–110). New York: Springer. doi:10.1007/978-1-4020-8864-3_4

Coiro, J. (2011). Predicting reading comprehension on the Internet: Contributions of offline reading skills, online reading skills, and prior knowledge. Journal of Literacy Research, 43(4), 352–392. doi:10.1177/1086296X11421979

Coiro, J., & Castek, J. (2011). Assessment frameworks for teaching and learning English language arts in a digital age. In D. Lapp & D. Fisher (Eds.) Handbook of research on teaching the English language arts (3rd ed., pp. 314–321). New York: Routledge.

Geertsen, H.R. (2003). Rethinking thinking about higher-level thinking. Teaching Sociology, 31(1), 1–19. doi:10.2307/3211421

Hopson, M.H., Simms, R.L., & Knezek, G.A. (2001). Using a technology-enriched environment to improve higher-order thinking skills. Journal of Research on Technology in Education, 34(2), 109–119.

Kiili, C., Laurinen, L., Marttunen, M., & Leu, D.J. (2012). Working on understanding during collaborative online reading. Journal of Literacy Research, 44(4), 448–483. doi:10.1177/1086296X12457166

Kirsch, I., Braun, H., Yamamoto, K., & Sum, A. (2007). America's perfect storm: Three forces changing our nation's future. Princeton, NJ: Educational Testing Service. Retrieved December 9, 2012, from www.ets.org/Media/Research/pdf/PICSTORM.pdf

Lankshear, C., & Knobel, M. (2006). New literacies (2nd ed.). Maidenhead, Berkshire, England: Open University Press.

Leu, D.J., Ataya, R., & Coiro, J. (2002). Assessing assessment strategies among the 50 states: Evaluating the literacies of our past or our future? Paper presented at the National Reading Conference, Miami, FL.

Leu, D.J., Forzani, E., Kulikowich, J., Sedransk, N., Coiro, J., McVerry, G., et al. (2012). Developing three formats for assessing online reading comprehension: The ORCA project year 3. Washington, DC: American Educational Research Association.

Leu, D.J., Jr., Kinzer, C.K., Coiro, J.L., & Cammack, D.W. (2004). Toward a theory of new literacies emerging from the Internet and other information and communication technologies. In R.B. Ruddell & N.J. Unrau (Eds.), Theoretical models and processes of reading (5th ed., pp. 1570–1613). Newark, DE: International Reading Association. doi:10.1598/0872075028.54

Leu, D.J., Kinzer, C.K., Coiro, J., Castek, J., & Henry, L.A. (2013). New literacies: A dual level theory of the changing nature of literacy, instruction, and assessment. In D. Alvermann, N.J. Unrau, & R.B. Ruddell (Eds.), Theoretical models and processes of reading (6th ed., pp. 1150–1182). Newark, DE: International Reading Association.

Leu, D.J., Kulikowich, J., Sedransk, N., & Coiro, J. (2009). Assessing online reading comprehension: The ORCA Project (Research grant funded by the U.S. Department of Education, Institute of Education Sciences). Retrieved December 9, 2012, from www.orca.uconn.edu/orca-project/project-overview/

National Governors Association Center for Best Practices & Council of Chief State School Officers. (2010). Common Core State Standards for English language arts and literacy in history/social studies, science, and technical subjects. Washington, DC: Authors. Retrieved from www.core standards.org/assets/CCSSI_ELA%20 Standards.pdf

Organisation for Economic Co-operation and Development. (2011). PISA 2009 Results: Students on line: Digital technologies and performance (Vol. 6). doi:10.1787/9789264112995-en

PIAAC Expert Group on Problem Solving in Technology-Rich Environments. (2009). PIAAC problem solving in technology-rich environments: A conceptual framework (OECD Education Working Paper No. 36). Retrieved December 9, 2012, from www.oecd.org/officialdocuments/displaydocumentpdf/?cote=edu/wkp(2009)15&doclanguage=en

Reich, R.B. (1992). The work of nations: Preparing ourselves for 21st-century capitalism. New York: Vintage.

Rouet, J.-F. (2006). The skills of document use: From text comprehension to Web-based learning. Mahwah, NJ: Erlbaum.

Smith, M.C., Mikulecky, L., Kibby, M.W., Dreher, M.J., & Dole, J.A. (2000). What will be the demands of literacy in the workplace in the next millennium? *Reading Research Quarterly, 35*(3), 378–383. doi:10.1598/RRQ.35.3.3

U.S. Department of Commerce National Telecommunications and Information Administration. (2002). *A nation online: How Americans are expanding their use of the Internet.* Washington, DC: Author. Retrieved December 9, 2012, from www.ntia.doc.gov/legacy/ntiahome/dn/nationonline_020502.htm

Zawilinski, L. (2012). *An exploration of a collaborative blogging approach to literacy and learning: A mixed method study.* Unpublished doctoral dissertation, University of Connecticut, Storrs.

CHAPTER 17

Research Foundations of the Common Core State Standards in English Language Arts

P. David Pearson

The Common Core State Standards (CCSS; National Governors Association Center for Best Practices & Council of Chief State School Officers [NGA Center & CCSSO], 2010a) for English Language Arts (ELA) have achieved remarkable "purchase" in the educational community in the two years of their existence (at the time when this chapter was composed in the late summer of 2012). Some 46 states have adopted them, and even the states that haven't are being pressured to make sure that their unique state standards "entail" everything covered in the Common Core. The U.S. federal government has made an enormous investment (about $350,000,000 as of fall 2012) in the development of assessments to measure whether students—and, by implication teachers and schools— can meet the performance measures laid out in the grade-by-grade outline of the Standards. The primary authors of the ELA Standards, Coleman and Pimentel, have crafted a document dubbed the *Revised Publishers' Criteria* (2012) to guide the educational publishing industry in shaping the materials it develops to help educators meet the Standards. And there seems to be an increasingly large, seemingly endless stream of commercial materials lined up to capture the "market" in helping states, districts, schools, teachers, and students meet the Standards. So as our colleagues and policymakers plunge headlong into that stream, I wanted to step back, take a deep breath, and ask, why are we all so engaged in and committed to this effort? What is it about the Standards that renders them so compelling? In particular, I wanted to ask about the evidentiary basis of the assumptions about teaching and learning that undergird the Standards in the hope that we might evaluate whether it is that underbelly of evidence that we find so appealing.

But before addressing these research foundations, I feel compelled to make it clear to all readers that I am not a neutral observer in the

---

Quality Reading Instruction in the Age of Common Core Standards, edited by Susan B. Neuman and Linda B. Gambrell. © 2013 by the International Reading Association.

CCSS effort. I was a member of the Validation Committee that, in the year before the release of the CCSS in June 2010, was charged with the task of reviewing several drafts, providing feedback to the writers of the Standards and the sponsoring agencies (the NGA Center for Best Practices and the CCSSO), offering suggestions for revisions both major and minor, and ultimately blessing the release of the published version of the Standards with our vote of confidence. So, in a sense, I have placed my signature of approval on them as they currently exist. Even more important, I have—while continuing to criticize them for shortcomings that I hope will be fixed in a "revised edition"—championed their cause as vastly superior in concept and execution to any of the myriad of state standards that preceded them. I am not an innocent bystander in this effort; to the contrary, I have high hopes and high expectations for these Standards. Readers of this chapter deserve to know that.

Two features of these Standards in particular compel me to support them: (1) their vision of what it means to be an accomplished reader and (2) their outlook of how the Standards should (or should not) shape instruction at the school and classroom level. Their view of the accomplished reader, unpacked at the very outset of the Standards document, is a description of an active, engaged reader endowed with agency:

> Students who meet the Standards readily undertake the close, attentive reading that is at the heart of understanding and enjoying complex works of literature. They habitually perform the critical reading necessary to pick carefully through the staggering amount of information available today in print and digitally. They actively seek the wide, deep, and thoughtful engagement with high-quality literary and informational texts that builds knowledge, enlarges experience, and broadens worldviews. (NGA Center & CCSSO, 2010a, p. 3)

And their view of the role that Standards should play in the classroom suits my moral and ethical values about teachers and teaching. The body politic has the right to set the ends or goals for our schools and students, but teachers must have the prerogative to determine the means of achieving those ends:

> By emphasizing required achievements, the Standards leave room for teachers, curriculum developers, and states to determine how those goals should be reached and what additional topics should be addressed. (NGA Center & CCSSO, 2010a, p. 4)

These Standards then, at least in their idealized form, leave a little room for players at every level in the educational system to place their "signature" on the Standards. This is a model that treats teachers as the professionals that they are and ought to be.

My plan is straightforward: I will list what I take to be the key assumptions underlying the Standards and ask, for each, whether the research base is strong enough to merit our support and our commitment to implement them. This is not a meta-analysis or even a classic review of the literature. It is my personal and professional reading of the research.

Analyzing the Assumptions

My reading of the CCSS yields five key assumptions:

1. We know how reading develops across levels of expertise.
2. Literacy is best developed and enacted in the service of acquiring disciplinary expertise.
3. Standards establish ends or goals; teachers and schools control the means.
4. Students read better and learn more when they experience adequate challenge in the texts they encounter.
5. Comprehension involves building models of what a text says, what it means, and how it can be used.

As I examine each assumption, I will employ both theoretical and empirical lenses to gauge its validity. I realize that such evidence is a high bar to set for education standards, which more often than not invoke professional consensus (agreement among experts) or best practices (practices enacted by exemplary teachers or standards currently employed by high-performing countries or states) as the most important criteria in evaluating the validity and relevance of a new set of standards. Even so, empirical and theoretical evidence provide a useful touchstone, especially for the basic principles (i.e., assumptions) that underlie a set of standards. Why? Because such evidence represents the highest aspirations we can hold for the standards to which we hold our students, teachers, and schools accountable.

Assumption #1: We Know How Reading Develops Across Levels of Expertise

The CCSS for ELA Reading Standards consist of 10 College and Career Readiness Anchor Standards that represent common practices that students should be capable of enacting when they leave high school for higher education or the workplace. In addition, the CCSS document provides grade-level enactments of each of these Anchor Standards for both literary and informational texts and, from grades 6 through 12, there are also Standards for Literacy in History/Social Studies, Science, and Technical Subjects. It is across the grade-level Standards that we encounter the assumptions about what develops across time within disciplines. Implicit, if not explicit, in such a framework are learning progressions that underlie the standards—what students can or should do at every stage along the way.

It is no accident that learning progressions have been a key part of modern test development; with their emphasis on defining what students know and can do at each successive grade or level of expertise, they map readily onto item specifications that form the development of test items for various subtests that might comprise a longitudinal (cross-grade, for example) assessment system. Learning progressions are judged to be "validated" when the tests that are developed from them confirm that student performance conforms to the hypothesized progressions; that is, students can do A before B before C before D, but not D before B or C. It seems a natural and logical step to move from validated learning progressions to curricular "scope-and-sequence" charts. And in an idealized world of standards, assessments, and curricula, precisely these relationships would prevail.

Do the CCSS represent such an idealized world? Do the progressions for each of the 10 Anchor Standards for Reading represent "validated" stages of student development that logically and empirically precede and follow one another? Do we know, for example, that the second-grade version of Reading Standard 3 for Literature logically or empirically precedes the third-grade version and logically follows the first-grade version? In Table 17.1, I have listed the versions of CCSS Reading Standard 3 (Key Ideas and Details) from the Literature (L) and Informational (I) Text strands for K–5 (NGA Center & CCSSO, 2010a, pp. 11–14).

What is the basis of these progressions? First, for literary texts, from LK (Literature Standard 3 at kindergarten level) to L1 (Literature Standard 3 at grade 1), the difference is (a) scaffolding and (b) the number of things to be described (notice that in L1, one has to describe the entities using key details, but in LK, the entities only have to be identified). From L1 to L2, the focus shifts to characters, as the discussion of events and settings is dropped, as is the term "key details" (NGA Center & CCSSO, 2010a, p. 11). From L2 to L3, the emphasis on characters is retained, the infrastructure of the construct of character is expanded to include inner phenomena, and the requirement is added that those inner phenomena

Table 17.1. Progression of CCSS Reading Standard 3 for Literature and Informational Texts Across Grades K–5

Grade	Literature	Informational
K	With prompting and support, identify characters, settings, and major events in a story. (p. 11)	With prompting and support, describe the connection between two individuals, events, ideas, or pieces of information in a text. (p. 13)
1	Describe characters, settings, and major events in a story, using key details. (p. 11)	Describe the connection between two individuals, events, ideas, or pieces of information in a text. (p. 13)
2	Describe how characters in a story respond to major events and challenges. (p. 11)	Describe the connection between a series of historical events, scientific ideas or concepts, or steps in technical procedures in a text. (p. 13)
3	Describe characters in a story (e.g., their traits, motivations, or feelings) and explain how their actions contribute to the sequence of events. (p. 12)	Describe the relationship between a series of historical events, scientific ideas or concepts, or steps in technical procedures in a text, using language that pertains to time, sequence, and cause/effect. (p. 14)
4	Describe in depth a character, setting, or event in a story or drama, drawing on specific details in the text (e.g., a character's thoughts, words, or actions). (p. 12)	Explain events, procedures, ideas, or concepts in a historical, scientific, or technical text, including what happened and why, based on specific information in the text. (p. 14)
5	Compare and contrast two or more characters, settings, or events in a story or drama, drawing on specific details in the text (e.g., how characters interact). (p. 12)	Explain the relationships or interactions between two or more individuals, events, ideas, or concepts in a historical, scientific, or technical text based on specific information in the text. (p. 14)

Note. From National Governors Association Center for Best Practices & Council of Chief State School Officers. (2010). *Common Core State Standards for English language arts and literacy in history/social studies, science, and technical subjects* (pp. 11–14). Washington, DC: Authors. Available at www .corestandards.org/assets/CCSSI_ELA%20Standards.pdf

provide explanatory fabric for the plot structure of the narrative. At L4, we see an expansion to other elements of the story besides character (e.g., setting or event) that might be described and a parallel expansion to more character detail types (thoughts, words, or actions) that might be used to do the explaining. Then in grade 5, students are asked to do what they were asked to do in L4, but for two or more story elements (NGA Center & CCSSO, 2010a, p. 12).

A similar progression appears in the Reading Standards for Informational Text. The IK (Informational Text Standard 3 at kindergarten level) is just like the LK except for the difference in the entities that get connected (NGA Center & CCSSO, 2010a, p. 13). From IK to I1, students lose the prompting but the connection criterion remains. The move from I1 to I2 brings in disciplinary perspectives: events (in the general sense) move to *historical* events, ideas move to *scientific* ideas, and "pieces of information" is replaced by *technical procedures*. The move from I2 to I3 entails the use of discipline-specific discourse for the ideas; the "language that pertains to time, sequence, and cause/effect" are required (NGA Center & CCSSO, 2010a, p. 14). In I4, two elements are added: description is replaced by explanation, and the reader is required to base responses on the information in the text. Finally, in I5, the requirement for explanation moves from the individual entities to relationships and interactions between and among the entities—although what counts as an entity is a bit different in I4 (events, procedures, ideas, or concepts) than in I5 (individuals, events, ideas, or concepts).

So where did these sequences of Standards come from? What are their intellectual foundations? They certainly do not resemble any learning progression that I have ever seen from a test-development effort. They vaguely resemble what we might see in a scope-and-sequence chart from a basal reader. They appear to rely on common sense notions of how task complexity increases across grade levels. I found five distinct types of grade-to-grade shifts for the Reading Standards for K–5:

- Change in the level of **support**—the removal of scaffolding when moving from K to grade 1 for both L and I texts.

- Change in the **number** of entities involved in the process—in moving from L3 to L4, the number of entities increases—from characters in L3 to characters, settings, or events in L4.

- Change in the **type** of entities—in moving from I1 to I2, there is a change from general to discipline-specific entities. In moving from I4 to I5, the change is from explaining entities to explaining relationships and interactions.

- Increase in the **cognitive** demand(s) of the **process**—there is a change from description to explanation in moving from L2 to L3 and from I3 to I4; also moving from explanation to comparison in L4-L5.

- Addition of **evidentiary** requirements—represented in the move from I3 to I4.

Is there an evidence base for these progressions? Personally, I know of few, if any, studies that actually document the progression of performances for particular standards, such as summarizing, explaining details, inferring the meanings of unknown words, or comparing texts on a set of dimensions. The research base to document any given progression from K through grade 12 simply does not exist.

How, then, did the designers come up with these progressions? As I examine these progressions and the grade-to-grade changes, they have the look and feel of a professional consensus process in which knowledgeable experts in the field got together and used all of the intellectual resources available to them—research (in cases where there was relevant evidence—e.g., that even kindergartners can retell stories), best practices (in this case, exemplary standards documents from high-performing states and countries), and experience (and the judgment that comes with it)—to settle on a course of action for defining the progressions, particularly in areas in which the available research evidence was spotty.

I was able to document just such an account of the process by contacting the designers of the ELA Standards—David Coleman and Susan Pimentel—and the Math Standards (NGA Center & CCSSO, 2010c)—Phil Daro—who corroborated the process I have described (Daro, personal communication, 2012; Pimentel, personal communication, 2012). It was a consensus process, and those involved in the consensus did employ these three resources in coming to agreement about the specific version of each Anchor Standard at each grade level. So the degree to which these progressions are research based is a function of the degree to which those who designed and reviewed the Standards brought their knowledge of and commitment to the relevant research bases to their work.

Reliance on professional consensus to determine the specific nature of standards does not distinguish the CCSS from a host of other standards efforts. For decades, various professions have used the process of requiring an authoritative body to reach consensus on (a) the particular standards that the profession will impose on its members, (b) what counts as evidence that they have been achieved, and/or (c) what level of performance on some assessment is required to meet a particular standard. Sometimes that authoritative body comprises scholars in the field (e.g., legal scholars for the bar exam or educational scholars for standards like these), sometimes it comprises end users of the standards (e.g., teachers and administrators), and sometimes it includes ordinary taxpayers or policymakers (folks whose lives will be affected by the professionals who are accountable to the standards).

But professional consensus is not an independent, empirically validated research base. So, in a literal sense, the progressions in the CCSS for ELA do not have a rich and elaborate research base to support them—at least to support every transition in an Anchor Standard from one grade to the next.

However, in invoking a professional consensus process, the Standards tacitly admit to the "fallibility" of professional judgment and, by inference, to the need to review the Standards periodically to make sure that new knowledge, research, and best practices—as well as insights gained in trying to implement the Standards—are used to revise the Standards on a continuing basis. As a participant in the consensus process, I look forward to the regular revision of them in light of these developments. The idea of a set of standards as a living document that is constantly scrutinized for its validity, as opposed to one that is carved in stone for eternity, is a welcome image for the future.

Assumption #2: Literacy Is Best Developed and Enacted in the Service of Acquiring Disciplinary Expertise

The CCSS for ELA are all about the acquisition of knowledge, particularly disciplinary knowledge of the sort that one acquires in rigorous coursework in the sciences, social sciences, and humanities. In fact, in the introductory description of the accomplished reader, the authors emphasize knowledge acquisition as a major goal of the CCSS: "Students establish a base of knowledge across a wide range of subject matter by engaging with works of quality and substance" (NGA Center & CCSSO, 2010a, p. 7). Content acquisition requires, rationalizes, and enhances the use of literacy and language tools, such as reading, writing, and talking. As such, this doubly integrated view (among the language arts and between the language arts and the disciplines) presents a sharp contrast with the encapsulated view of reading as an independent subject, to be taught and measured on its own terms, as in the era of No Child Left Behind (NCLB). (Please note that the ideas in this section first appeared, in modified form, in a book chapter by Pearson & Hiebert [2013].)

Integration of language processes around literature has always been a staple in the K–12 language arts curriculum, but when disciplinary content (via history, science, or the arts) is added to the mix, the nature of instruction takes quite a different form. A disciplinary view of literacy recognizes that literacy is an essential part of any disciplinary practice and that different skills, knowledge, and reasoning processes are privileged as one moves from one discipline to the next (Heller & Greenleaf, 2007;

Shanahan & Shanahan, 2008). One of the most obvious ways in which literacy demands differ across disciplines is in the nature of the text (van den Broek, 2010). Texts that students encounter in history are quite different from those they encounter in chemistry or literature. Another transparent difference is in vocabulary (each discipline has its own jargon), but syntax is also different, as evident in a mathematical equation and a historical document. But differences exist on the processing side as well. Shanahan and Shanahan (2008) found that experts in different disciplinary areas approached the reading of texts in unique ways, and these unique approaches to reading reflect differences in the values, norms, and methods of scholarship within disciplines.

There is a growing body of research documenting the efficacy of a discipline-based approach to ELA curricular practices, with science leading the way (see Pearson, Moje, & Greenleaf, 2010). In general, integrated approaches have outperformed "encapsulated" approaches on a variety of measures (Cervetti, Barber, Dorph, Pearson, & Goldschmidt, 2012; Pearson et al., 2010; Greenleaf et al., 2011). While the research in social studies is not as extensive, what little exists favors integrated approaches (De La Paz & Felton, 2010; Halvorsen et al., 2012; Williams et al., 2007).

All things considered, this assumption seems moderately well documented in the research. Ironically, however, it is not well embedded in K–12 instruction. Reading instruction is still the province of literary study, both in the primary grades—where informational texts are truly marginalized (Duke, 2000), and in secondary schools—where reading is assigned to the English curriculum and poorly represented and seldom taught in other disciplines (Pearson et al., 2010). The CCSS for ELA provide hope that a disciplinary lens will be focused on literacy instruction in the years to come.

A corollary of Assumption 2 is that the responsibility for developing literacy should be shared by ELA and disciplinary teachers. And the implicit (if not explicit) message throughout the CCSS for ELA is that disciplinary teachers will have to share responsibility with English teachers in implementing, teaching, and measuring mastery of these Standards. The CCSS for ELA, then, are staking out a moral position about who bears responsibility for reading. But a moral imperative is not a reality, and it remains to be seen whether the mantle of disciplinary literacy, as intriguing and well documented as it is, will be taken up by educators over the next several years. The research base to support this assumption exists. Even a core set of instructional practices exists (e.g., Schoenbach, Greenleaf, & Murphy, 2012). But we still don't know whether professional expertise and professional practice will exist in the degree required to transform this moral imperative into a classroom reality. That will be one of the stiffest challenges these Standards face.

Assumption #3: Standards Establish Ends or Goals; Teachers and Schools Control the Means

The Standards tell a good tale of teacher and school empowerment. The quote from page 4 of the Standards (NGA Center & CCSSO, 2010a) that appears early in this chapter is as clear a commitment to teacher prerogative as one is likely to find in this era of accountability. And that commitment to prerogative and professional judgment is raised again on page 6 in discussing what is *not* covered by the Standards, specifically the need for schools and teachers to accommodate individual differences among students. Another index of the commitment of the CCSS to teacher learning is symbolized in the triadic model of text complexity. Two sides of the triangle are quantitative indexes of complexity (e.g., lexiles or readability) and qualitative (close examination of the linguistic demands of the text). These two are clearly the purview of technical analysts, but the third—reader and task considerations—is set squarely on the shoulders of teachers, as indicated in this statement in CCSS Appendix A:

> While the prior two elements of the model focus on the inherent complexity of text, variables specific to particular readers (such as motivation, knowledge, and experiences) and to particular tasks (such as purpose and the complexity of the task assigned and the questions posed) must also be considered when determining whether a text is appropriate for a given student. Such assessments are best made by teachers employing their professional judgment, experience, and knowledge of their students and the subject. (NGA Center & CCSSO, 2010b, p. 4)

The "deal" in this view of Standards is that the larger body politic (the nation, the profession, the state, the district, or the school) gets to set the goals (the signposts to guide the way), but teachers, either individually or collectively, get to determine the means by which they meet the goals. This is the view of standards championed in their initial instantiation in the late 1980s, when standards-based accountability was first proposed as a model of school reform at the historic Governors Conference in Charlottesville, VA, in 1989. And it certainly held sway for the decade of the 1990s, only to be replaced by a model, via the NCLB Act of 2001, that fixed both the ends of instruction (through state standards and accountability practices) and the means of instruction (through requirements that teachers follow officially sanctioned curricula) to a high degree of fidelity (Pearson, 2007).

The great irony of reform in this era is that research-based pedagogical practices for students (i.e., based on the Report of the National Reading Panel [National Institute of Child Health and Human Development, 2000]) were delivered to teachers using an approach (top-down external delivery of mandates) that essentially ignored the past 30 years of research on teacher learning. The research base on teacher learning (e.g., Lieberman & Wood, 2003; Richardson & Placier, 2002; Wilson & Berne, 1999) documents the efficacy of approaches to school change that (a) situate teacher learning within communities formed to support teacher learning and change efforts, (b) provide teachers with authority in determining the curricular practices they will implement, and (c) allow teachers to set the professional development agenda and deliver a substantial amount of the professional development activities within their own community. Top-down goals for curricular reform, it seems, can only achieve lasting realization when they are delivered through bottom-up approaches to change. The mechanism is the transparent commitment to change that individuals and groups develop when they have a stake in the effort, when they have placed their own "signatures" on the goals and the efforts to achieve them (Lieberman & Wood, 2003).

The question for the CCSS is whether they will deliver on their promise to cede to teachers the authority (or at least some of the authority) to determine how they will help their students meet the CCSS within their school settings. The Standards say, "yes, they will." But a recent document coming out of the CCSS movement says, "maybe not."

The publication of a recent document on the CCSS website, *Revised Publishers' Criteria for the Common Core State Standards in English Language Arts and Literacy, Grades 3–12* (Coleman & Pimentel, 2012), leads me to wonder whether the letter and spirit of the Standards document has been sacrificed in the service of influencing published programs and materials. The Standards, as I have argued twice, are noteworthy for the degrees of freedom that they cede to the local level, even classroom teachers. Again, the Standards "leave room for teachers, curriculum developers, and states to determine how those goals should be reached and what additional topics should be addressed" (NGA Center & CCSSO, 2010a, p. 4). But consider in Table 17.2 the sequence of verbatim passages from the *Revised Publishers' Criteria* illustrating how they undermine the promise of teacher choice in the Standards themselves. These directives to publishers directly contradict the commitment to teacher prerogative promised in the Standards. If publishers are persuaded to follow these

Table 17.2. Excerpted Directives From the *Revised Publishers Criteria* for the CCSS

Regarding the nature of tasks to guide discussion	A significant percentage of tasks and questions are text dependent…. Rigorous text-dependent questions require students to demonstrate that they not only can follow the details of what is explicitly stated but also are able to make valid claims that square with all the evidence in the text. Text-dependent questions do not require information or evidence from outside the text or texts; they establish what follows and what does not follow from the text itself. (p. 6)
Regarding the sequences of questions and tasks	The Common Core State Standards call for students to demonstrate a careful understanding of what they read before engaging their opinions, appraisals, or interpretations. Aligned materials should therefore require students to demonstrate that they have followed the details and logic of an author's argument before they are asked to evaluate the thesis or compare the thesis to others. (p. 10)
Regarding the need to stay close to the text	Materials make the text the focus of instruction by avoiding features that distract from the text. Teachers' guides or students' editions of curriculum materials should highlight the reading selections…. Given the focus of the Common Core State Standards, publishers should be extremely sparing in offering activities that are not text based. (p. 10)

Note. From *Revised Publishers' Criteria for the Common Core State Standards in English Language Arts and Literacy, Grades 3–12*, by D. Coleman & S. Pimentel, 2012. Washington, DC: National Governors Association Center for Best Practices and Council of Chief State School Officers. Available at www.corestandards.org/assets/Publishers_Criteria_for_3-12.pdf.

criteria, they will turn out scripts, not broad options. Unless teachers reject materials from the marketplace, teacher and school choice about how to "deliver the curriculum" will be markedly reduced, perhaps to the point that there is no real choice among the commercial alternatives. So teachers are promised choice and prerogative in the Standards only to learn that all of the materials available to them to deliver the curriculum are cut from the same cloth. I worry that if the *Revised Publishers' Criteria* prove effective, teachers will become cynical about the choices offered by the Standards.

Assumption #4: Students Read Better and Learn More When They Experience Adequate Challenge in the Texts They Encounter

The rationale for the increase in text complexity called for in the CCSS (e.g., see Anchor Standard for Reading 10, NGA Center & CCSSO, 2010a, p. 10) is straightforward: the gap between reading competence at the end of high school and the beginning of college is so great that we must begin a gradual increase in the level of complexity students encounter in grades 2 and 3 so that we can close what amounts to a gap of about a grade level and a half at the end of high school. The commitment is stated clearly in Appendix A of the CCSS: "Students need opportunities to stretch their reading abilities" (NGA Center & CCSSO, 2010b, p. 9).

Perhaps no feature of the CCSS is a greater challenge to the conventional wisdom in teaching reading than the text complexity commitment. Over the past 70 years, beginning with Betts (1946), we have converged on a theory of reader–text match that strives to find the optimal level of challenge for each reader, resulting in constructs such as independent (what I as a reader can manage on my own) and instructional (what I can manage with the help of a teacher or coach) levels. The goal has always been to maximize the amount of time that students spend reading in that "Goldilocks" zone—where books are neither too easy nor too hard, but "just right"—so that they help students achieve growth by requiring them to continually reach just beyond their grasp. But with the CCSS, we are told that such an approach, if implemented throughout the elementary and secondary years of schooling, will not provide enough challenge to ensure that students will leave our secondary schools ready for the literacy challenge of college or workplace careers.

In a recent essay, Hiebert and Mesmer (in press) have noted that the text complexity initiative of the CCSS rests on three key assumptions (the first two are assumptions of fact, and the last is a recommendation to remedy the situation):

1. Many current high school graduates are not prepared to read the texts of college and the workplace.
2. K–12 texts have decreased in complexity.
3. Increasing the complexity of texts from the primary grades onward can close the gap between the levels of texts in high school and college. (Hiebert & Mesmer, pp. 3–4)

The evidence in support of the first assumption is compelling. Williamson (2006, 2008) has undertaken extensive analysis of the level of complexity and difficulty in the texts required in high schools and college. Measuring complexity in Lexile levels, he found that the gap between 12th grade (1220L) and the first year of college (1350L) is about 130L. The typical grade-to-grade increase in the secondary years is about 50L; thus, if we want students to enter college or the workplace ready for the texts they meet, we will have to close about an 80L gap, or about 1.6 grade levels, on a readability scale.

Evidence for the second assumption is not quite as extensive but is certainly suggestive of a decline over time. Chall, Conrad, and Harris (1977) examined the 6th- and 11th-grade textbooks of the era to determine whether they were challenging our students as they had in the past. Using the Dale-Chall (1948) formula, which was validated on the textbooks in place during the 1940s and 1950s, Chall and colleagues found that the high school texts of the 1960s and 1970s did not measure up to those in earlier decades: 11th- and 12th-grade texts scaled in the 9th- and 10th-grade readability bands, thus providing a piece of the explanation for the puzzling decline in SAT scores in that era. Hayes and his colleagues (Hayes, Wolfer, & Wolfe, 1996) examined an extensive corpus of K–8 school texts in three eras to determine whether there had been a decline in text difficulty across the eras (1919–1945, 1946–1962, and 1963–1991). They did document a decline in text challenge for the later periods, but the decline was more consistent in the higher grades. Curiously, there was no decline for grade 3 texts. They could not conduct as systematic an analysis of high school texts across eras, but they did find that the average difficulty of grade 12 literature selections in the last era was lower than the average for 7th- and 8th-grade texts in the pre–World War I era. Thus, there is reason to believe, as the CCSS Appendix A asserts, that text complexity is on the decline—and, more important, is not up to the level required for success with postsecondary performance.

The third assumption, that we can get students back on track for college and career readiness by gradually increasing the linguistic complexity of texts required of students in grades 2–12, is, of course, the unknown; it awaits empirical evaluation. Certainly those who favor this approach can point to the predictive power of school-text complexity in explaining exit indicators, such as SAT scores (Chall et al., 1977; Hayes et al., 1996), as evidence in support of the recommendation to up the ante on text complexity throughout the grades. And there is at least a preliminary piece of evidence that an intervention based on this principle works: With Learning Oasis, developed by Hanlon and colleagues, students experience a sequence of ever more complex texts as they progress through a planned sequence of complexity (MetaMetrics, 2010). In essence, what Hanlon and colleagues have tried to do is embed the scaffolding that we usually cede to teachers within the digitally delivered text environment.

The big question for me (Pearson & Hiebert, 2013) is, What makes us think that we can improve things by expecting students to read *above*-grade-level texts when, in the current environment, we cannot manage to help our students handle texts that are *at* grade level? Unless something changes, I cannot imagine that the exhortation to teachers and students to try harder will succeed where serious efforts to bring students up to grade-level expectations have failed. A recent examination of the impact of text complexity and text length on comprehension (Mesmer & Hiebert, in press)—in particular the gap between student ability (as measured in Lexile units) and text complexity (again calibrated in Lexile units)—suggests that stretching the gap between ability and text challenge may be harder than we might imagine, at least in situations in which no teacher scaffolding is provided. For me, teacher scaffolding (what the CCSS authors refer to as reader-task elements) focused on making accessible texts that would otherwise fall into students' frustration level zone is both the key to making this recommendation work as well as the big unknown in the equation. The body of scholarship on rendering difficult texts accessible is small. We know that it can be done. In a sense that is what the comprehension strategies and text discussion are intended to do: help students approach and gain knowledge from challenging texts. But I have seen little research focused on the differential effects of a range of text-accessibility scaffolds on the understanding of texts that range in both linguistic and conceptual complexity.

So what is the final word on the research foundations of this assumption? It is a mixed message. There is certainly good reason to conclude, based on trustworthy scholarship, that the level of challenge in texts used in schools today is not what it *needs* to be—that our current diet of school texts is not paving the way to college and career readiness. And there is reason to believe that text challenge is not what it *used* to be either. Finally, I agree that it is critical to support teachers and students in their attempts to meet a more challenging portfolio of texts. There is some support for engineering scaffolding into instructional learning materials and environments. And there is a lot of research to document teacher efficacy: Teachers can do much, via ambitious instruction and rich text discussions, to support access to difficult texts. What we do not know, and need to conduct research to learn, is whether these sorts of scaffolds will eventually enable students to manage complexity on their own. And self-sufficient learners and workers is the only acceptable outcome for college and career readiness.

Assumption #5: Comprehension Involves Building Models of What a Text Says, What It Means, and How It Can Be Used

Key Components of a C-I Model. My initial reading of the Standards, particularly the introduction and the 10 Anchor Standards for Reading, led me to conclude that the writers of the Standards had paid attention to the cognitive research of the past 40 years. By all accounts, the Standards take seriously the view of reading comprehension emanating from the cognitive revolution, particularly the construction-integration (C-I) models elaborated in the past 15 years by scholars such as Kintsch (1998), van den Broek, Young, Tzeng, and Linderholm (1999), and Perfetti (1999).

In a C-I model (e.g., Kintsch, 1998), two levels of representation are critical—the text base and the situation model. For Kintsch, the *text base* involves an accurate reading of the text for the purpose of getting its key ideas into working memory. But even in building this accurate rendition of the text, knowledge plays a key role. We use our knowledge of the world, along with our knowledge of how language and text work, to make all the local inferences required to connect the sentences to one another— to build, if you will, a coherent representation of "what the text says." Consider the following sentences:

1. Henry desperately wanted to buy a baseball glove.

2. He took a job delivering newspapers in his local neighborhood.

Connecting pronouns to their antecedents is one kind of linking inference (for example, figuring out that the *he* in sentence 2 refers to *Henry* in sentence 1). Another kind of local inference is making logical connections among ideas or events in the text. In the example sentences, this means that a local inference is involved in figuring out that wanting a new baseball glove was a key motive in prompting Henry to take the job delivering newspapers.

The kind of reading involved in constructing a text base is what is called for in CCSS Anchor Standard for Reading 1: "read closely to determine what the text says explicitly" (NGA Center & CCSSO, 2010a, p. 10). It is also central to Reading Anchor Standards 2 (central ideas) and 3 (idea development), and to certain degrees, Standards 5 (text structure) and 8 (evaluate arguments).

A second level of representation is the *situation model.* The situation model is the coherent mental representation of the events, actions, and conditions in the text. Readers integrate information from the text base (the initial representation of the words, sentences, and paragraphs) with available and relevant prior knowledge retrieved from long-term memory and integrate it all into an emerging situation model that represents meaning of the text at that point in the process. If the text base is an account of what the text *says*, then the situation model can be thought of as an account of what the text *means.* A compelling situation model requires readers to meet two standards: (a) the model has to be consistent with the current text base (up to that point in the reading), and (b) it must be consistent with the store of relevant prior knowledge activated up to that point.

When readers build a situation model, they rely even more heavily on background knowledge and inferential processes than in building a text base. In the scenario with Henry and the baseball glove, for example, readers might infer, even on the basis of minimal information from the text base, that Henry is a self-motivated, independent person who understands that he has to work for what he wants in life. They might also have to connect the idea of a newspaper deliverer with their schema for newspaper delivery in different neighborhoods, and they might infer that the neighborhood in which Henry lives is more suburban than urban or rural. At a simpler level, a first grader who reads that George Washington chopped down a cherry tree will infer that he used a hatchet or an axe to perform the act. And writers of narratives often omit the motives that drive characters to particular actions in a story on precisely the grounds that readers can and will use their knowledge of stories, life experiences, and human nature to infer those motives. In the scenario for Henry, we would have to infer, based on our own experiences, why Henry was so desperate for a new glove: perhaps his old glove was worn out, or maybe he had made an all-star team, or it could be that his old glove was embarrassingly out of date.

Constructing a situation model is central to reading comprehension. It is the mechanism that allows readers to integrate what they already know with what they read—and, equally as important, it is on the pathway to building new knowledge structures; these new knowledge structures will modify or replace those currently in long-term memory.

Just as knowledge drives comprehension, so does comprehension drive knowledge production and refinement. This is the kind of reading that is emphasized in CCSS (NGA Center & CCSSO, 2010a, p. 10) Anchor Standards for Reading 7 (synthesize and apply information presented in diverse ways) and 9 (compare texts) , and it is implicated in Standards 4 (interpret words and phrases) and 6 (assess point of view). One can build a strong argument that situation model construction is entailed in, if not licensed by, Standards 1–3; verbs such as *analyze, summarize, develop,* and *interact* are the essence of integrating ideas across texts, sentences, ideas, and experiences.

The Standards Research Base Mapping. When I read the Standards before they were released, I recognized that the authors of the Standards did not portray everything in precisely the same way that I would have. For example, the CCSS allocate more attention to "constructing" a text base—and a bit less attention to building an "integrated" situation model—than I would have. I thought they gave minimal attention to the sociocultural context in which reading occurs and comprehension is enacted; readers—as I knew and the research documented—read and understand differently as a function of the purpose (where, when, and why one is reading) and academic traditions (personal response, an authorial reading, or a critical reading) that the context brings to the reader. But the family resemblance between the model implicit in the Standards and my reading of the research base was clear. Indeed, there was so much to like about the focus on understanding and knowledge building (that's what happens when the information in the situation model seeps back into a reader's long-term memory and expands the reader's knowledge base), that it seemed appropriate to cut the Standards a little slack on a few minor points of disagreement.

And for at least a year after their initial publication, I felt as though I could say, in good conscience, that the CCSS for Reading were based on a fair recognition of the cognitive research base in reading—with at least a tip of the hat to an ever-expanding sociocultural research base. And I felt that if teachers at all grade levels would worry about the twin goals of building a solid *text base* and equally solid *situation model*, we would be helping students figure out what texts "say" and what they "mean" in their quest for an expanded knowledge base. That for me was the point of this whole effort—and what merited our strong support as a profession.

Revised Publishers' Criteria. But all that changed for me with the publication of the *Revised Publishers' Criteria* (Coleman & Pimentel, 2012), which I already cited as compromising the CCSS promise of teacher prerogative and the research documenting the key role of teacher aegis in curriculum reform. I think the *Revised Publishers' Criteria* document represents an equally strong betrayal of the view of comprehension that undergirds the Standards themselves.

As I suggested and documented earlier, the Standards themselves tell a comprehension story characterized by balance between the text and the reader in determining legitimate interpretations or readings of text. Several Anchor Standards for Reading (1, 2, 3, 5, and 8) privilege close readings of the content "on the page," while others promote integration (2, 7, and 9), and still others privilege analysis and interpretation of the text (4, 6, and 8).

Not so with the *Revised Publishers' Criteria*. There is a bit of waffling. For example, in the first quote, the phrase "make valid claims that square with all the evidence in the text" (Coleman & Pimentel, 2012, p. 6) implies that the claim could come from outside the text. An example might be a word or phrase to describe a character's values or character (he's a real villain!) that, while not *in* the text, is licensed by the text. But the quote goes on to say, "Text-dependent questions do not require information or evidence from outside the text" (Coleman & Pimentel, 2012, p. 6), a position that would seem to block inferences to prior knowledge. The second quote in Table 17.2 seems to argue that text-based reading should be logically precedent to either evaluation or comparison, two processes that presumably invoke prior knowledge. And the third quote in Table 17.2 is a kind of consumer warning about the seductive character of knowledge-based activities.

My suspicion is that Coleman and Pimentel (2012) were persuaded that many of the "building background prior to reading" segments of basal lessons or the personally witnessed versions of prereading picture walks and discussions of relevant knowledge and experiences were pushing the text out of reading lessons. I have witnessed my share of 40 minutes of experience swapping followed by 3 minutes of eyes on print as well. I agree that these sorts of extravagances and distortions of the "new to known" principle of learning deserve our whole-hearted critique. But the remedy is not, I think, to eradicate or minimize the role of knowledge in comprehension and discussion but rather to balance it vis-à-vis the text. It is the constant orchestration of *constructing* a text base and *integrating* it, along with knowledge, into a situation model, that we want to promote. And we must always keep in mind the advantage that readers accrue once information is encoded in the situation model: It stands ready to be incorporated into our existing store of knowledge in long-term memory, where it can serve in a knowledge role in the next cycle of comprehension and knowledge building.

Misconstruing the Comprehension Process. But the main reason to object to the "keep prior knowledge at bay" principle that pervades the *Revised Publishers' Criteria* is that it reveals a fundamental misunderstanding of the comprehension process. It is not as though prior knowledge was an "optional" cognitive move that one could turn on or turn off at will. A reader cannot build a text base or a situation model without invoking relevant prior knowledge; there is nothing voluntary about it.

Recall the scenario about Henry and the baseball glove. The knowledge base had to be accessed to make all the links between anaphora (pronouns and the like) and the referents (names and verbs) to which they point. And knowledge (about what drives people to different actions) was the primary resource for making the logical inferences between Henry's actions and motives, such as wanting the glove and getting a job.

But the links from text to knowledge go even deeper in building a text base. Individual words encountered in the text base in the current construction cycle determine which schemata will be called up from prior knowledge, and until those schemata are activated, there is no text base construction—and no comprehension.

One of the most telling quotes from the *Revised Publishers' Criteria* (Coleman & Pimentel, 2012), which focuses on the primacy of text and close reading, implicates this issue of what counts as the text in building a text base:

> The Common Core State Standards place a high priority on the close, sustained reading of complex text, beginning with Reading Standard 1. Such reading focuses on what lies within the four corners of the text. (p. 4)

The four corners metaphor is very appealing (after all, it implies close reading that is both comprehensive and deep), but it introduces a puzzlement. Does it refer to the four corners of the page? Or could it be a folio (2-page spread)? A section or a chapter? And when one stays within the four corners of the page, does that evoke a different close-reading process than the close-reading process that is evoked when one stays within the four corners of, say, a chapter—where some of the "text" is not easily available for ready inspection and reference? Is linking the ideas in two adjacent sentences the same as linking the ideas in two sentences that are four sentences apart? How about four pages apart?

We don't have basic research available to answer these questions, but they raise a fundamental dilemma: as a reader moves across successive cycles of construction, integration, and restructuring one's knowledge base, at what point does information that was in the first sentence or two of processing vacate the text and become a part of the knowledge base that one uses in later C-I cycles? Is there a real difference between an idea that entered my knowledge base from reading I did three weeks ago, three pages back, three minutes ago, and three seconds ago? The slope between the text base and the knowledge base is indeed slippery.

Finally, knowledge is implicated in the ongoing "monitoring" process in which a reader asks, "Does this all make sense?" because the only standard available for sense-making is a reader's cumulative knowledge store about what normally happens in the sorts of situations described in the text. Now just as surely, the other standard for sense-making is the text base one has constructed up to that point in the reading. In fact, what drives comprehension is the perception that one's account of the current situation model meets the joint constraints of one's relevant prior knowledge (Is this consistent with what I know to be true of the world?)

and the current text base (Does this square with the message I am getting from the text?). Text and knowledge are the standards by which the validity of comprehension is judged.

Asking students to resist appealing to prior knowledge as they try to understand text is like asking leaves not to fall or dogs not to bark. Leaves fall and dogs bark; it's in their nature. And it's in the nature of comprehension to use knowledge to carry out the various aspects of the process: constructing meaning, integrating new with known information, and monitoring for meaning. Ceding the point that as a profession we have overindulged at the trough of prior knowledge (too much building background at the expense of active reading of text), the remedy is to balance its role, not eliminate it. One hope is that the next revision of the *Publishers' Criteria* will be better aligned with the knowledge base for reading comprehension. The Standards are likely to need less revision on this assumption.

Conclusions

So what is the bottom line on the CCSS for ELA in terms of their research foundations? Are the Standards based upon substantial and up-to-date findings from research about teaching, learning, and reading? If so, is that research transparently represented in the public presentation of the Standards? Finally, based on an analysis of current developments in the Standards movement, is there reason to believe that the implementation of the CCSS will remain true to their intentions and to the research on which they are based?

As a way of summarizing the points elaborated in the preceding pages, I have organized the major points in Table 17.3. I have rated the research base on three of the assumptions in the "strong" category— disciplinary grounding, teacher prerogative, and comprehension model. Among those three, I viewed their clarity in the Standards as high or moderately high. Text complexity was rated moderate on the research base but very strong on the clarity of representation: whatever it is we know about text complexity is *in* the Standards. When it comes to my assessment of the likelihood of implementation, it varies, but for different reasons. I think that disciplinary literacy and text complexity are likely to be implemented as described in the Standards. Why? Because the research is transparent and the press for each assumption is distributed across a wide range of current movements, such as deeper learning, project-based learning, and a variety of efforts to increase the challenge of curriculum (e.g., National Research Council, 2012). I have rated the other

Table 17.3. Evaluation of the Assumptions Underlying CCSS-ELA

Assumption	Strength of Research Base	Clarity of Representation in the Standards	Likelihood of High-Fidelity Implementation
Learning Progressions	Very Weak	Low	Low
Disciplinary Grounding	Strong	High	High
Teacher Prerogative	Moderately Strong	High	Low
Benefits of Text Complexity	Moderate	Very High	High
Comprehension Model	Strong	Moderately High	Low

three assumptions—learning progressions, teacher prerogative, and the comprehension model—as unlikely to be implemented with fidelity to the research base.

Learning progressions *will* be implemented; that is for certain—but not with fidelity to any research base but with fidelity to the consensus-based progressions that are in the Standards. In short, students, teachers, and schools will be held accountable to a set of plausible, perhaps even reasonable, but thoroughly untested progressions; the question that only time can answer is whether these progressions will promote growth on the cognitive processes that they are supposed to index.

Teacher prerogative and the comprehension model, two assumptions that are strongly represented in the Standards and clearly based on research, will not, in my view, be implemented with a high degree of fidelity, because the guidelines in the *Revised Publisher's Criteria* are likely to undermine the Standards as they are written. Only if schools can resist these guidelines and stay true to the version of the Standards in the original document do we have a hope of a high-fidelity implementation of what we know about reading comprehension and about teacher learning within school-change efforts.

These deep concerns and misgivings notwithstanding, I have supported and will continue to support the CCSS movement. Why? For three reasons. First, compared with their alternative—the confusing and conflicting world of 50 versions of state standards—the CCSS are clearly the best game in town. Second, with any luck, these will prove to be "living Standards" that will be revised regularly so that they are *always* based on our most current knowledge. Third—and most important—my reading of the theoretical and empirical scholarship on reading comprehension and learning lead me to conclude that these Standards are definitely a move in the right direction—toward (a) deeper learning, (b) greater accountability to careful reading and the use of evidence to support claims and reasoning in both reading and writing, and (c) applying the fruits of our learning to improve the world beyond schooling and text.

TRY THIS!

- Use a discussion web to help students consider relevant and irrelevant information in math story problems. For example, in the center of the page draw a circle and write this question: "Which information is needed to solve the problem?" Then, draw an arrow from the left of the circle and label that column "Irrelevant." Draw an arrow from the right side of the circle and label that column "Relevant." Finally, draw an arrow from the bottom of the circle and label the box "Solution." In this way, students can differentiate between sources of information needed to solve the problem.

- Use the guided reading procedure to emphasize a close reading of any text of your choice. This procedure requires that students gather information and organize it around pertinent ideas, and helps students develop a strong factual base, as follows:

  1. Prepare students for reading by clarifying key concepts, building background knowledge, and providing direction for reading.

  2. Assign a reading selection and provide a general purpose for reading, such as "Read to remember all you can."

  3. As students finish reading, have them turn books face down, and ask them to tell what they remember by writing things they remember on the whiteboard.

  4. Help students realize if they have missed some important information or remembered some incorrectly.

  5. Redirect students to their books and review the text selection to correct inconsistencies and add more important information.

  6. Organize the new information into some kind of outline.

  7. Question students to stimulate their analysis of the material and synthesis with previous material.

  8. Provide immediate feedback, such as a short quiz, as a reinforcement of short-term memory.

DISCUSSION QUESTIONS

1. According to Pearson, literacy practice occurs best within content area disciplines where students are given the opportunity to engage in literacy strategies that enhance their understanding of the content. However, in many schools, literacy instruction is most often tied directly to literature and falls within the purview of ELA teachers only. How can students' levels of expertise in reading increase if content area teachers embrace the idea that literacy practices occur when students interact with authentic texts in content-specific disciplines?

2. One of the selling points of the CCSS is the autonomy the Standards award teachers (that is, the CCSS afford teachers the leeway to form their own instructional plans and assessments in order to achieve the Standards). However, as Pearson notes, the release of the *Revised Publisher's Criteria* may impede any autonomy ceded by the CCSS. Locate the *Revised Publisher's Criteria* and skim the document to evaluate its purpose. Then, decide how it could limit the freedom established by the CCSS.

3. In Table 17.3, Pearson evaluates the assumptions underlying the CCSS. Discuss how each component is (or is not) addressed in the CCSS, and decide your stance on the implementation of the CCSS. How will this decision impact your own personal adoption of the primacy of the role of the CCSS in your classroom?

REFERENCES

Betts, E.A. (1946). *Foundations of reading instruction, with emphasis on differentiated guidance.* New York: American Book Company.

Cervetti, G.N., Barber, J., Dorph, R., Pearson, P.D., & Goldschmidt, P.G. (2012). The impact of an integrated approach to science and literacy in elementary school classrooms. *Journal of Research in Science Teaching, 49*(5), 631–658. doi:10.1002/tea.21015

Chall, J.S., Conrad, S.S., & Harris, S.H. (1977). *An analysis of textbooks in relation to declining SAT scores.* Princeton, NJ: College Entrance Examination Board.

Coleman, D., & Pimentel, S. (2012). *Revised publishers' criteria for the Common Core State Standards in English Language Arts and Literacy, grades 3–12.* Washington, DC: National Governors Association Center for Best Practices & Council of Chief State School Officers. Retrieved from www.core standards.org/assets/Publishers_Criteria_for_3-12.pdf

Dale, E., & Chall, J.S. (1948). A formula for predicting readability. *Educational Research Bulletin, 27*(2), 11–20, 28. Retrieved December 11, 2012, from www.jstor.org/stable/1473669

De La Paz, S., & Felton, M.K. (2010). Reading and writing from multiple source documents in history: Effects of strategy instruction with low to average high school writers. *Contemporary Educational Psychology, 35*(3), 174–192. doi:10.1016/j.cedpsych.2010.03.001

Duke, N.K. (2000). 3.6 minutes per day: The scarcity of informational texts in first grade. *Reading Research Quarterly, 35*(2), 202–224. doi:10.1598/RRQ.35.2.1

Greenleaf, C.L., Litman, C., Hanson, T.L., Rosen, R., Boscardin, C.K., Herman, J., et al. (2011). Integrating literacy and science in biology: Teaching and learning impacts of Reading Apprenticeship professional development. *American Educational Research Journal, 48*(3), 647–717. doi:10.3102/0002831210384839

Halvorsen, A.L., Duke, N.K., Brugar, K.A., Block, M.K., Strachan, S.L., Berka, M.B., et al. (2012). Narrowing the achievement gap in second-grade social studies and content area literacy: The promise of a project-based approach. *Theory & Research in Social Education, 40*(3), 198–229. doi:10.1080/00933104.2012.705954

Hayes, D.P., Wolfer, L.T., & Wolfe, M.F. (1996). Sourcebook simplification and its relation to the decline in SAT-Verbal scores. *American Educational Research Journal, 33*(2), 489–508.

Heller, R., & Greenleaf, C.L. (2007). *Literacy instruction in the content areas: Getting to the core of middle and high school improvement.* Washington, DC: Alliance for Excellent Education.

Hiebert, E.H., & Mesmer, H.A. (in press). Upping the ante of text complexity in the Common Core State Standards. *Educational Researcher.*

Kintsch, W. (1998). *Comprehension: A paradigm for cognition.* Cambridge, England: Cambridge University Press.

Lieberman, A., & Wood, D.R. (2003). *Inside the National Writing Project: Connecting network learning and classroom teaching.* New York: Teachers College Press.

Mesmer, H.A., & Hiebert, E.H. (in press). *How far can third graders be stretched?* Santa Cruz, CA: TextProject.

MetaMetrics. (2010). Learning Oasis. [Digital learning platform and interactive application software]. Retrieved from alearningoasis.com

National Governors Association Center for Best Practices & Council of Chief State School Officers. (2010a). *Common Core State Standards for English language arts and literacy in history/social studies, science, and technical subjects.* Washington, DC: Authors. Retrieved from www.corestandards.org/assets/CCSSI_ ELA%20Standards.pdf

National Governors Association Center for Best Practices & Council of Chief State School Officers. (2010b). *Common Core State Standards for English language arts and literacy in history/social studies, science, and technical subjects: Appendix A: Research supporting key elements of the Standards and glossary of key terms.* Washington, DC: Authors. Retrieved

from www.corestandards.org/assets/ Appendix_A.pdf

National Governors Association Center for Best Practices & Council of Chief State School Officers. (2010c). *Common Core State Standards for Mathematics.* Washington, DC: Authors. Retrieved from www.corestandards.org/assets/CCSSI_ Math%20Standards.pdf

National Institute of Child Health and Human Development. (2000). *Report of the National Reading Panel. Teaching children to read: An evidence-based assessment of the scientific research literature on reading and its implications for reading instruction* (NIH Publication No. 00-4769). Washington, DC: U.S. Government Printing Office.

National Research Council. (2012). *Education for life and work: Developing transferable knowledge and skills in the 21st century.* Washington, DC: The National Academies Press.

Pearson, P.D. (2007). An endangered species act for literacy education. *Journal of Literacy Research, 39*(2), 145–162.

Pearson, P.D., & Hiebert, E.H. (2013). Understanding the Common Core State Standards. In L.M. Morrow, T. Shanahan, & K.K. Wixson (Eds.), *Teaching with the Common Core Standards for English Language Arts, preK–2* (pp. 1–21). New York: Guilford.

Pearson, P.D., Moje, E., & Greenleaf, C. (2010). Literacy and science: Each in the service of the other. *Science, 328*(5977), 459–463. doi:10.1126/science.1182595

Perfetti, C.A. (1999). Comprehending written language: A blueprint of the reader. In C.M. Brown & P. Hagoort (Eds.), *The neurocognition of language* (pp. 167–208). New York: Oxford University Press. doi:10.1093/acprof:oso/9780198507932.003 .0006

Richardson, V., & Placier, P. (2002). Teacher change. In Richardson, V. (Ed.), *Handbook of research on teaching* (4th ed., pp. 905–947). Washington, DC: American Educational Research Association.

Schoenbach, R., Greenleaf, C., & Murphy, L. (2012). *Reading for understanding: How Reading Apprenticeship improves disciplinary learning in secondary and college classrooms* (2nd ed.). San Francisco: Jossey-Bass.

Shanahan, T., & Shanahan, C. (2008). Teaching disciplinary literacy to adolescents: Rethinking content-area literacy. *Harvard Educational Review, 78*(1), 40–59.

van den Broek, P. (2010). Using texts in science education: Cognitive processes and knowledge representation. *Science, 328*(5977), 453–456. doi:10.1126/science.1182594

van den Broek, P., Young, M., Tzeng, Y., & Linderholm, T. (1999). The landscape model of reading: Inferences and the online construction of memory representation. In H. van Oostendorp & S.R. Goldman (Eds.), *The construction of mental representations during reading* (pp. 71–98). Mahwah, NJ: Erlbaum.

Williams, J.P., Nubla-Kung, A.M., Pollini, S., Stafford, K.B., Garcia, A., & Snyder, A.E. (2007). Teaching cause–effect text structure through social studies content to at-risk second graders. *Journal of Learning Disabilities, 40*(2), 111–120. doi:10.1177/00222194070400020201

Williamson, G.L. (2006). *Aligning the journey with a destination: A model for K–16 reading standards—A white paper from The Lexile Framework for Reading.* Durham, NC: MetaMetrics.

Williamson, G.L. (2008). A text readability continuum for postsecondary readiness. *Journal of Advanced Academics, 19*(4), 602–632.

Wilson, S.M., & Berne, J. (1999). Teacher learning and the acquisition of professional knowledge: An examination of research on contemporary professional development. In A. Iran-Nejad & P.D. Pearson (Eds.), *Review of research in education* (pp. 173–209). Washington, DC: American Educational Research Association. doi:10.3102/0091732X02400117

AUTHOR INDEX

A

Academy, Voice, 214
ACT, 205
Adams, M.J., 208, 210, 214
Afflerbach, P., 109
Afflerbach, P.A., 222, 224
Allington, R.L., 64, 109, 158
American Speech-Language-Hearing
    Association, 213
Anderson, D.R., 182
Anderson, L.W., 222
Anderson, R.C., 130, 150
Anderson, T.H., 5
Archer, A.L., 127
Arguelles, M.E., 50
Armbruster, B.B., 5
Aro, M., 211
Association of American Publishers, 190
Ataya, R., 225
August, D., 64, 92, 94, 95, 102, 122
Australian Curriculum, Assessment and
    Reporting Authority, 219
Autor, D.H., 205

B

Baca, L., 107
Baker, E.A., 219
Baker, S., 102
Baker, S.K., 49
Barber, J., 245
Barnett, W.S., 2, 19, 97
Barr, R., 180
Baumann, J.F., 126
Beal, C.R., 181
Beck, I.L., 7
Becker, W.C., 124
Bell, S., 111
Bell, S.M., 65, 66
Belt-Beyan, P.M., 80
Benner, S., 111
Bennett, S., 225
Bennett-Armistead, V.S., 4
Berne, J., 247
Betts, E.A., 137, 249
Bialystok, E., 96, 97
Biancarosa, G., 108–109, 211
Biemiller, A., 182, 183
Billman, A.K., 49
Bishop, Beverly, 28
Blanco, D., 97
Blewitt, P., 183
Boote, C., 182, 183
Bos, C., 65

Boulay, B., 65
Boyle, O.F., 129
Boynton, S., 192
Bradley, B.A., 5
Brasseur-Hock, I.F., 211
Braun, H., 220
Brenner, D., 157
Brown, J.S., 196
Brueck, J., 178, 193, 195
Bruschi, B.A., 60
Buckleitner, W., 193, 198
Buenger, A., 125
Buly, M.R., 115
Burns, M.S., 60, 122
Burstein, K., 195, 196, 197, 198
Bus, A.G., 176, 177, 178, 179, 180, 181, 182, 183,
    184, 185, 186, 193, 195, 212
Butler, S., 125
Butler, Y.G., 99

C

Cabell, S.Q., 195
Calderón, M., 121, 122
Calkins, L., 116
Calkins, L.M., 63
Cammack, D.W., 224
Campbell, J.R., 209
Carlisle, J.F., 156
Carlo, M., 122
Carlson, C.D., 94
Carolan, M.E., 2
Carpenter, P.A., 156
Cassidy, J., 116
Castek, J., 222, 224
Catterson, J.H., 3
Caughlan, S., 56
Celano, D.C., 10
Centers for Disease Control and Prevention,
    67
Cervetti, G.N., 156, 245
Chall, J.S., 250
Char, D., 65
Chard, D.J., 49, 108–109
Cheung, A., 97
Chhabra, V., 64
Chinn, C.A., 130
Chiong, C., 177, 195, 196
Cho, B.-Y., 222, 224
Christian, D., 92
Clark, A., 130
Clark, R.E., 5
Coburn, C.E., 62
Coiro, J., 222, 224, 225, 226

Leftwich, S.A., 50
Lehman, C., 116
Lenhart, L.A., 26
Lesaux, N.K., 121, 123–124
Leu, D.J., 9, 224, 225, 226, 227, 231
Leung, C.B., 123
Levy, B.A., 184
Levy, F., 205
Li, Y., 130
Lieberman, 247
Linderholm, T., 252
Lindhold-Leary, K., 92
Lindsay, M., 154
Logan, J.W., 52
Lonigan, C.J., 97, 176, 213
Loots, B.K., 39, 41
Loveless, D., 116
Lynch-Brown, C., 155

M

Mahoney, K., 97
Makaryk, I.R., 142
Malloy, J.A., 4, 5
Marinak, B., 4
Martin, N.M., 56
Martin, S.D., 61
Martin-Beltran, M., 127, 129
Martineau, J.A., 50
Marttunen, M., 225
Mashburn, A.J., 115
Mather, N., 65
Maton, K., 225
Mazzoni, S.A., 4
McCallum, R.S., 65
McCardle, P., 64
McDonald, M., 31
McGill-Franzen, A., 109, 111, 113, 115
McKenna, M.C., 181, 198
McKeon, D., 121
McKeown, M.G., 7
McLaughlin, M., 116, 117
McLeod, S., 192
McLuhan, M., 9
McMaken, J., 93
McMaster, K.L., 129
McNamara, D.S., 207
McNamara, P., 60
McRae, A., 55
McRae, A.C., 170
Mesmer, H.A., 150, 249, 251
MetaMetrics, 250
Meyer, A.G., 123
Millard, R.T., 150
Miller, D., 204
Miller, R.J., 60
Mitchell, M.A., 123
Moje, E., 245
Mol, S.E., 176
Montecillo, C., 123

Moody, A.K., 181, 195, 198
Moreno, R., 183
Morrow, L.M., 61, 71
Muentener, P., 180
Murnane, R.J., 205
Murphy, L., 245

N

Nagy, W.E., 35
Nandakamar, R., 123
National Assessment Governing Board, 44, 45
National Association for the Education of
    Young Children, 2, 22
National Center for Education Statistics, 122,
    150, 206, 207
National Council of Teachers of English,
    121–122
National Employment Law Project, 205
National Governors Association Center for
    Best Practices and the Council of Chief
    State School Officers, 1, 2, 3, 13, 14, 16,
    26, 27, 36, 44, 46, 59, 60, 63, 75, 90, 95,
    96, 98, 99, 102, 107, 121, 123, 125, 127,
    128, 129, 130, 136, 138, 139, 140, 142,
    149, 152, 155, 162, 167, 176, 190, 192,
    197, 204, 206, 219, 223, 226, 237, 238,
    240, 241, 242, 243, 244, 246, 247, 248,
    249, 252, 253, xiv
National Institute for Literacy, 14
National Institute of Child Health and Human
    Development, 64, 124, 210, 247
National Research Council, 19, 257
Nelson, P., 213
Nelson, P.B., 213
Ness, M., 124
Neuman, S.B., 4, 7, 9, 10, 101, 114, 130, 186
Neuman, W.R., 9
Nichols, P.D., 3
Nichols, W.D., 52
Norton, D.E., 192
Norton, S., 192

O

O'Brien, C., 195
Ochshorn, S., 23
Ogle, D., 117
Omanson, R.C., 7
Oranje, A., 209
O'Reilly, T., 207
Organisation for Economic Cooperation and
    Development, 225
Osterag, J., 5

P

Paivio, A., 130, 180
Pappas, C., 48
Parikh, M., 22
Paris, S.G., 55
Payne, R.L., 113, 115

SUBJECT INDEX

for practitioners, 68–70; speaking and listening standards, 26–34; technology, 9–10; text complexity, 3–4

Improving Reading Comprehension in Kindergarten Through 3rd Grade practice guide, 126

independent reading time, 157–158

informational texts: as boring, 162–163; focus on, 207–209; instructional strategies with, 48–51; reading and writing, standards for, 46–47; recommendations for using, 51–55; recommended distribution of, 44–45; shift in emphasis on, 4–5; types of, 46

information sheet sample, 88

input theories, 91

instructional level, 3

instructional strategies with informational texts, 48–51

integrated model of literacy, 15–16

integration of knowledge and ideas, challenges of, 6–9

Integration of Knowledge and Ideas Standards, xiv, 47, 53

interactivity in enhanced e-books, 181–184, 192, 193

interdisciplinary units: example of, 170–172; for literacy engagement, 167–170; research on, 173

J–K

Japanese Lesson Study, 69

Joan Ganz Cooney Center, 177

key ideas, recounting or describing, 28–29

Key Ideas and Details Standards, xiv, 16, 46–47, 52

kindergarten: instructional strategies with informational text, 48–49; vignette for Presentation of Knowledge and Ideas standard, 33–34

Kindergarten Early Assessment, 20

Kirkus Reviews, 193

Knowledge of Language standard, 35

K-W-L strategy, 117–118

L

language standards: development of throughout day, 41–42; overview of, 35–36; Vocabulary Acquisition and Use, 35–36, 38–41, 95–96. *See also* Conventions of Standard English standard

language structure, importance of, 93–95

learning-from-text instruction, 138–141

Learning Oasis, 250

learning progression of skills, 2–3, 240–243, 258

leveled texts, 3

Lexile Framework, 149

limited English proficient (LEP) students, 122

line sets sample, 87

linguistic awareness skills, 123, 128–129

literacy: of African American males, 76–80; disciplinary, 5–6, 244–246; early, 14, 26; integrated model of, 15–16. *See also* early literacy research; new literacies

literacy engagement: designing classrooms for, 163–167; of ELs, 101–102; interdisciplinary units for, 167–172; research on, 172–174; text complexity and, 162–163

literary texts, recommended distribution of, 44–45

locating information, assessment of, 227–229

M

media skills, 17. *See also* online research and comprehension

motivation: of ELs, 101–102; of teachers, 113–114. *See also* literacy engagement; motivation supports

motivational scaffolds, 55–56

motivation supports: in classroom design, 164–166; in interdisciplinary units, 168–169

multidimensional reading model, 83–84, 85–88

multimedia additions to e-books, 176, 193

multimedia support for ELs, 130–131

Multiple Choice format assessment, 227

music in e-books, 180–181

N

National Assessment of Educational Progress (NAEP): Reading Framework, 44; results of, 206, 207; special study on fluency, 209; Writing Framework, 25

National Council on Teacher Quality, 65

National Early Childhood Accountability Task Force, 20

National Reading Panel, 64, 65, 124

National Reading Technical Assistance Center, 125

NCLB (No Child Left Behind), 59, 60, 246

New Criticism, 142

new literacies: assessment of, 226–233; as blended into CCSS, 225–226; CCSS and (*See* Common Core State Standards for English Language Arts); described, 219; of online research and comprehension, 222, 224–225

90-10 phenomenon of vocabulary distribution, 150–153

No Child Left Behind (NCLB), 59, 60, 246